RACIAL PROFILING: FROM RHETORIC TO REASON

BRIAN L. WITHROW, PH.D.

Wichita State University

Upper Saddle River, New Jersey 07458

Library of Congress Cataloging-in-Publication Data

Withrow, Brian L.
    Racial profiling : from rhetoric to reason / Brian L. Withrow.-- 1st ed.
        p. cm.
    Includes bibliographical references and index.
    ISBN 0-13-127379-5
    1. Racial profiling in law enforcement--United States. 2. Police-community relations--
United States. 3. Criminal justice, Administration of--United States. I. Title.

HV8141.W58 2006

363.25'8--dc22   2005004733

Executive Editor: Frank Mortimer, Jr.
Assistant Editor: Mayda Bosco
Executive Marketing Manager: Tim Peyton
Editorial Assistant: Kelly Krug
Managing Editor: Mary Carnis
Production Liaison: Brain Hyland
Production Editor: nSight, Inc.
Director of Manufacturing and Production: Bruce Johnson
Manufacturing Manager: Ilene Sanford
Manufacturing Buyer: Cathleen Peterson
Design Director: Cheryl Asherman
Senior Design Coordinator: Miguel Ortiz
Cover Design: Marianne Frasco
Cover Photo: Getty Images/Thinkstock
Composition: Laserwords
Printing and Binding: Courier Stoughton

Pearson Education LTD.   Pearson Educacion de Mexico, S.A. de C.V.
Pearson Education Australia PTY, Limited   Pearson Education—Japan
Pearson Education Singapore, Pte. Ltd.   Pearson Education Malaysia, Pte. Ltd.
Pearson Education North Asia Ltd.   Pearson Education, Upper Saddle River, New Jersey
Pearson Education Canada, Ltd.

10 9 8 7 6 5 4 3 2 1
ISBN 0-13-127379-5

To Mauverine, who taught us to value acceptance, fairness, and laughter.

TABLE OF CONTENTS

4

EXPLAINING THE DISPARITY   **111**

7

SOLUTIONS   **203**

8

WHAT'S NEXT?   **227**

PREFACE

There are probably no more than half a dozen good reasons to commit the time necessary to write a book. Certainly there are some financial incentives, and academic recognition is important to someone like me. But the most important reason to write a book such as this is having something important to say. Racial profiling is an emerging issue. It is by all accounts the most critical issue facing American policing today. It tears at the heart of our sense of fairness and social equity. It threatens to adversely affect the legitimacy of our entire legal system.

Unfortunately, most of what we know or think we know about racial profiling comes to us from rather suspicious sources. The controversy is highly influenced by individuals and groups with alternative political and social agendas. A finding of racial disparity in police stops may lead one researcher to conclude racial profiling is rampant in the community, while another researcher, looking at the same data, may conclude the opposite. Some disagreement among scholars is understandable. There are considerable differences in how scholars are trained to approach social science research. It is even likely that disagreement among scholars substantially advances science and is therefore good for the growth of knowledge. But much of the conflict in the current controversy has nothing to do with academic training, the peer review process, or the advancement of scientific knowledge. It is about advancing a particular political or social agenda under the umbrella of legitimate social science inquiry, and that is offensive to all of us who care deeply about the inherent rights of individuals and the importance of policing by consent.

The purpose of this book is to move the racial profiling controversy from its current rhetorical base into a reasoned argument. It is my objective to move racial profiling inquiry away from exaggerated and overreaching conclusions and into the realm of bona fide scientific investigation. In doing so, I have purposely limited the use of anecdotal stories from victims of racial profiling. While these stories provide a human richness to the issue and have likely advanced the media's attention on the controversy, they do little to improve our understanding of why minorities are overrepresented in police stops. The uniqueness of this book, compared to others available today, lies in its lack of a priori assumptions about the nature of American policing and police officers. The book neither attempts to indict the police nor support them. Instead, the focus of this book is on the scientific investigation of racial profiling. It has been my desire to offer an objective view of the evidence, so far, as well as a thorough treatise of what we do not know. It is my sincere hope that political leaders, police administrators, training academy instructors, scholars, and, of course, students will find the information in these pages useful as they grapple with the difficult political, administrative, and methodological issues associated with the racial profiling controversy.

Any author who writes on a topic like racial profiling assumes some risk of offending readers over his use of terms. Throughout the text I use the term *Black* to describe African American, *Hispanic* to describe Latino or Mexican American, *White* to describe Caucasian, *Asian*, and *Native American*. The use of the term *Black* is likely controversial. It is intended to describe all individuals with black skin, regardless of their national origin or ethnicity. The term, albeit imprecise as an indicator of race, is consistent with my understanding of the racial profiling controversy in that it is the perception of race, rather than an individual's actual race, that allegedly influences a police officer's decision to stop. The term *Hispanic* is used to describe an individual's ethnicity. While some researchers consider Hispanic a race, it is more commonly considered an ethnicity. There is substantial variation in skin color throughout the Hispanic ethnicity. The terms *minority* and *minorities* are used throughout the text to describe groups of individuals (usually defined by race or ethnicity) who represent a numeric minority within a given population.

Throughout the text I refer to racial profiling as a "controversy." This in no way should be considered evidence that the author discounts the work of other researchers. Instead, in using this term I intend to express that racial profiling, as an issue or research agenda, is still in its infancy. A controversy in this sense is intended to mean a discussion characterized by the expression of alternative views. While some consistency of findings is evident in the literature, there is still considerable disagreement on the meaning of the term *racial profiling*, how to measure who gets and doesn't get stopped, and the appropriate manner in which to interpret the analytical findings of a study. It is admittedly quite likely that even when these issues are addressed in the future, racial profiling will continue to be a controversial topic.

The text consists of eight chapters. Chapter One, An Emergence, discusses how six seemingly unrelated issues and practices coalesced over the past decade into what is commonly referred to as the racial profiling controversy. Chapter Two, What We Know and Don't Know, reports on the findings of a representative sample of racial profiling studies. Chapter Three, Critical Methodological Issues, outlines the important methodological issues that have so far hampered our understanding of racial profiling. Chapter Four, Explaining the Disparity, identifies and critically evaluates various theoretical explanations for the overrepresentation of minorities among individuals stopped by the police. Chapter Five, The Political and Legal Response, discusses how political leaders should manage the racial profiling controversy to their advantage in their communities. This chapter also outlines and evaluates the potential legal remedies for addressing the practice of racial profiling. Chapter Six, Conducting Racial Profiling Studies (Best Practices), outlines and discusses the important steps for successfully conducting a racial profiling study. Chapter Seven, Solutions, offers ten potential solutions to the racial profiling controversy. Chapter Eight, What's Next?, attempts to predict the future of the racial profiling controversy. In addition, this chapter discusses the relevance of the racial profiling controversy to our national war against terrorism.

President Lyndon B. Johnson had a habit of starting contentious meetings with the phrase "Come, let us reason together." I hope to encourage participants in this controversy to do the same. The racial profiling controversy is not new to America. Indeed, racial issues have been at the forefront of American society since the early days of the republic. They are endemic, intractable, and complicated, but not insurmountable. The way out of the abyss of racial profiling is through reason, not rhetoric.

Brian L. Withrow, Ph.D.
Bel Aire, Kansas

ACKNOWLEDGMENTS

In 1999, a polite young man entered my university office with a simple request. He wanted me to act as his mentor in our university's Shadow a Scholar program, part of the McNair Scholars Program at Wichita State University. What Henry Jackson (now a Ph.D. student at Kansas State University) wanted to do was study racial profiling. I agreed, and over the next months we evaluated dozens of anecdotal stories from victims of racial profiling. Eventually, our paper was one of about two dozen chosen from the thousands submitted to appear in the *National McNair Journal*. Henry lit a spark of scholarly curiosity in me that continues to burn brightly. This book, and my interest in writing it, comes from my experience working with Henry, more than anyone else. He taught me how to read between the lines of the stories and understand what he calls "the Black experience." I am immensely indebted to Henry for his guidance. It is possible for the professor to learn from his student.

Later that year Deputy Chief Terri Moses of the Wichita Police Department asked me to assist her department in its first comprehensive racial profiling study. By the time she asked, the plans for conducting the study were well underway. My role was to analyze the data and write the final report. I agreed to do so as a community service. It was an immensely rewarding experience. The Wichita Stop Study launched an entire research agenda resulting in the publication of no less than half a dozen technical reports and scholarly articles. Ultimately, this experience led me to the conclusion that a more comprehensive treatise on the subject was necessary. Along the way I encountered an individual who would become one of my closest friends. Chief Norman D. Williams is one of the most committed and caring community leaders I have ever met. His commitment to community involvement in policing was established long before community oriented policing became fashionable. As a young patrol officer he distinguished himself in the community through his regular practice of walking a beat and engaging at-risk youth in productive activities. Today, the Wichita community is actively involved in nearly every major administrative issue facing the Wichita Police Department. I am indebted to him for his support of my scholarly activities and appreciative of his friendship.

Finally, an endeavor of this magnitude is not possible without the support of many others. Dr. Paul Cromwell, Director of the School of Community Affairs, and my boss, has offered his unqualified support of me and my research from the very first day I joined the faculty at Wichita State University. He is a competent scholar, a skilled administrator, and a good friend. Dr. Anna Chandler, Chair of the Ethnic Studies Department at Wichita State University, and my friend, has graciously allowed me access to her considerable knowledge and experience as I have struggled to understand the meaning of race in America. Kerry Weible and Christina Circle, my graduate assistants, never complained about my numerous requests of them to "get a copy of this article," "double check my numbers," or "read over this and tell me what you think."

Thanks to these reviewers: Tim Berard, Kent State University; Tod W. Burke, Radford University; Corrine Koepf, MLS, University at Buffalo; Ken Novak, University of Missouri-KC; Ernest Uwazie, and Tom O'Connor.

I am immensely appreciative of the guidance, support, and, of course, motivation of Korrine Dorsey and Mayda Bosco, my editors at Prentice Hall. Without their guidance, it is unlikely this text would have ever made it to market.

Finally, it is important that I acknowledge the people who mean the most to me, my family. My wife Lisa is an elementary school teacher. She is good enough to work at any elementary school in Wichita. She chooses to work with impoverished children at an inner city school, and I applaud her commitment as a teacher and social activist. Our children, Kathryn (a sophomore at the University of Kansas), Emma (a freshman at Wichita State University), Audrey (a junior at Wichita Heights High School), and Evan (an eighth grader at Resurrection Catholic School) continue to amaze and delight us. Lisa and I are immensely proud to be their parents and are enjoying their transition into adulthood.

Brian L.Withrow, Ph.D.
Bel Aire, Kansas

chapter 1

AN EMERGENCE

OBJECTIVE

To discuss how six seemingly unrelated issues and practices coalesced over the past decade into what is commonly referred to as the racial profiling controversy.

CHAPTER OUTLINE

Introduction
The Police and the Minority Community
    Police Abuse and the Minority Community
    The Influence of Race in Police Decision Making
    Differential Community Support for the Police
    The Promise and Peril of Community Policing
Profiling as an Enforcement Tool
    Profiling Defined
    Hijacker Profiling
    Criminal Profiling
    Drug Courier Profiling

INTRODUCTION

Prior to the mid-1990s the term *racial profiling* had very little meaning, at least to the general public. The term first appeared in the *San Diego Union Tribune* on October 8, 1987, in a story about a major drug seizure by the Utah state police. The term was used next in a similar story on December 25, 1987, in the *Washington Post*. The use of the term within the context of "routine" police practices first appeared in an article in the *Omaha World Herald* on October 24, 1994, and then in the *Patriot Ledger*, a New Jersey publication, on December 23, 1994. The similar term *driving while Black* was originally coined by Henry Louis Gates in an article appearing in the *New Yorker* on October 23, 1995 (Heumann and Cassak 2003).

By the mid-1990s racial profiling had become one of the most, if not the most, important issue in American policing. Accusations of racial profiling came at a time when the police were enjoying consistent reductions in crime (Fridellet al. 2001). Beginning in 1990, all of the major indexes of crime reported reductions, some substantial, in the rates of reported crime and criminal victimization. These drops in crime were largely attributed to proactive policing strategies that focused the attention of street officers on relatively minor quality of life infractions and aggressive directed patrol strategies. During the mid-1990s police departments throughout the nation were being credited with making communities safer. Beginning in the late 1980s American policing experienced fundamental organizational and philosophical change. Police leaders throughout the nation embraced the principles of community involvement and proactive problem solving.

Arguably, the police were making substantial improvements in their relationships with previously disenfranchised groups within their communities. Even some of the more ardent critics of the police began to acknowledge the efficacy of these new policing paradigms.

Almost immediately after the racial profiling controversy developed traction in the popular media, and especially after the first legal challenges were initiated, police departments throughout the nation retrenched and tagged it is a media myth. They vehemently denied the accusation that their officers are inappropriately influenced by an individual's race or ethnicity while making routine enforcement decisions. Police chiefs typically scoffed at the notion that their enforcement programs, most notably routine traffic stops and searches, had any disparate effect with respect to race. Very few, however, could produce evidence in their own defense. Until very recently little was known about how traffic stops and searches were conducted, and even less was known about the kinds of individuals whom the police stop. The police charged that their critics used the terms *racial profiling* and *driving while Black* to distort the nature of their routine procedures (Buerger and Farrell 2002) and unfairly cast them as little more than racist thugs. Early on, few departments were willing to acknowledge that they had a racial profiling problem (Fridell et al. 2001) and even fewer were willing to voluntarily conduct in-depth studies. That, of course, has changed. To date, more than 400 police agencies have collected traffic stop data either voluntarily, in response to a statutory requirement, or court order. Twenty-three states have passed legislation requiring the collection of traffic stop data or racial profiling studies (Amnesty International USA 2004; McMahon et al. 2002).

A nationwide telephone poll of 2,006 individuals conducted in 1999 by the Gallup organization erases any doubt that racial profiling has become well known to the general public. This poll finds that 56 percent of Whites and 77 percent of Blacks believe racial profiling is a widespread practice in police departments throughout the United States. Six percent of Whites, 42 percent of Blacks, and nearly 75 percent of young Black males surveyed report that they are victims of racial profiling. Amnesty International USA (AIUSA 2004) estimates there are 32,000,000 victims of racial profiling and that 87,000,000 individuals are at high risk of victimization during their lifetimes. While racial profiling appears to adversely affect the Black community primarily, it is also an important issue among Hispanics, and post-9/11, Arabs and Muslims (AIUSA 2004; Harris 2002; Heumann and Cassak 2003). Recent research (Withrow 2004a) indicates that in some cases (e.g., in predominately Black neighborhoods) Whites are stopped at disproportionately higher rates than minorities. Racial profiling is not simply a traffic enforcement issue. Meeks (2000) alleges that racial profiling is a common practice among shopping mall security guards and taxicab drivers. During a series of nationwide hearings, Amnesty International USA (2004) received public testimony from individuals alleging to be victims of racial profiling while driving, walking, shopping, traveling through airports, going to church, and even in the privacy of their own homes. The perception of racial profiling is now so pervasive that minority parents routinely counsel their teenage children shortly after they start driving on how to respond to a racially motivated traffic stop (Meeks 2000; Harris 2002).

At its heart, racial profiling is a human rights issue (Fridell et al. 2001). It is complex, transcends whether or not the police are discriminatory, and includes "factors related to social psychology, occupational socialization, and law" (Carter and Katz-Bannister 2004, 236). Race profiling is not new. Race and ethnicity have always played a significant and divisive role in the American society and, in particular, the administration of justice. Nearly half of the individuals in prison today are Black, even though Blacks represent only 12 percent of the overall population in America. Forty percent of the individuals currently on death rows throughout the nation, and 53 percent of the individuals executed since 1930 are Black (Walker, Spohn, and DeLone 2000). While equality under the law is a fundamental precept of our nation's system of justice, "the administration of criminal law—whether by the officer on the beat, the legislature, or the Supreme Court—is in fact predicated on the exploitation of inequality" (Cole 1999, 5).

While the issue of racial profiling got its legs in the mid-1990s, its roots are as old as the republic. A series of seemingly unrelated events merged during the 1990s that essentially created a controversy that has become far more than the sum of its parts. The purpose of this chapter is to explore how six seemingly unconnected events coalesced into what is now arguably the most important issue facing American policing and indeed potentially affecting the legitimacy of the entire American legal system.

The Wichita Eagle, March 17, 2004, used by permission.

The Police and the Minority Community

A substantial part of the racial profiling controversy is directly related to the historically contentious relationship between the police and the minority community. There is a long history of police abuse involving minorities. As a result, support for the police within the minority community is consistently lower than the overall level of public support for the police. Despite attempts to engage the minority community and the police in a meaningful dialogue, the conflict remains. There is even evidence that recent problem-oriented policing programs may have further eroded police-minority relationships.

Police Abuse and the Minority Community

To say that the 1960s were socially turbulent is indeed an understatement. Very few urban centers or university campuses escaped protests of civil injustice or opposition to the Vietnam War during this decade of social upheaval. Following a series of particularly deadly and destructive urban riots, the Kerner Commission attempted to determine the cause of civil insurrection within the chronically economically disadvantaged and politically disenfranchised inner cities of America. The commission concluded, "Our nation is moving towards two societies, one black, one white—separate and unequal" (Magee 1994, 162). This finding suggests that American society was at one time, prior to the 1960s, a singular society. Nothing could be farther from the truth. American society has always been plural, separated by race, national origin, class, religion, gender, and many other factors. The vilification of various racial and ethnic groups has been the basis for enslavement, segregation, and the denial of full participation in American society, but no group has suffered more than the Black community. "Racial bigotry has been and remains a significant pollutant within the administration of criminal justice" (Kennedy 1997, 21).

The differential, that is harsher, treatment of minorities by the police is not new. It is the latest chapter in a long history of tension between the police and the minority communities and has a direct effect on police-minority relationships today (Batton and Kadleck 2004; Fridell et al. 2001; Jernigan 2000; O'Reilly 2002). As early as the 1600s the Philadelphia courts authorized citizens to arrest any Blacks they found loitering. In the mid 1700s South Carolina adopted a policy that allowed warrantless searches of Blacks while at the same time White colonists were vehemently protesting similar civil liberties abuses committed by the English crown (Jernigan 2000). Even after the Supreme Court ruled on the unconstitutionality of the separate but equal doctrine in 1954 (*Brown v. Board of Education*), the police actively participated in the enforcement of laws that facilitated segregation. Even the passage of the Civil Rights Act of 1964 did not deter police departments from supporting a dominant system of Jim Crow laws, effectively disenfranchising minorities (Batton and Kadleck 2004; Buerger and Farrell 2002).

The Influence of Race in Police Decision Making

For most of the twentieth century, and especially during the last quarter, scholars and students of American policing were interested in how the police make decisions, particularly the decision to arrest. One of the earliest studies (Westly 1953) finds that the police are typically quicker to respond physically when the suspect exhibits a lack of respect for them. Goldman (1963) reports that the police are influenced by the race, national origin, and class of juvenile suspects when deciding on whether to respond formally (arrest or summons) or informally (verbal or written warning). Piliavin and Briar (1964) observed police officer contacts with juvenile suspects and identified wide variations in the use of discretion. While race alone does not appear to play a significant role in police decision making, they found that Black more often than White youths, in the opinion of the police officers they observed, exhibit characteristics (e.g., grooming and demeanor) more likely associated with juvenile delinquents.

In the 1970s several attempts were made to identify the extralegal factors that influence police officers (Bittner 1970; Black 1971, 1976, 1980; Black and Reiss 1970; Quinney 1980; Rubinstein 1973; Smith and Visher 1981; Van Maanen 1974). While race consistently appears to have some influence on an officer's decision making, its importance appears to be quite small, especially when contrasted with other situational factors like demeanor, social class, the perceived social distance between the victim and suspect, the level of discretion available to the officer, the visibility of the enforcement context, and the dispositional demands of the complainant. In later research Powell (1981) finds differences in the level of discretion used by the police between types of neighborhoods. The police in predominately Black urban centers exercise the highest level of discretion and are slightly more punitive toward White suspects than Black suspects. Conversely, the police in predominantly White urban centers and suburbs are considerably more punitive toward Black than White suspects.

At first glance the current research on racial profiling beginning in the mid-1990s appears to be a logical extension of this prior research (Engel, Calnon, and Bernard 2002). There are, however, two critical differences. First, all of the prior research is conducted within the scope of a police-citizen contact. It attempts to determine how the police make a decision after the initial contact has been made. The contemporary racial profiling research focuses on the factors that influence officer decision making prior to the initial contact. This is an important difference. Police-citizen contacts are discrete events from which important information (most notably the race of the individual) can be determined with a reasonable level of accuracy. This establishes a relatively accurate baseline or population upon which comparative outcomes can be based. For example, the researchers in the 1970s were able to compare the proportional racial representation of individuals contacted versus those arrested by the police. Contemporary racial profiling researchers do not have an acceptable benchmark upon which to compare the results of stop information.

Second, the prior research focuses primarily on the behavior of individual officers during the context of a police-citizen encounter. The contemporary research tends to be more systems oriented. It draws its conclusions from the outcomes of system processing rather than direct observations of individual police-citizen encounters. Donzinger (1996) is typical of the contemporary research. He begins his research by observing a five to one ratio of Black to White arrests. He then predicts that if the criminal justice process (postarrest) were race neutral, the ratio of Blacks to Whites would remain essentially the same (5:1) throughout the criminal justice system. The ratio of Blacks to Whites in prison, however, is seven to one. Prosecutors are much less likely to reduce or drop charges for Black defendants and more willing to enhance charges for Blacks, particularly if the defendant is White. Furthermore, Blacks are more likely to be jailed pending adjudication, less likely to be successful during plea negotiations, and more likely to receive the death penalty. From these findings Donzinger concludes that "there is evidence that discrimination exists at every stage in the criminal justice process" (114).

Differential Community Support for the Police

Contrary to a popularly held perception, police departments enjoy overwhelming support from a broad spectrum of individuals across their communities (MacDonald 2003). Most people, when asked, are generally confident in the ability of their police department to prevent crime, apprehend law breakers, and make their communities safer. Most people believe that the police will treat them fairly and professionally. Furthermore, levels of public confidence in the police have remained relatively stable for more than three decades, even during periods of intense social unrest caused by police misconduct (Walker, Spohn, and DeLone 2000).

This, however, does not mean that this level of support is consistent in every part of the community. There is strong evidence that within minority communities, and in particular Black communities, the police are viewed less favorably. While generally more favorable than less, the level of public confidence in the police appears to be consistently lower within minority communities (Walker, Spohn, and DeLone 2000). Blacks, Hispanics, and other minorities are consistently less likely to view police stops as legitimate (Cole 1999; Lundman and Kaufman 2003; Ramirez, McDevitt, and Farrell 2000; Weitzer and Tuch 2002; Withrow and Jackson 2002). Minorities allege that they are singled out by the police, stopped more frequently, and detained for longer periods of time than nonminorities (Tomaskovic-Devey, Mason, and Zingraff 2004). Minorities believe that their encounters with the police are more punitive than encounters involving nonminorities (Lundman and Kaufman 2003). Furthermore, minorities appear more willing to interpret negative aspects of traffic stops, such as officer rudeness, as racially motivated (Fridell et al. 2001; Withrow and Jackson 2002).

There is, however, some evidence that as the social context of cities changes, the connection between race and attitudes toward the police may also change. Frank, Brandl, and Cullen (1996) conducted a telephone survey of 516 residents of Detroit, Michigan. Their results contradict the previously outlined literature. In this city Black residents had more favorable attitudes toward the police and were less likely to perceive a police officer's behavior negatively than Whites. There is some evidence that this change is due to the appointment and election of prominent Black leaders to positions of high visibility and authority.

During the 1970s many police departments embarked on ambitious programs to improve their relationships with minority communities. Throughout our nation's history citizens groups, in cooperation with police departments, have enjoyed limited success at reducing specific crime problems and generally improving the quality of life in a community (Farrell, McDevitt, and Buerger 2002). Unfortunately, there is no evidence that police community relations programs do much to improve long-term relationships within the minority community (Walker, Spohn, and DeLone 2000). Police department attempts to engage the Black community are for the most part ineffective and fail to overcome the stigma of past abuses and brutality (Asim 2001).

The Promise and Peril of Community Policing

For more than a decade the rate of crime has dropped consistently, and in some cases precipitously, in nearly every city in the nation. Because of the complexity of crime, it is difficult, if not impossible, to empirically explain why the both the rate of crime as well as the rate of victimization have dropped so consistently over the past decade. The aging out of the youngest members of the Baby Boomer population, the imposition of longer prison sentences, and low rates of unemployment are all considered possible explanations.

One explanation however, cannot be overlooked. Beginning in the late 1980s policing in America experienced a sort of paradigm shift. In an effort to reduce the incidence of corruption, police leaders for most of the twentieth century adopted a professional efficiency model of policing. This philosophy of policing placed substantial controls on police officers and in a significant way created strong barriers between the police and their communities (Cohen, Lennon, and Wasserman 2000; Wilson and Kelling 1982). Patrol officers were encouraged to remain on routine patrol and respond quickly to calls for service. During a call the police were taught to conduct their business quickly and return to patrol as soon as possible, leaving little time for community engagement and problem solving. This approach to policing pervaded every aspect of the police organization, even its language. Police available for call, that is, on routine patrol, were said to be "in service," but while interacting with the public they were said to be "out of service."

Then in the late 1980s the police began to rethink their role. The police began to realize that their relatively narrow law enforcement objective was not producing acceptable reductions in crime. Simply responding to repeated calls for service at the same locations was doing little to effect real change. The police began to explore other styles of policing. The community policing, problem oriented policing (see Goldstein 1990), and the *Broken Windows* (see Wilson and Kelling 1982) philosophies provided police leaders with the first real models for effective organizational change in decades. These approaches to policing are credited with steep drops in crime as a result of community involvement in pubic safety, systematic problem solving, and a renewed focus on quality of life issues (Cleary 2000; MacDonald 2003).

While most people tend to view the recent change in policing philosophy favorably, at least one author argues that these new approaches may adversely affect the minority community (Harris 2002). The *Broken Windows* philosophy is particularly suspect. The authors (Wilson and Kelling 1982) use the term *broken windows* as a metaphor. They propose that if a window in a building is broken and not immediately repaired, then soon all the other windows in the building will be broken. "Untended property becomes fair game for people out for fun or plunder" (Wilson and Kelling 1982, 360). The same is true of untended behavior. The perpetrator perceives that if nobody cares, then he can be assured of anonymity while breaking the other windows or committing more serious violations. This approach to policing encourages the police to focus on relatively minor infractions of the law. These include quality of life issues like vagrancy, loitering, and drunk in public violations. This, the proponents argue, will deter likely perpetrators from more serious criminal behaviors like burglary, robbery, and assault. Harris (2002) alleges that this approach is the impetus behind an increased use of stop and frisk encounters that require very little or no probable cause and may adversely affect the minority community.

Community involvement is the hallmark of the community policing and problem oriented policing approaches. Typically the police are confronted with community representatives and asked to focus their attention on a particular issue, like drug dealing, prostitution, gangs, and other relatively specific crime problems. In some instances the police are proactive and make the initial contact with the community in an effort to enlist their support during the problem solving process. In either case, a plan for addressing the problem more often than not includes a directed or saturation patrol strategy targeting a specific behavior in an attempt to either deter or displace future offending. While the police and the community are often quite successful at effecting real and sustained reductions of criminal behavior, these strategies sometimes result in a disproportionately high representation of minorities in official police statistics.

An overrepresentation of minorities in police-citizen contacts may also be caused by the emphasis or context of an enforcement program. The police are deployed principally to deter crime that occurs on the street. Comparatively, very few police resources are allocated to white collar or corporate crime. If certain racial or ethnic groups are more likely to commit crime on the street, as opposed to the corporate suite, then they are more likely to be observed by the police and therefore confronted. The fictional story in Box 1.1 illustrates how well-intended policing programs can ultimately be perceived to be racist.

BOX 1.1   THE PROMISE AND PERIL OF COMMUNITY POLICING

Author's note: The following story, although fictitious, is a compilation of similar stories that have played out in many communities throughout the nation in recent years. The story demonstrates how an effective crime fighting tool can result in what appears to be discriminatory activities.

When it was built in the 1950s, the Windsor Heights neighborhood was the most desired place to live in a mid-sized Midwestern community. Its close proximity to shopping centers, entertainment facilities, and quality schools made it one of the best places to live, work, and raise a family. The neighborhood lies in close proximity to the city's core area, providing its residents easy access to places of employment. Beginning in the mid-1960s many of the neighborhood's predominantly White residents moved to the suburban areas springing up around the city's perimeter. These residents were replaced primarily by lower income Black residents. The proximity of Windsor Heights to the downtown area and the availability of public transportation made this neighborhood particularly appealing to its new residents.

Unfortunately, nearly immediately after the neighborhood transitioned, many merchants divested and moved to the more financially lucrative sections of town. Because of their lack of education, many of the new Windsor Heights residents were unable to find gainful employment in the nearby downtown area. Poverty, and all the social maladies associated with it, became rampant. Crime, a consistent correlate with poverty, increased substantially. The neighborhood spiraled down into the abyss of inner city blight.

Today, Windsor Heights is among the least desirable places to live in the city. It has the highest rate of crime, poverty, drug addiction, domestic violence, and proportion of rental properties in the city. Even though it accounts for less than 5 percent of the city's population nearly 80 percent of the crime and citizen calls for service originate from this neighborhood.

By the late 1980s the residents had had enough and organized an informal neighborhood association. During one of their first meetings they identified crime, specifically drug trafficking, as the most present threat to the safety of the residents. A subcommittee was appointed to approach the police department and demand some action. The police were receptive to the neighborhood associations demands. The formalized the neighborhood association, organized a neighborhood watch system, and assigned a highly effective beat team of officers to address the crime problems.

The beat team determined that drug trafficking (in the context of crack houses), gang violence, and prostitution were the most serious crimes affecting the community. Their response relied on an aggressive saturation patrol strategy and health and building code enforcement. Foot and bicycle patrols were deployed to address quality of life violations like public urination, vagrancy, loitering, public drunkenness, and graffiti. Officers routinely attended neighborhood association meetings and offered residents advice on how to secure their homes and vehicles. The police aggressively enforced the city's new juvenile curfew law and pressured the local electric company to repair existing and erect additional street lighting.

In what seemed a very short time the neighborhood rebounded. Crime rates and citizen calls for service fell precipitously. Deteriorated properties were either repaired or removed. The city even built two new playgrounds and a swimming pool. The neighborhood association began meeting regularly in the new storefront police station built in an abandoned strip mall. Routine citizen surveys revealed a new level of hope among the residents. It would appear that the neighborhood's problems had been solved.

Within about a year after the police and the neighborhood declared victory in their war on crime and inner-city blight a routine departmental audit noticed a rather strange occurrence. The number of stops and searches involving minorities far exceeded their proportional representation in the city. Blacks were the subject of 30 percent of the stops, yet they accounted for less than 10 percent of the city's overall population. Blacks, when stopped, the study found, were three times more likely to be searched than Whites. The local chapter of the NAACP issued a scathing press release condemning the police for targeting

(Continues)

(Continued)

Blacks for enforcement. They, along with the state chapter of the ACLU, threatened to file a class action suit to stop the "obviously racist pattern of law enforcement by the police." In an attempt to defend themselves, the police pointed to their success in the Windsor Heights neighborhood. They argued that the stop numbers are skewed because of the aggressive patrol programs initiated in this predominantly Black neighborhood. Eventually the NAACP and the ACLU opted not to file a class action law suit. The police, now made timid by the accusations, decided to terminate many of the aggressive enforcement programs credited with reducing crime in Windsor Heights. In time, crime rates returned to their pre-intervention levels, and Windsor Heights is again one of the worst places in the city to live.

PROFILING AS AN ENFORCEMENT TOOL

The use of profiles as an enforcement tool is not new to policing. Police officers have for a long time used commonalities in criminal behaviors to increase their odds of identifying and apprehending suspects or to deter future offending. One of the earliest proponents of a profile was Major General Sir Llewellyn W. Atcherly, the Chief Constable of West Riding of Yorkshire in Wakefield England. In 1913, Sir Atcherly encouraged the use of criminal profiles based on the *modus operandi*, or method of operation, of criminals. For example, if a serial burglar consistently used a narrow basement window to enter a home, then the police should focus their attention on small framed individuals or children. In 1921, August Vollmer, the Chief of Police in Berkley, California, and an early proponent of the use of science in policing, found that criminals tend to specialize and develop expertise. Vollmer proposed that the knowledge of these specific behaviors, traits, and methods of operation may enable the police to focus their investigatory resources more efficiently (Fredrickson and Siljander 2002).

Profiling Defined

Profiling is the use of a combination of physical, behavioral, or psychological factors that, after being subjected to careful analysis, improves the probability of identifying and apprehending a suspect. Profiling is a dynamic process that includes a broad range of practices. Investigators use crime scene clues and evidence to develop lists of traits that describe the type of individual most likely to have committed the crime. Collectively these traits are referred to as a profile. Profiles are used to focus the attention of an investigation either away from or toward a particular type of person in the hopes of increasing the odds of apprehending the suspect (Carter and Katz-Bannister 2004; Cleary 2000; Harris 2002; Heumann and Cassak 2003).

Profiles have both static and dynamic components (Fredrickson and Siljander 2002). Males and youths are consistently viewed as more likely to engage in criminal behavior than females and the elderly. Profiles, however, change when new intelligence information is received that suggests a change in criminal offending methods. For example, courier profiles were amended when drug dealers began enlisting the assistance of older drivers of recreational vehicles as drug couriers.

Profiles can either be formal of informal. Formal profiles are based on documented empirical or statistical evidence and are subjected to rigorous analytical review. Informal profiles, which are used more commonly, represent the "street sense," personal experiences, and strongly held beliefs of the officers that use them (Harris 2002).

Hijacker Profiling

It is hard to believe now, but at one time a person could enter an airport, buy a ticket, and board an airplane without ever having to walk through a metal detector, have carryon luggage scanned, or submit to a cursory pat down search. Prior to the late 1960s security at most American airports was, by today's standards, nonexistent. However, in 1968, the number of annual airplane hijackings tripled. In an effort to equip airport security personnel with the tools necessary to identify potential hijackers, an extensive series of psychological, sociological, and statistical analyses were conducted. These analyses were designed to identify the "characteristics by which skyjackers appeared to differ from ordinary air travelers" (Heumann and Cassak 2003, 30). The resulting profiles were considered highly effective. It is, however, unclear whether the use of other target hardening techniques (e.g., metal detectors) was more effective than the use of hijacker profiles at reducing the number of air piracy incidents.

In some ways hijacker profiles are fundamentally different from criminal profiles. First, criminal profiles are primarily reactionary. They are developed after an incident has occurred. Hijacker profiles are proactive tools designed to detect ongoing or predict future criminal behavior. Second, the more contemporary criminal profiles are developed and used primarily by individuals highly trained in psychology, sociology, statistics, criminology, and other empirically based disciplines. Hijacker profiles were developed for and used primarily by street-level law enforcement officers.

Criminal Profiling

Criminal profiling is a judgmental process wherein highly qualified scientists trained in psychology, sociology, criminology, and forensics create behavioral outlines of the types of individuals who are most likely to have committed a crime in a particular manner. This process involves the use of both obvious and subtle behavioral characteristics as well as the situational context of the criminal event (Fredrickson and Siljander 2002; Heumann and Cassak 2003).

The most well-known type of criminal profiles are developed to identify serial murderers and rapists. This type of profiling was made popular by the movie *Silence of the Lambs* and remains an active interest of the general public. The practice of criminal profiling matured in the Behavioral Sciences Unit of the Federal Bureau of Investigation during the 1970s and 1980s. The process is highly interdisciplinary and collaborative. It is also inherently reactionary, meaning that profiles are developed to respond to events that have already happened.

While criminal profiles have a long, legitimate, and successful history in policing (Fredrickson and Siljander 2002), they have never been subjected to rigorous empirical testing (Harris 2002) to determine their accuracy after the suspect is apprehended and convicted. Actual profiles developed and used by police agencies are seldom publicized unless the police need the public's help in locating a suspect. Most criminal profiles known to the public are presented by various "profilers" and medial consultants. The most recent example of this is the profile presented during the

Washington, DC–area sniper case. Most profilers suggested that the suspect was White, former military, and acting alone. It is true that the adult member of the sniper team had served in the military. But nobody suspected an African-American team of snipers that included a juvenile.

Drug Courier Profiling

During a campaign speech in 1968, President Richard M. Nixon equated the increase in use of illegal drugs with increases in crime and thereby began what was to eventually become the War on Drugs. The creation of the United States Drug Enforcement Agency (DEA) in 1973 initiated a series of cooperative arrangements between federal, state, and local policing organizations with the singular focus of reducing the supply of illegal drugs through rigorous enforcement. By 1974, drug courier profiles had been developed for use by street level officers in the nation's airports. DEA agents Paul Markone and John Marcello are considered by many to be the individuals responsible for developing profiles to proactively identify potential drug couriers (Harris 2002; Heumann and Cassak 2003). These agents argue that in the hands of a trained officer, drug courier profiles are an effective enforcement tool.

The transference of drug courier profiles used in airports to highway interdiction was a predictable next step. Operation Pipeline, a collaborative effort of the DEA and the Florida Department of Motor Vehicles, was designed to address drug smuggling in southern Florida. In 1984, the Florida Highway Patrol found that drug couriers appeared to have common characteristics. Trooper Paul Vogel, later elected the sheriff of Volusia County, became quite effective at distinguishing between potential drug couriers and innocent motorists on Interstate Highway 95 near Daytona Beach. In 1985, the Florida Department of Highway Safety and Motor Vehicles developed one of the nation's first formal drug courier profiles in a set of guidelines titled "The Common Characteristics of Drug Couriers" (Engel, Calnon, and Bernard 2002; Harris 2002; Heumann and Cassak 2003).

The proliferation of drug courier profiles is dependent on three law enforcement realities. First, for more than four decades drugs have been considered the most serious threat to our public safety. A commonly held perception is that drugs are the root of nearly all evil in our society. Political leaders jumped at the opportunity to attach themselves to the law and order crowd by increasing the resources available to police agencies for the interdiction of drugs. From 1976 to 2002 the budget for the DEA grew from 2.9 billion to 18.8 billion. The results of this are an aggressive policing strategy and an incentive structure that rewards officers for making large drug seizures (Engel and Calnon 2004a). Few drug seizures of any size go unnoticed by the local media (Covington 2001). Asset seizure laws provide greater incentives for police departments and encourage the use of any tools that could increase the number of drug seizures (Blumenson and Nelson 1998; Harris 2002).

Second, as a result of a series of Supreme Court rulings, beginning with *Terry v. Ohio* (1968), the police have almost unfettered authority to stop motorists without probable cause. Once the motorist has stopped, the police can chose from a variety of techniques to conduct warrantless searches of individuals and vehicles. Drug courier profiles allegedly provide the police with an efficient means for deciding who to stop based on who is more likely to be carrying drugs. Third, most individuals are not aware that they have a constitutional right to deny a police officer access to their vehicle. Some individuals even believe that if they quickly give consent to search, the officer will conclude they have nothing to hide and will abandon the desire to search. Nothing could be farther from the truth. The use of a drug courier profile only attempts to differentiate between couriers and noncouriers. The actual case is made after a consensual search at the side of the road.

Covington's (2001) review of various manuals, interviews with police officers, and court testimony reveals the following common characteristics of drug courier profiles.

- Minorities driving expensive cars
- Minorities driving old cars
- Blacks and Hispanics in neighborhoods in which they do not belong
- Motorists carrying religious paraphernalia to deflect suspicion
- Leased vehicles

- Use of air fresheners
- Young black females with long nails, hair weaves, and Fendi bags
- Motorists with maps from cities where drugs originate
- Motorists with only one key in the ignition
- Long drives with infrequent stops
- Refusal to look trooper in the eye
- High mileage on late model cars
- Too much or too little baggage

While a 1999 evaluation of Operation Pipeline reveals little change in the written factors listed on the profile since the 1980s (Webb 1999), drug courier profiles appear to be quite dynamic and subject to change (Heumann and Cassak 2003). Critics of drug courier profiles allege that they were developed with very little empirical evidence (Engel, Calnon, and Bernard 2002; Heumann and Cassak 2003) and that they are a "scattershot hodge-podge of traits and characteristics so expansive" that potentially anybody and everybody could be considered a potential courier (Cole 1999, 47). The generic profile in Box 1.2 illustrates how loosely connected most drug courier profiles are.

How Race Became a Part of the Profile

Although there is very little empirical support for it, race became an explicit factor in most drug courier profiles beginning in the mid 1980s. No single event occurred that encouraged officers to look more suspiciously at racial minorities. Instead a series of subtle, seemingly race neutral suggestions were made through training programs and intelligence circulars that over time appear to have resulted in the disparate treatment of racial minorities (Cole 1999; Donzinger 1996; Harris 2002; Leitzel 2001; Tonry 1995; United States General Accounting Office 2000; Walker, Spohn, and DeLone 2000). Additionally, there is some evidence that individual officers began in the mid-1980s to truncate the profiles developed by the DEA for Operation Pipeline, isolating selected variables at the expense of equally important indicators (Carter and Katz-Bannister 2004). In the mid-1980s the DEA began focusing more enforcement attention on source countries, suggesting that nationals from these

BOX 1.2   GENERIC DRUG COURIER PROFILE

- Factors relating to the exterior of the vehicle
  - License plates from high drug distribution states
  - Rental cars
  - Vehicles with large trunks
  - Tinted or blacked-out windows
  - Numerous antennas
  - Decals or bumper stickers supporting police organizations or opposing drug use
  - Air shocks
- Factors relating to the interior of the vehicle
  - Large quantities of food wrappers and other trash in the car indicating long periods on the road
  - Newspapers and motel or gas receipts indicating departure from high drug distribution cities
  - Large amounts of cash in plastic bags or on the driver
  - Scanners, radar detectors, and portable radios
  - One key in the ignition
  - Little or no luggage
  - Duct tape
  - Plastic garbage bags
  - Drugs and drug paraphernalia
  - Odor maskers and air fresheners
- Factors relating to couriers
  - Multiple cars driving in tandem
  - Use of cell phones
  - Nervousness when spotting the police patrol car
  - Driver failing to look officer in the eyes
  - Driver taking a long time to pull over
  - Driver exiting car and coming to the police immediately after stopping
  - Driver being overly friendly to the police
  - Driver adhering strictly to traffic laws after spotting the police

countries were more likely to be carrying drugs. Many of these source countries are inhabited by individuals considered racial and ethnic minorities in the United States (Heumann and Cassak 2003). Training videos made available to New Jersey state troopers led officers "to believe that violent Jamaican gangs were primarily responsible for transporting drugs and these violent gangs could easily disguise themselves as professional black males by sporting suits and short hair" (Covington 2001, 37). The Office of National Drug Control Policy reported that crack dealers in Trenton, New Jersey, are mainly African-American, and dealers in powder cocaine and marijuana are mostly Latinos and Jamaicans (Covington 2001; Harris 2002).

Collaboration with the DEA and local officers led to perceptions that "minorities were carrying most of the drugs." (MacDonald 2003, 16). Even though the DEA may not explicitly say that race was a factor, they used other race specific factors like dreadlocks as indicators of potential drug traffickers (Harris 2002). In a drug interdiction training video used to train New Mexico state troopers all of the individuals playing the roles of the drug dealers are Hispanic (Harris 2002; Heumann and Cassak 2003). A Maryland State Police criminal intelligence report in 1992 suggests that crack cocaine dealers are predominately Black males and females (Meeks 2000). Another profile included drivers who wear lots of gold, drivers who do not "fit" the vehicle, and ethnic groups that are associated with the drug trade (ACLU 1999). "They claim to be focusing on factors other than race in their decision making—such as driving violations and suspicious activities—and assert that if their results are racially disproportionate, this is only because these other factors are present in disproportionate amounts among various racial groups" (Cleary 2000, 9).

Arguments for Including Race in the Profile

Profiles are an integral part of contemporary American policing. Whether formal or informal, they serve an important purpose by allowing officers to focus their attention and other limited resources in areas that are the most likely places where crime occurs or on people who are the most likely offenders. Police departments use profiles for one simple reason: they catch criminals. "Although not a panacea, profiling [in general] has been shown to be a successful supplement to older and more fundamental police

strategies" (Cleary 2000, 5). Using traits as indicators is an efficient way of making decisions about other people. For example,
someone with a law degree can be assumed to have an understanding of the law (Batton and Kadleck 2004; Carter and Katz-
Bannister 2004; Kennedy 1997). But are profiles that are overly
influenced by race or ethnicity accurate? Do they produce consistent results? Do they really improve the efficiency of police procedures like search hit rates?

One of the most compelling arguments for the use of race as
an indicator of suspiciousness is based on the differential arrest
and victimization rates with respect to race and ethnicity. There is
no denying that Blacks are arrested at substantially higher rates
than Whites. The ratios are five to one for misdemeanors and three
to one for violent crimes (Donzinger 1996). In 1990, one of four
Black men between the ages of 18 and 28 was under some type of
criminal justice sanction or control. By 1995, one in three Black
men was under some type of supervision of the criminal justice
system (Harris 2002). "Statistics abundantly confirm that African-
Americans—and particularly young Black men—commit a dramatically disproportionate share of street crimes in the United
States. This is a sociological fact, not a figment of the media's (or
the police's) racist imagination." (Kennedy 1999, 30). Blacks and
Hispanics experience consistently higher rates of personal victimization. Black males in particular face a substantially higher risk
of being victims of homicide (Walker, Spohn, and DeLone 2000).
Given that a sizeable portion of crime appears to be intra-racial,
one could conclude that this supports the notion that Blacks are
more likely engaged in criminal behavior. Unfortunately, the data
are not sufficient to support such a notion.

Thus, it is understandable why the police would conclude that
Blacks are more likely to commit crime than Whites (Davis 1997;
Meeks 2000). Anecdotal interviews with officers and similar studies indicate that many police believe minorities are more likely to
be engaged in criminal behavior, most notably drug related, and
therefore the police feel completely justified in focusing their attention on them (Cleary 2000; Goldberg 1999; Herszenhorn 2000;
Heumann and Cassak 2003; Kennedy 1997, 1999; Taylor and Whitney 1999). Barlow and Barlow (2002) observed that police officers
view racial profiling as an acceptable method of policing. Although
they may not use that particular term, the police believe they are

doing what is expected of them. "Police defend the use of criminal profiles that target minorities…as a means of reaching likely criminal behavior" (Garrett 2000, 1815–16). The police, including many minority officers and administrators, defend the use of race profiles as "an effective way to focus their limited resources on likely law breakers. They maintain that profiling is based not on prejudice but probabilities" (Cohen, Lennon, and Wasserman, 2000, 12). Bernard Parks, the chief of the Los Angeles Police Department, defends the use of race in some limited forms of police decision making. For example, if intelligence reports indicate that Columbians are robbing jewelry stores, then a Columbian male outside a jewelry store would and should attract the attention of a police officer. Even the most ardent critics of the police would likely support the use of race in this instance (Banks 2001).

Arguments Against Including Race in the Profile

While the previous findings are compelling, do they justify the use of race as an indicator of suspiciousness and in turn support the police practice of racial profiling? Harris (1999a) agrees that victimization rates are higher for racial minorities but argues that these are measures of victim-based crimes like burglary, robbery, and assault. These are the crimes that are most likely to be reported. Drug crimes are largely victimless and likely not reported. Most racial profiling is about drug interdiction, and the statistics consistently indicate that minorities are not more likely than nonminorities to possess drugs. In fact, during some years the self-report studies indicate that minorities are less likely than nonminorities to possess drugs. The National Household Survey of Substance and Drug Abuse finds that the same proportion of Blacks and Whites (12 percent to 13 percent, respectively) say they use illegal substances. This same survey indicates that among users of crack cocaine; 71.3 percent are White, 17.3 percent are Black, and 7.9 percent are Hispanic. The United States Sentencing Commission (2000) reports that arrestees for crack cocaine are 5.7 percent White, 84.2 percent Black, and 9.0 percent Hispanic. The National Household Survey of Substance Abuse finds that among users of powder cocaine, 81.3 percent are White, 7.70 percent are Black, and 8.5 percent are Hispanic. The United States Sentencing Commission reports that arrestees for powder cocaine are 18.2 percent White, 30.3 percent Black and 50.5 percent Hispanic. The difference may lie in where the drugs are sold or consumed. Blacks tend to sell and use crack cocaine and heroin on the street, where police surveillance is likely more intense (STATS 1999).

The perception that minorities are more likely to be drug couriers is also not supported by the empirical evidence. The reason more Blacks are arrested is that more are being searched (Ramirez, McDevitt, and Farrell 2000). There is no credible or objective data that legitimize police attention on one racial group (Covington 2001). Arrest and conviction rates are not measures of criminality. They are measures of police activity (Harris 2002; STATS 1999). In addition, it is true that "Blacks are over-represented among offenders in each category of aggressive crime . . ." and that "Blacks are at highly increased risk" for victimization, but 73 percent of criminal episodes are committed by Whites and 27 percent are committed by Blacks (Pallone and Hennessy 1999, 1).

Hit rates for highway searches are not consistently higher for minorities than nonminorities. In some cases hit rates are higher for nonminorities. Recent data from Maryland finds that race is not an important indicator for drug carrying potential (Knowles, Persico, and Todd 1999). Citing data from 2001, Wise (2003) argues that although Blacks are twice as likely as Whites to have their cars stopped and searched, the police are actually twice as likely to find evidence of illegal activity in cars driven by Whites. Furthermore, he argues that if race were an important indicator, then why don't the police focus on Whites while enforcing crimes that are committed predominantly by Whites like driving under the influence, binge drinking on college campuses, and child sexual molestation? "Racial profiling doesn't work as a crime-fighting tactic. Focusing on minorities does not, as many believe, give police better odds of apprehending criminals in possession of drugs or guns" (Harris 2002, 145).

MacDonald (2001) disagrees. "The fact that hit rates for contraband tend to be equal across racial groups, even though Blacks and Hispanics are searched at higher rates, suggests that the police are successfully targeting dealers, not minorities" (p. 9). Similarly, Taylor and Whitney (1999) observe that young people and males are more dangerous than old people and females. "Why then must we pretend that statistics regarding race differences in violent crime, are to be ignored? It is surely understandable that police should take these statistics into account when searching for suspects, and that they may wish to take more precautions when entering some neighborhoods than others" (p. 508).

In 2000, Professor David Harris, appearing before a United States Senate subcommittee hearing, argued that the use of race in profiles leads to racial and ethnic disparities throughout the criminal justice system. The misconception that Blacks are more likely to be involved in drug crimes becomes a self-fulfilling prophesy. Based on this misperception, the police will more aggressively look for drugs among Black drivers and ignore drivers of other races and ethnicities. This will ultimately result in a disproportionately higher representation of minorities at every step in the criminal justice process, thus perpetuating the same falsehood. In effect, racial profiling produces the very statistics that are used to justify the use of race in police decision making (Engel, Calnon, and Bernard 2002). When the police use race in a profile, based on a presumed statistical probability of criminal behavior, they contribute to the very statistics they use as the justification for using race in the first place. This produces an insidious and viscous cycle (Barlow and Barlow 2002; Harris 2002; Susskind 1994).

MacDonald (2001) disagrees. "The circularity argument is an insult to law enforcement and a prime example of the anti-police advocates' willingness to rewrite reality. Though it is hard to prove a negative—in this case, that there is not a large cadre of white drug lords operating in the inner cities." She argues that the percentage of Blacks killed in homicides during drug turf wars (64 percent) closely approximates the percentage of Blacks in prison (67 percent) for drug offenses. "Unless you believe that White traffickers are less violent than Black traffickers, the arrest, conviction, and imprisonment rate for drug charges appears consistent with the level of drug activity in the Black population" (pp. 6–7). The idea that "there are lots of heavy-duty White drug dealers sneaking by undetected contradicts the street experience of just about every narcotics cop you will ever talk to" (MacDonald 2001, 8).

Probably one of the most compelling indictments against the ability of profiles to identify potential criminals occurred shortly after a series of deadly school shooting incidents. Educational administrators asked police departments to assist them with developing profiles or traits that could identify a student as a possible shooter. Using these commonalities, they argued, would encourage school counselors, teachers, and administrators to identify potential shooters and intervene with proactive prevention steps. The Federal Bureau of Investigation, a pioneer in the development of criminal profiles, disagreed. They argued that developing such a profile would expose innocent individuals to scrutiny. Furthermore, many of the behaviors exhibited by school shooters are too broad to offer any real chance of singling out a particular person at risk of such behavior (Harris 2002).

There is a great deal of concern that the events following the terrorists' attacks on September 11, 2001, may put Arabs or Muslims at greater risk of racial profiling. There is some preliminary evidence that this may in fact be occurring, particularly in airports. While the empirical evidence is lacking, the anecdotal evidence is substantial (AIUSA 2004). A more thorough discussion on post-9/11 profiling involving Arabs and Muslims appears in the final chapter of this book.

THE DYNAMICS OF THE TRAFFIC STOP

Police officers enjoy a tremendous level of discretion in the exercise of their official duties, most of which are conducted outside the purview of supervisory oversight (Cole 1999). The police are the gatekeepers of the criminal justice system. Without a traffic stop, there is little likelihood of an arrest, much less a conviction. "No scenario better exemplifies both the benefits and drawbacks of this discretionary arrest power than the traffic stop" (Davis 1997, 427). The effectiveness of a drug interdiction program, and indeed most crime suppression programs, is dependent upon making a lot of traffic stops. Once the stop is made, officers have at their disposal an assortment of legally approved techniques that enable them to conduct searches of individuals and vehicles to look for evidence of criminality that is likely not at all related to the original reason for the stop. Furthermore, the courts tend to defer to the judgment of the police when deciding on the legality of stops and police-citizen contacts (Harris 1999a; Hemmons and Levin 2000; Heumann and Cassak 2003; O'Reilly 2002). The efficacy of traffic stops as the primary enforcement tool for most American police departments is dependent on three factors.

First, there is an inordinately large number of probable cause–generating events available to the police that enable them to legally initiate traffic stops. In a literal sense there are thousands of things a person can do with, in, or to a car that legally justifies the attention of a police officer. Most departments don't have written directives on how to use discretion. Officers typically develop their own enforcement criteria, and these standards are rarely documented. Furthermore, very few officers or departments are held accountable for their discretionary enforcement decisions (Ramirez, McDevitt, and Farrell 2000). After the violation has been observed, regardless of how important it may be, the officer has complete authority to effect a traffic stop. While the police may argue that they enforce all laws equally, the practical reality is that they do not. No department has the resources to enforce all laws at all times, and no responsible administrator would allow it if they did. As a result, discretion becomes an important factor in police decision making (Davis 1975, 1997).

Second, a violation of a traffic law is nearly inevitable. Most police officers readily admit that because of the comprehensiveness of the traffic code, they can usually find some reason to stop almost any car. Traffic laws are designed to enhance traffic safety. Most traffic regulations are readily recognizable as important to an effective traffic safety program. For example, a substantial portion of traffic accidents are caused by speeding and driving under the influence. Even the most ardent critics of the police support the judicious enforcement of these regulations. Some violations, however, border on the arcane. Although the statistics are not available, it is unlikely that dirty license plates or windshields obstructed by air fresheners cause many accidents. Furthermore, very few of us can honestly argue that we have never violated a traffic law. In fact, most people do routinely. "In the most literal sense, no driver can avoid violating some traffic law during a short drive, even with the most careful attention" (Harris 1997, 545).

Third, consent searches of motorists and their equivalent stop and frisk searches of pedestrians are relatively easy to do and constitutionally permissible. The courts consistently rule in favor of the police when the legality of a search is questioned if the defendant consented to the search. Furthermore, the courts generally refuse to consider the police officer's actual motivation for requesting a search. Consent searches are by and large neither voluntary nor informed. Most individuals do not know they have a right to refuse consent and believe that even if they refuse they will be searched anyway (Harris 2002; Jernigan 2000). Most searches are conduced as the result of a friendly and courteous request for consent. Even if the motorist refuses, by virtue of a twenty-year expansion of their authority to search vehicles, drivers, and their passengers, the police have virtually unfettered authority to conduct a search using dogs or the plain view exception (Harris 1999a). Officers are not required to inform motorists of their right to refuse to give their consent. This creates "a very coercive environment" (Oliver 2000, 1420), and exploits the ignorance of citizens.

THE STORIES AND MEDIA ATTENTION

Nothing communicates like a good story, especially one where an innocent person is fighting against all odds to beat the system. During the mid-1990s newspapers across the nation began to feature stories on minorities who had been stopped by the police. The articles were typically human interest stories written from the victims' perspectives. Later, as the issue of racial profiling matured, the stories became more in-depth and probing. Stories on racial profiling studies are now more often than not lead items in most local media outlets.

The stories can be classified into four distinct categories. First, known juvenile gang members complain that they are stopped and searched frequently by the police for what appears to be no valid reason or for at least relatively minor or subjective reasons. While these stories certainly add to the debate and keep the issue at the front of the news, they are easily discounted by both the police and, more importantly, the public. The police tend to respond to these stories by saying that they are doing what they have been asked to do, that is, aggressively interrupting potential gang activity. They argue that confronting known gang members frequently is an important part of their policing strategy for making communities safer. This patrol method is evidence of the police investment in the Broken Windows philosophy. The communities, and even a substantial portion of the minority community, generally support aggressive policing of known gang members and drug dealers. Generally, the public, and in particular individuals with limited exposure to the criminal justice process, are quick to discount the veracity of the victims' accounts and have little sympathy for them. As a result, these types of stories do little to add substantially to the racial profiling controversy.

Second, the stories most effective for raising our consciousness of racial profiling are those involving minority professionals. These stories tend to have wide appeal and make a significant impact in the public's perception of racial profiling. The typical scenario is a young Black man, normally a moderately successful professional, who reports being stopped and searched frequently. These men are typically well respected in the wider community and have overcome many barriers on their way to economic success. In some cases these men are stopped dozens of times in a single year. Nearly always they are driving relatively expensive cars in neighborhoods populated predominately by Whites. The justifications for the stops, if stated at all, are relatively minor violations of the traffic code. Because most people routinely commit the same sorts of violations, a greater portion of the public can identify with the victims and therefore better understand the level of harassment they feel. In most cases the stops include a simple request to search the vehicle, and most comply. Those that do not are usually surprised that the police simply let them go without seeking a warrant. This adds to the perception that the police are conducting pretextual stops. The most damning feature of these stories, at least to the image of the police, is that many do not result in the issuance of a citation. Those of us who are rarely stopped would consider getting a verbal warning a lucky break. Individuals who are repeatedly stopped, however, have a different perspective. Many question whether or not the stop was really necessary. In short they ask, "If the violation was important enough to be stopped, then why didn't I get a ticket?"

Third, in quite a few of these stories the police initially justify the stop by saying that the driver or the vehicle fit a description of a known suspect for a recent crime. While this in most cases is undoubtedly true and a justifiable reason for making a stop, in a few of these situations it is simply not. In these situations, when pressed for details, the police cannot demonstrate the similarities between the description of the suspect or vehicle and the person or vehicle stopped. In a few of these situations the differences have been quite remarkable. The effect of these stories is profound and fosters an image of an abusive and brutal police force. We don't like it very much when our police lie.

Fourth, the stories involving seemingly honorable individuals go a long way toward personalizing the issue to a broad spectrum of the population. These stories involve Black men and youths who are stopped on the way home from a sporting event or church social. The fact that an inventory search reveals little more than sports equipment and a Bible causes us to question whether or not the police really needed to focus on these individuals. These stories are effective because most of us identify with the victims. Many of us would be pleased to have any of them as our own sons. When we read of these stories we are sometimes angered that the police would treat these young men so harshly and wonder whether or not the victims will be discouraged.

All of these stories have common themes and features that have meaning in large audiences and effectively broaden public awareness of racial profiling and its effect on the minority community. First, in many cases the stops are decidedly harsher and more punitive than the situations seem to justify. Minorities consistently argue that their encounters with the police are more punitive than encounters involving nonminorities (Lundman and Kaufman 2003). These stories attempt to communicate, and many clearly do, that minority experiences with the police are quite different. "If you happen to be a little old white lady, who has never been considered a likely suspect for a crime, has never been harassed because you look like someone else who could've committed a crime, well then, I can understand why you could see the police" as objective, impartial, unbiased, and helpful (Johnson 2001, 88).

Second, most police-citizen encounters last less than five minutes, do not involve searches, and do not include separate interrogations of the driver and passengers. Nearly all of the media reports of stops involving minorities describe lengthy (some for hours) contacts wherein searches and intensive interrogations routinely occur. Often these encounters do not result in the issuance of a citation, much less an arrest. The most effective of these stories are those that describe the heavy handedness of the police, the unfairness of their behavior, and importantly, their inability to justify the use of their time.

Third, most of us can count on one hand the number of times we have been stopped by the police. Even among particularly errant youths, the number of times they report being stopped seldom exceeds more than half a dozen encounters per year. In many of the racial profiling stories the victims report being stopped dozens of times a year. Most of us are not particularly offended when we are stopped by the police. We may be angry, frustrated, or embarrassed. We may even believe that the police stop is unjustified and want to look at the radar. Eventually we get over it, pay the ticket, and consider ourselves lucky that we don't get stopped more often. The racial profiling stories communicate a different perspective. The frequency of these stops leads us to ask questions like "What kind of car do you drive?", "How fast do you drive?", or "Did you do something to piss off the police?". When we find out that the victims, except for their skin color, are really more like us than not, we begin to question the fairness of the police. When that happens the story has had its intended effect.

Media attention to racial profiling increased steadily until 1998, and then it exploded. Eventually the volume and frequency of the stories as well as their commonalities left the public with the perception that racial profiling was more than the result of a few rogue cops (Harris 1999a). A number of organizations like the American Civil Liberties Union (ACLU) and the National Association for the Advancement of Colored Persons (NAACP), skilled in managing the media, began to actively discuss the issue (O'Reilly 2002). The ACLU chapter in Northern California developed an Internet-based Driving While Black or Brown questionnaire and encouraged individuals who believed themselves victims to complete the questionnaire (ACLU 1999).

At some point, by virtue of the intensity of the media coverage, the issue expanded beyond its drug courier context and expanded into other policing contexts. It became more than a minority issue. Large segments of the general public began to question the fairness and objectivity of the police. More importantly, elected officials, recognizing the volatility of the issue, began to ask questions of their police representatives. The issue became so intense that a police dog in Pennsylvania was accused of racial profiling when it attacked a Black child (Heumann and Cassak 2003).

WHREN ET AL. V. UNITED STATES

Of all the court cases affecting criminal procedure, none is more important to the racial profiling issue than *Whren*. Decided in 1996, it is the seminal case that most experts agree heightened our awareness of the potential abusiveness of police procedures and how they can result in the disparate treatment of minorities. Here are the facts from the Supreme Court decision. On the evening of June 10, 1993, plainclothes vice squad officers of the District of Columbia Metropolitan Police Department were patrolling a "high drug area" of the city in an unmarked car. Their suspicions were aroused when they passed a dark Pathfinder truck with temporary license plates and youthful occupants waiting at a stop sign. The truck remained stopped at the intersection for what seemed an unusually long time—more than twenty seconds. When the police car executed a U-turn in order to head back toward the truck, the Pathfinder turned suddenly to its right, without signaling, and sped off at an "unreasonable" speed. The policemen followed, and in a short while overtook the Pathfinder when it stopped behind other traffic at a red light. They pulled up alongside, and Officer Ephraim Soto stepped out of his car, approached the driver's door, identified himself as a police officer, and directed the driver (Brown) to put the vehicle in park. As Officer Soto approached the driver's window, he immediately observed two large plastic bags of what appeared to be crack cocaine in the passenger's (Whren's) hands. The occupants were arrested, and quantities of several types of illegal drugs were retrieved from the vehicle. The defendants were charged in a four-count indictment with violating various federal drug laws.

At a pretrial suppression hearing, they challenged the legality of the stop and the resulting seizure of the drugs. They argued that the stop had not been justified by probable cause, or even reasonable suspicion, to believe that petitioners were engaged in illegal drug dealing activity and that Officer Soto's grounds for approaching the vehicle—to give the driver a warning concerning traffic violations—was pretextual. The District Court denied the suppression motion, concluding that "the facts of the stop were not controverted," and "[t]here was nothing to really demonstrate that the actions of the officers were contrary to a normal traffic stop." The defendants were convicted of the charges. The Court of Appeals affirmed the convictions, holding with respect to the suppression issue that, "regardless of whether a police officer subjectively believes that the occupants of an automobile may be engaging in some other illegal behavior, a traffic stop is permissible as long as a reasonable officer in the same circumstances *could have* stopped the car for the suspected traffic violation." The Supreme Court agreed with the Court of Appeals.

It is important to note that the Court's decision in *Whren* did not create the practice of pretextual stops. Instead it validated this long standing police practice that is even encouraged by police administrators. Neither was the *Whren* decision unpredictable. It is the result of more than a decade of decisions wherein the courts were unwilling to consider the legality of the use of race in law enforcement decision making (Harris 1997; Heumann and Cassak 2003). The *Whren* decision gave the police virtually unlimited authority to stop anyone for any reason if a traffic violation had occurred (Harris 1999a). As discussed earlier, that means everyone who drives. The Court was not persuaded to apply a reasonable officer standard. Using this standard, a court would have to ask whether or not a reasonable officer *would have* made the stop. In this case a reasonable officer would clearly not have made the stop, at least for the reason they articulated. The officers were plain-clothes vice officers and as such would likely object if their supervisor told them they had to make routine stops for traffic violations. Instead the Court imposed an objective, or could-have, test. What this means is that an officer, any officer, is legally justified in making a stop for any reason, assuming a traffic violation has occurred. Furthermore, assuming no Constitutional violation occurs following the stop, any and all evidence arising from the stop is admissible, regardless of whether or not it relates to the stated reason for the stop. In many cases the traffic violation simply goes away in deference to the more serious violation, which is likely the real reason for the stop. In effect, if an officer has nothing more than a mere hunch that someone has committed a burglary, he need only follow the person a short distance and make a legal stop on the basis of an inevitable traffic violation. Once the person is stopped, the officer need only make a few interrogatory statements, courteously ask to search the car, or separately question the occupants of the car to identify incongruities in their stories in a thinly veiled effort to obtain evidence of the possible burglary.

Harris (1997) agrees that the Court's decision to impose the could-have test makes the administration of justice easier for the lower courts. The would-have test might result in more rigorous judicial scrutiny of police department regulations and practices and substantially complicate suppression hearings. However, in doing so, the Court provides too much discretion to police officers (Harris 2002; Jernigan 2000) and allows the police to circumvent the Fourth Amendment safeguards against unreasonable search and seizure (Barlow and Barlow 2002). The Court's failure to consider the effect of race on police decision making encourages racial profiling and drastically limits the effectiveness of the Fourth Amendment for the minority community (Batton and Kadleck

2004; Heumann and Cassak 2003; Jernigan 2000; Oliver 2000; O'Reilly 2002)

NEW JERSEY: RACIAL PROFILING'S GROUND ZERO

Starting in the late 1980s a series of events occurring in New Jersey substantially contributed to the creation of the racial profiling issue. While complaints of racial discrimination in traffic enforcement had been heard and investigated in other states at roughly the same time (the Wilkins case in Maryland is a notable example), none captured our attention like New Jersey. In the late 1980s and early 1990s minorities began to bitterly complain that the New Jersey State Police were unfairly targeting them as they drove on the New Jersey Turnpike. Each time they complained, the state police responded that there was no evidence that minorities were being unfairly targeted. The police were at that time correct: the police didn't keep any records that could either support or reject the allegations of unfairness.

That all changed in 1990, when a group of lawyers challenged the state through a series of suppression hearings. This case eventually became *State v. Pedro Soto*. The legal proceedings began in 1994, before State Superior Court Judge Robert Francis. The court hired Dr. John Lamberth, formerly of Temple University, to conduct what was to become the first credible racial profiling study in the nation. Using field observations to establish a baseline, Dr. Lamberth concluded that the police were targeting minorities. Specifically, he found that the proportion of minorities stopped and searched is substantially higher than the proportion of minorities who are actually on the roadway and that these differences could not be attributed to random chance. As if this were not enough, the court conducted a separate inquiry into the state police records and found that the troopers had received a clear message to target minorities through various training exercise and criminal intelligence circulars (Harris 2002). Eventually the court found substantial credibility in the plaintiff's arguments and ruled against the state.

Shortly after this case was decided, three other events occurred that essentially sealed the fate of the state police. In 1998, two troopers on the New Jersey Turnpike stopped a van containing four Black youths. The initial justification for the stop was a speeding violation. During the stop the van inadvertently rolled forward. The startled troopers opened fire on the youths and seriously wounded most of them. Eventually, an inquiry revealed that the patrol car used by the troopers was not even equipped with radar. Next, the superintendent of the New Jersey State Police, Colonel Carl Williams, made a public statement in defense of his troopers' use of race as an indicator of potential criminality. He stated, "Two weeks ago the President of the United States went to Mexico to talk to the President of Mexico about drugs. He didn't go to Ireland. He didn't go to England" (quoted by Heumann and Cassak 2003). In doing so, he suggested that the drug courier problem was primarily a problem involving Hispanics. He was fired by Governor Christine Whitman the next day. Finally, the New Jersey Attorney General, who had previously defended the state police, issued a comprehensive report critical of the police and essentially agreeing with the court's decision. Among other things, Attorney General Peter Verniero acknowledged that the state police reward system encouraged big drug busts and that the police, in response to this enticement, attempted to maximize their hit rates by inappropriately using race as an indicator of criminal drug possession.

Eventually, the state police were forced by the United States Department of Justice to accept one of the most comprehensive consent decrees ever imposed on a police agency. This decree, discussed in detail in Chapter 5, effectively controls nearly every facet of the New Jersey State Police organization. As a result, political leaders and police administrators became quite concerned that a similar series of events could occur in their own jurisdictions.

SUMMARY

Until about a decade ago the term *racial profiling* was largely unknown in the popular American lexicon. In about the mid-1990s, during the height of the war on drugs, minorities increasingly began to question the disparate effect caused by the use of drug courier profiles in routine police decision making. Six important factors coalesced into what is now commonly referred to as the racial profiling controversy. First, the protection of minority rights has been a critical issue in American society since the very beginnings of the republic. Historical evidence of police abuses are numerous and have created an adversarial relationship between the police and the minority community. While race has not proven to be a critical factor in police decision making, it is evident that race does play some role, and usually not to the advantage of minorities. Efforts by the police to proactively engage the minority community in a productive dialogue have been largely ineffective. Even the promising programs that fall under the general classification of community-oriented policing have some potential for adversely affecting the minority community.

Second, during the 1960s the police began to recognize the value of offender profiles within their law enforcement function. Hijacker profiles are credited with reducing the frequency of airline hijackings during the late 1960s. Criminal profiling is recognized as a valuable investigatory tool. To capitalize on the success of these strategies, many police departments, with the guidance of federal law enforcement agencies, developed drug courier profiles. These profiles were a part of an overall enforcement emphasis of the nation's war on drugs. Eventually, race and ethnicity were included in profiles. The inclusion of race and ethnicity, whether explicitly or implicitly, was intended to increase officers' efficiency by allowing them to recognize common factors among potential drug couriers. Unfortunately, there is little empirical support for the inclusion of these factors in a profile. As a result, it appears that routine drug interdiction efforts have resulted in a disparate effect.

Third, the traffic stop is one of the most effective enforcement tools available to the police. There are literally thousands of traffic laws that act as probable cause–generating events producing a legal justification for a stop. This, coupled with the inevitability of violation, affords the police the flexibility to stop virtually anyone at any time. Furthermore, because most citizens are not aware that they can refuse an officer's request for consent to search, the police have a nearly limitless ability to conduct invasive searches of citizens without reasonable suspicion. Fourth, in the mid-1990s the media began to focus its attention on stories from individuals alleging to be victims of racial profiling. Advocacy organizations, well skilled at managing the media, successfully created an image of the police as little more than racist thugs. Fifth, in 1996, the United States Supreme Court handed down a unanimous decision in *Whren* that validated the use of pretextual stops. A pretextual stop occurs when the police stop an individual for one reason (usually a minor traffic violation) but actually intend to conduct a more thorough investigation because they believe (usually without reasonable suspicion) that the person is engaged in a more serious criminal activity. The Court applied an objective test to the officers' behavior and ruled that as long as the officers had a reasonable suspicion that the person violated the traffic laws, then the stop and the resulting consensual search do not violate the Fourth Amendment protections against unreasonable search and seizure.

Finally, New Jersey is ground zero of the racial profiling controversy. Minorities in New Jersey were successful in convincing a court that they had been targeted for enforcement by the state police on the New Jersey Turnpike. The court commissioned what was to become the first full-scale racial profiling study in the nation. The results of this study were convincing, and eventually the state police were forced to accept an unprecedented level of external supervision in the form of a comprehensive consent decree.

DISCUSSION QUESTIONS

1. Which of the six issues or practices discussed in this chapter contributed the most to the racial profiling controversy, and why?
2. Given the disproportionately higher representation of minorities under supervision by the criminal justice system, are the police justified in focusing patrol resources in minority neighborhoods?
3. Despite the risk, should the police continue aggressive crime suppression activities in known high crime areas even though these strategies may result in an overrepresentation of minorities in police stops?
4. How does an individual's race affect his or her attitudes toward the police?
5. In what ways could the police improve relations with the minority community?
6. To what extend did the United States Supreme Court's decision in *Whren* encourage racial profiling, or did it?

CASE STUDIES

1. The police chief has been approached by a neighborhood association from a predominately Black neighborhood and asked to address a recent increase in daytime robberies occurring in

convenience stores, gas stations, liquor stores, pawn shops, banks, and other retail locations. The crime analyst has offered the following options for addressing this crime problem:

a. Neighborhood watch

b. Crime prevention through environmental design

c. Training of clerks

d. Surveillance

e. Saturation patrol

Discuss each of these enforcement alternatives with respect to their potential for a disparate effect with respect to race.

2. A recent intelligence report indicates that a Jamaican gang is expanding its drug trafficking operation in a mid-sized Midwestern community. Discuss how this information should be disseminated to officers. Specifically outline how you would authenticate the validity of the intelligence and the steps you would take to avoid a potential overrepresentation of all Blacks in enforcement activities.

3. During a public meeting of the local chapter of the National Association for the Advancement of Colored People you (a police chief) are asked by an African-American mother how she should prepare her teenage son for racial profiling. How would you respond?

chapter **2**

WHAT WE KNOW AND DON'T KNOW

Are Incidents Involving Physical Resistance and Confrontation
More Frequent?

Do Officer Characteristics Matter?

Overall Limitations of the Research

Summary

Discussion Questions

Case Studies

INTRODUCTION

When awareness of racial profiling began during the early 1990s
more than a few police administrators and scholars were surprised
that not a great deal was known about police patrol procedures.
Despite the prominence of the patrol function within policing programs, very little research had been conducted that could describe,
much less explain, its procedures and specifically what motivates
patrol officers to initiate a traffic stop or citizen contact. Even less
was known about the effect of race on police decision making
within the context of traffic stops. The most comprehensive study
(Gardiner 1969) largely ignores race and does not address how
police officers make the decision to stop. The remaining studies of
national significance focus primarily on how driving habits affect
enforcement patterns (Walker 2001).

In 2001, the United States Department of Justice (Bureau of
Justice Statistics) issued the results of a comprehensive nationwide
study of police-citizen contacts that includes extensive descriptive
information about traffic stops. They report that 10.3 percent of all
licensed drivers are stopped at least once by the police, and 2.1
percent are stopped two or more times. Of those stopped, 77 percent are White, 11.6 percent are Black, 8.4 percent are Hispanic,
and three percent are another race. Age and gender appear to
increase an individual's chance of being stopped. Among teenage
drivers 18.3 percent are stopped at least once. Nearly 61 percent of
all individuals stopped are male. Most stops (54.2 percent) result
in the issuance of a ticket, citation, or summons to appear.
Searches are conducted in 6.6 percent of the stops. The police
handcuff 3.1 percent and arrest 3 percent of all individuals
stopped. Force, characterized as excessive by the citizen, occurs in
0.5 percent of all stops. Although the focus of the Bureau of Justice
Statistics report is not on racial profiling per se, the researchers

conclude that the police are more likely to conduct a search if the driver is young, male, and Black (Langan et al. 2001).

The next major national attempt to define the racial profiling issue came a year later when the United States General Accounting Office published a survey of the literature on racial profiling. The authors conclude that each of the five quantitative studies available at that time have significant methodological problems that cause them to question the validity of the analysts' findings. In addition, the authors conclude that no nationwide sources of information are available to determine if race is an important factor in the police decision on whom to stop (United States General Accounting Office 2000). The first and most instructive research on racial profiling came from the early court cases filed in New Jersey, Maryland, and Illinois. In these situations the courts either commissioned outside researchers to conduct research or accepted research conducted by the plaintiffs on the effect of race or ethnicity on police decision making during highway drug interdiction programs. While this research was clearly sufficient to convince the courts to rule in favor of the plaintiffs, and to some degree increase the general public's awareness of the issue, it produced more questions than answers. Many of these questions remain unanswered today. This early research has been criticized because it focuses on a relatively narrow enforcement context (highway drug interdiction), and the researcher's findings were not subjected to rigorous peer review (Walker 2001).

The purpose of this chapter is to outline the research on racial profiling. Since the mid 1990s as many as 400 racial profiling studies have been conducted throughout the nation. Nearly every major city has conducted some sort of racial profiling study. While this survey of the literature is by no means definitive, it is representative of the research. It includes findings of research conducted in every region of the nation, by every type of department, and within every enforcement context. In addition, this survey is representative of the various methodological techniques used by racial profiling researchers.

DEFINITIONS AND MEASURES

As racial profiling matures into a distinct research agenda, more attention is being given to its key definitions and measures. The controversy is now at a critical juncture, and serious debates are occurring on how to develop conceptual and operational definitions of racial profiling and measure its extent within police procedures. While a universally acceptable definition has not yet surfaced, there is some agreement within the field. Closely related issues have emerged on how to measure who gets stopped and, more importantly, who is available to be stopped. Determining the racial proportions of individuals stopped by the police, while a relatively straightforward measurement process, is potentially inaccurate. Finding an acceptable benchmark or baseline with which to determine the racial proportions of individuals who are available to be stopped is the most important methodological issue in the racial profiling research agenda. The following sections discuss these issues briefly. A more detailed discussion on the methodological issues facing the racial profiling research agenda is offered in a later chapter.

Definitions

Researchers struggle with an acceptable definition of the term *racial profiling*. Some prefer to use broader terms like *race based policing* (Cordner, Williams, and Zuniga 2000, 2002; Withrow 2002) or *race biased policing* (Fridell et al. 2001), arguing that the term *racial profiling* is too restrictive and does not fully communicate the importance of the issue, that is, the effect of race on overall police decision making. In addition, Fridell, et al. (2001) argues that the term *profiling* confuses the issue with other legitimate and effective methods of policing. These terms are not interchangeable. Consumers of this literature should be cautious and determine exactly what social phenomenon the researcher is attempting to evaluate. Racial profiling may be an issue limited to street level enforcement. Race biased policing may suggest racial bias on the part of an administrator while developing deployment strategies or disseminating intelligence information.

A few authors have attempted to develop definitions suggesting levels or degrees of racial profiling. MacDonald (2003) distinguishes between soft and hard profiling. She defines soft profiling as the use of race as one of many factors in police decision making. Hard profiling occurs when race is used as the only factor in a police officer's decision to make a stop. Cleary (2000) recognizes the lack of consensus on the definition among researchers and identifies two levels of racial profiling: narrow and broad. Narrow profiling "occurs when a police officer stops, questions, arrests, and/or searches someone solely on the basis of the person's race or ethnicity" (p. 5). Broad profiling "occurs when a law enforcement officer uses race or ethnicity as one of several factors when deciding to stop, question, arrest, and/or search someone" (p. 6). Emerging from these definitions is the notion that in some situations the use of race in police decision making may be acceptable and even appropriate. Even the most ardent critics of the police would not deny them the use of race as part of a physical description of a known criminal suspect. It is the routine use of race, ethnicity, and national origin by the police as a general indicator of criminal suspiciousness that appears to cross the threshold into racial profiling.

While many researchers attempt to develop specific definitions of racial profiling, a surprising number merely imply a definition within the context of their discussion (Batton and Kadleck 2004). Most definitions of racial profiling can be classified into one of two general categories. The first, and most common, category defines racial profiling within the context of the police decision making process and its inappropriate use of race, ethnicity, or national origin as a general indicator of criminal suspiciousness. Within this category the most popular definition used in the literature was developed by Ramirez, McDevitt, and Farrell (2000) in a resource guide published by the United States Department of Justice intended to provide researchers with the information necessary to conduct racial profiling studies. They define racial profiling as "any police-initiated action that relies on the race, ethnicity, or national origin rather than the behavior of an individual or information that leads the police to a particular individual who has been identified as being, or having been, engaged in criminal activity" (p. 3). Other examples within this category include

> ...whenever police routinely use race as a negative signal that, along with an accumulation of other signals, causes an officer to react with suspicion. (Kennedy, 1997, 11)
>
> ...the tactic of stopping someone only because of the color of his or her skin and a fleeting suspicion that the person is engaging in criminal behavior. (Meeks 2000, 4–5)
>
> ...the discriminatory practice by police of treating Blackness (or brownness) as in indication of possible criminality. (Muharrar 1998, 1)
>
> ...the practice of questioning Blacks in suspicious circumstances in disproportionate numbers in the expectation that

they are more likely than people of other races to be criminals. (Taylor and Whitney 1999, 507)

...any action taken by a state trooper during a traffic stop that is based on racial or ethnic stereotypes and that has the effect of treating minority motorists differently than non-minority motorists (Verniero and Zoubek 1999, 5)

The second category focuses on the overall disparate effect by race of a traffic enforcement program. For example, the Police Foundation's (2003) multi-jurisdictional study in Kansas argued that racial profiling occurs when minorities are stopped at disproportionately higher rates than they are represented within the benchmark that measures the proportional racial representation of actual roadway users. Other examples within this category include

...whether Blacks...were being stopped in numbers disproportionate to their presence in the driving population. (Harris 1999b, 281)

The racial representation of individuals stopped by troopers should be equal to the racial representation of the driving age population and of those involved in traffic collisions. (Washington State Patrol 2001)

The overall goal of the study was to determine if Maryland State Police stop and search Black motorists at a rate disproportionate to their numbers on the highway. (American Civil Liberties Union 2000, 1)

...the intentional consideration of race in a manner that disparately impacts certain racial minority groups, contributing to the disproportionate investigation, detention, and mistreatment of innocent members of those groups. (Banks, 2001, 1075–1076)

Normally a researcher is free to use whatever type of definition he or she chooses as long as it is clearly articulated within the text of the report. Of more concern here is whether or not the researcher actually collects information that is responsive to the definition. There is some evidence that the type of definition used by a researcher has a profound effect on the researcher's conclusions. This issue is discussed thoroughly in Chapter Three.

Measures

There are two principal measures in racial profiling research. The first, police stop data, measures the racial and ethnic proportions of individuals stopped by the police. In addition, most racial profiling researchers are interested in what happens to individuals once they are stopped and measure poststop occurrences like searches, arrests, and incidents of physical confrontation. Most research relies on data collected by the officers who conduct the stops. Because police departments do not routinely record information on stops in sufficient detail to support racial profiling research, the data collection processes are normally independent of and in addition to their routine record keeping systems. In other words, police officers are required to complete an additional form after each stop or citizen contact. As a result, data collection programs are intentionally temporary and terminated once sufficient data have been collected. Most police stop data is collected via machine-readable paper forms. Some departments collect police stop data using mobile display terminals, laptops, or pocket computers. In some studies stop data are collected by dispatchers. Because of the logistical complexities associated with collecting large numbers of forms or data from multiple sources, state level researchers tend to use existing police data. In more complex studies, such as those conducted in several cities of various sizes dispersed over a wide geographical area, researchers use an array of stop data collection methods (see Table 2.1).

There is some concern that the data collected by police officers, cognizant of the probability that the data will be used against them or their departments, will be inaccurate, incomplete, or false. In addition, there is some evidence that the data collection process interrupts routine enforcement and results in a process of disengagement or de-policing, wherein the police dramatically change their behavior during the data collection process. These and other critical methodological issues are discussed in detail in Chapter 3, and various solutions are offered in Chapter 6.

The second key measure is the racial and ethnic proportions of individuals available to be stopped by the police. This measure is normally referred to as a benchmark or baseline. Stop data information relating to the racial and ethnic proportional representation of individuals stopped by the police are all but meaningless unless compared against an acceptable benchmark that accurately

TABLE 2.1 Police Stop Data Collection Methods Used in Racial Profiling Studies

STUDY	DATA COLLECTION METHOD[a]
Anonymous (Meehan and Ponder 2002)	MDTs, laptops, PDAs/CAD records
California (CHP 2000)	Existing data
Connecticut (Cox et al. 2001)	Paper forms/MDTs, Laptops, PDAs
Denver, CO (DPD 2002)	Paper forms
Kansas (Police Foundation 2003)	Varied by department
Maryland (Lamberth 1996)	Existing data
Massachusetts (Farrell et al. 2004)	Existing data
Minnesota (MDPS 2003)	MDTs, laptops, PDAs
Missouri (Rojek, Rosenfeld, and Decker 2004)	Paper forms, MDTs, PDAs
Nevada (McCorkle 2003)	Paper forms
New Jersey Turnpike (Lamberth 1994)	Existing data
New York, NY (Spitzer 1999)	Paper forms
North Carolina (Zingraff et al. 2000)	Existing data
Overland Park, KS (Novak 2004)	CAD records
Richmond, VA (Smith and Petrocelli 2001)	MDTs, laptops, PDAs
Sacramento, CA (Greenwald 2003)	Paper forms
San Antonio, TX (Lamberth 2003a)	Paper forms
San Diego, CA (Cordner, Williams, and Zuniga 2000)	Paper forms
San Diego, A (Cordner, Williams, and Zuniga 2002)	Paper forms
San Jose, CA (Landsdowne 2002)	MDTs, laptops, PDAs
Sedgwick County, KS (Withrow 2003)	Paper forms
Texas (TDPS 2000)	Existing data
Washington (WSP 2001)	Existing data
Wichita, KS (Withrow 2002)	Paper forms

[a]CAD, computer aided dispatch; MDT, mobile display terminal; PDA, personal digital assistant (pocket computer)

measures the proportional racial and ethnic representation of individuals available to be stopped. For example, if a researcher finds that 15 percent of the individuals stopped are Black and 15 percent of the individuals available to be stopped are Black, then he is likely to conclude that racial profiling, or at least racial disparity, is not occurring in the routine enforcement program of that department.

By far the most popular benchmarks are based on population. Some researchers use the entire population (see Withrow 2002, 2003), but many use a subset of the population like individuals over sixteen years of age or licensed drivers (see Smith and Petrocelli 2001). In a few cases population-based benchmarks are adjusted by crime rates or calls for service (California Highway Patrol [CHP] 2000). Benchmarks based on field observations (Lamberth 1994, 1996) were among the first used by racial profiling researchers. Typically the researcher conducts a series of systematic observations and records the race, gender, and approximate age of drivers in selected locations. An emerging benchmark creating some interest within the academic community is based on accident rates (Alpert, Smith, and Dunham 2003; Washington State Patrol [WSP] 2001). Long used by traffic safety engineers as a means to determine the qualitative features of drivers, these benchmarks are based on the idea that not at fault drivers in two-vehicle accidents are randomly selected and therefore closely approximate the driving population. A relatively new trend among researches is to conduct studies using competing benchmarks in an effort to determine which are more valid or reliable (Withrow 2004b) (see Table 2.2).

Each of these benchmarks has advantages and disadvantages. None have received universal acceptance within the research or practitioner communities. A more comprehensive discussion on the utility of the various benchmarks used by racial profiling researchers is included in Chapter 3.

THE STRUCTURE OF RACIAL PROFILING INQUIRY

Racial profiling studies tend to be organized into two distinct analytical components. The first is a comparison of the proportional racial and ethnic representation of individuals stopped (as defined by the police stop data) with the proportional racial and ethnic representation of individuals available to be stopped (as defined by

TABLE 2.2   Basis for Benchmarks Used by Racial Profiling Researchers

STUDY	BENCHMARK
Anonymous (Meehan and Ponder 2002)	Field observations
California (CHP 2000)	Population, accidents, motorist assists
Connecticut (Cox et al. 2001)	Population
Denver, CO (DPD 2002)[a]	None
Kansas (Police Foundation 2003)	Field observations
Maryland (Lamberth 1996)	Field observations
Massachusetts (Farrell et al. 2004)	Population, citations
Minnesota (MDPS 2003)	Population
Missouri (Rojek, Rosenfeld, and Decker 2004)	Population
Nevada (McCorkle 2003)	Population
New Jersey Turnpike (Lamberth 1994)	Field observations
New York, NY (Spitzer 1999)	Population
North Carolina (Zingraff et al. 2000)	Population
Overland Park, KS (Novak 2004)	Population
Richmond, VA (Smith and Petrocelli 2001)	Population
Sacramento, CA (Greenwald 2003)	Population
San Antonio, TX (Lamberth 2003a)	Field observations
San Diego, CA (Cordner, Williams, and Zuniga, 2000)	Population
San Diego, CA (Cordner, Williams, and Zuniga 2002)	Population
San Jose, CA (Landsdowne 2002)	Population
Sedgwick County, KS (Withrow 2003)	Population
Texas (TDPS 2000)	Population
Washington (WSP 2001)	Population, traffic accidents
Wichita, KA (Withrow 2002)	Population

[a]The Denver study did not utilize a benchmark. As a result, they could not report whether minorities are over represented in traffic stops.

the benchmark). These portions of the studies tend to receive the most public attention. Often these findings are represented in simple tables, charts, and graphs and are more often than not the findings upon which analysts base their overall conclusions of whether racial profiling is occurring within a jurisdiction. Because of the importance of the police stop as a gate keeping function of the criminal justice process, the importance of these analyses cannot be overlooked. The most comprehensive studies account for factors like the reason for the stop, time of day, crime rate, neighborhood variables, and enforcement context of the stop in an effort to comprehensively describe how, when, and why stops occur. At least three studies have sufficiently robust data with which to conduct the multivariate analyses necessary to isolate the relative influence of various factors affecting the decision to stop (Novak 2004; Smith and Petrocelli 2001; Withrow 2002).

The second analytical component focuses on the features (searches, arrests, physical confrontations) that occur during and after the initial stop with respect to the race or ethnicity of the citizen. This portion of the analysis is potentially the most revealing and instructive of routine patrol operations. The general question asked is whether or not the stops differ qualitatively with respect to the race or ethnicity of the individual stopped. Are minorities stopped for different reasons than nonminorities? Are minorities searched or arrested more often than nonminorities? Are stops involving minority drivers more likely to include incidents of physical confrontation? These and many more features are typical. More sophisticated studies also take into account the demographic characteristics of officers and ask whether the race, age, gender, and experience of the officers make any difference in what occurs during a stop (Novak 2004; Smith and Petrocelli 2001; Withrow 2002).

SALIENT RESEARCH QUESTIONS

Racial profiling studies vary considerably with respect to their focus and comprehensiveness. Nearly all studies ask whether minorities are disproportionately overrepresented in traffic or pedestrian stops. Most collect information on poststop behaviors like searches, arrests, the duration of the stop, and incidents of physical confrontation. A few consider the impact of the demographic features of police officers. Throughout the literature seven salient research questions have emerged. These are outlined and discussed in the following sections. No doubt, as the racial profiling research agenda matures, many more questions and dimensions will be explored, but for now, the following questions appear to be the most important.

Are Minorities Stopped More Frequently?

Of the twenty-four studies analyzed here that ask this question, eighteen found that Blacks, eight found that Hispanics, and one found that other races are stopped at disproportionately higher rates than they are represented in the benchmark used by the researchers. Except for the Denver study, all of the studies ask this question with respect to Blacks, twenty ask it with respect to Hispanics, and only five ask it with respect to other races (see Table 2.3). This finding explains to some degree why racial profiling is often referred to as *driving while Black* or *driving while brown*.

Even though racial disparity is evident in police stopping behavior, particularly with respect to Blacks, not all researchers are willing to conclude that racial profiling occurs. In only six (Lamberth 1994, 1996; Meehan and Ponder 2002; Minnesota Department of Public Safety [MDPS] 2003; Police Foundation 2003; Spitzer 1999) of the eighteen studies finding disparity with respect to Blacks do the researchers conclude that racial profiling occurs. In only two (MDPS 2000; Police Foundation 2003) of the eight studies finding disparity with respect to Hispanics do the researchers conclude that racial profiling occurs. When they explicitly state it, these researchers define racial profiling within the context of the police decision making process and its inappropriate consideration of race, ethnicity, or national origin as a general indicator of suspiciousness. None of these researchers use the more operational definition that considers the disparate effect of an enforcement program as evidence of racial profiling. In effect, these researchers use the disparate effect of the enforcement program as *prima facie,* or conclusive, evidence of racial profiling in police decision making and make no attempt to measure the factors that influence a police officer's decision to stop.

Other researchers are more cautious, methodologically conservative, and cognizant of the complexities of the police decision making process. They recognize that any number of factors (e.g., crime rates, deployment, differential driving behavior) could produce a disparate effect with respect to race and do not appear

TABLE 2.3   Are Minorities Stopped More Frequently?

STUDY	BLACKS	HISPANICS	OTHER RACES	PROFILING?
Anonymous (Meehan and Ponder 2002)	Yes	NR	NR	Yes
California (CHP 2000)	No	No	No	No
Connecticut (Cox et al. 2001)	Yes	No	NR	No
Denver, CO (DPD 2002)[a]	NR	NR	NR	No
Kansas (Police Foundation 2003)	Yes	Yes	NR	Yes
Maryland (Lamberth 1996)	Yes	NR	NR	Yes
Massachusetts (Farrell et al. 2004)	Yes	Yes	NR	No
Minnesota (MDPS 2003)	Yes	Yes	Yes	Yes
Missouri (Rojek, Rosenfeld, and Decker 2004)	Yes	No	NR	No
Nevada (McCorkle 2003)	Yes	Yes	NR	No
New Jersey Turnpike (Lamberth 1994)	Yes	NR	NR	Yes
New York, NY (Spitzer 1999)	Yes	No	NR	Yes
North Carolina (Zingraff et al. 2000)	Yes	No	NR	No
Overland Park, KS (Novak 2004)	Yes	No	No	No
Richmond, VA (Smith and Petrocelli 2001)	Yes	Yes	NR	No
Sacramento, CA (Greenwald 2003)	Yes	No	NR	No
San Antonio, TX (Lamberth 2003a)	No	No	NR	No
San Diego, CA (Cordner, Williams, and Zuniga 2000)	Yes	Yes	NR	No
San Diego, CA (Cordner, Williams, and Zuniga 2002)	Yes	Yes	NR	No
San Jose, CA (Landsdowne 2002)	Yes	Yes	NR	No
Sedgwick County, KS (Withrow 2003)	No	No	No	No
Texas (TDPS 2000)	No	No	NR	No
Washington (WSP 2001)	No	No	NR	No
Wichita, KS (Withrow 2002)	Yes	No	No	No

[a]The Denver study did not utilize a benchmark. As a result they are not able to report whether minorities are over represented in traffic stops.
NR, not reported; No, no disparity found; Yes, disparity found.

willing to conclude racial profiling on the basis of a disparate effect alone (Cordner, Williams, and Zuniga 2000, 2002; CHP 2000; Cox et al. 2001; Denver Police Department [DPD] 2002; Farrell et al. 2004; Greenwald 2003; Landsdowne 2002; McCorkle 2003; Novak 2004; Rojek, Rosenfeld, and Decker 2004; Smith and Petrocelli 2001; Texas Department of Public Safety [TDPS] 2000; WSP 2001; Withrow 2002, 2003; Zingraff et al. 2000).

Are There Differences in the Reasons for Stops?

Nearly all state statutes and local ordinances mandating the collection of racial profiling data recognize the importance of collecting information on the reason for stops. Even in the absence of a statutory requirement, many researchers include this data in their studies. This information attempts to address two key issues in the racial profiling controversy. First, there are literally thousands of legal reasons a police officer may use to stop an individual. Some violations are quite serious (e.g., driving while intoxicated), and others are quite benign (e.g., dirty license plate), but all provide the probable cause necessary for a police officer to initiate a traffic stop. The critical part of this research question is whether minorities are stopped for relatively minor violations because the police, in alleged accordance with their alleged prejudicial beliefs, want to conduct a search for a violation of the law for which they do not have sufficient probable cause to initiate a search, in other words, a pretextual stop. If for example, a substantially larger proportion of minorities are stopped for relatively subjective reasons (e.g., inattentive driving), then one might conclude that the police are targeting them unfairly.

Second, many of the more comprehensive and sophisticated studies attempt to draw some correlation between the severity of the reason for the stop and the outcome of the contact. Ideally, there should be some positive correlation. For example, stops for relatively serious violations (e.g., driving under the influence) should result in more punitive outcomes (e.g., an arrest rather than a warning). If, however, a substantial proportion of minority drivers are ticketed for violations that nonminorities typically receive a warning for, then the researcher might conclude that the police are using minor traffic code violations to target minorities unfairly.

Of the twenty-four studies included in this portion of the analysis, thirteen include information on the reason for the stop (see Table 2.4). Of those, only five report substantial differences in the reason for the stop between racial groups (DPD 2002; Greenwald 2003; McCorkle 2003; Novak 2004; Withrow 2002). From these no pattern of abuse with respect to race or ethnicity has emerged. In most studies the attributes for this variable are relatively limited. For example, the Richmond, Virginia, study (Smith and Petrocelli 2001) and the Overland Park, Kansas, study (Novak 2004) only include three and four attributes, respectively. Typically, these include categories like moving violations, defective equipment, nonmoving violations, unsafe driving, or speeding. These overly broad categories substantially restrict most attempts at detailed analyses. In the Wichita, Kansas (Withrow 2002), and Sedgwick County, Kansas (Withrow 2003), studies the researcher included twenty-five attributes in this field. This enabled him to provide a more detailed analysis of the differences, if any, in the reason for the stop with respect to the race or ethnicity of the driver. He found no differences with respect to race or ethnicity in any of the offense categories. However, even in this case the attributes were nominal, so the researcher could not establish a numerical correlation between the severity of the reason for the stop and the punitiveness of the police response.

In a few cases (DPD 2002; Greenwald 2003; Withrow 2002) the researchers were able to determine the level of discretion available to the officer based on the indicated reason for the stop. For example, Withrow (2002) considered stops involving traffic accidents, serious traffic violations, and in response to citizen calls for assistance to be relatively low discretion, that is, more likely to require some action by the police officer. On the other hand, stops involving officer-observed nonhazardous violations, nonserious equipment violations, or suspicious circumstances are considered high discretion, that is, allowing the officer the option to take no action. The most serious analytical concern is that all researchers measure the reason for the stop nominally. In doing so, they eliminate any opportunity at finding a numerical correlation between the relative seriousness of the reported reason for the stop and the relative punitiveness of the stop's disposition. As a result, researchers are forced to develop findings from imprecise cross tabulations.

TABLE 2.4   Are There Differences in the Reasons for the Stops?

Study	Reason for Stop Reported?	Differences with Respect to Race/Ethnicity?[a]
Anonymous (Meehan and Ponder 2002)	No	NA
California (CHP 2000)	No	NA
Connecticut (Cox et al. 2001)	Yes	No
Denver, CO (DPD 2002)	Yes	Whites appear more likely to be stopped for moving violations
Kansas (Police Foundation 2003)	No	NA
Maryland (Lamberth 1996)	No	NA
Massachusetts (Farrell et al. 2004)	No	NA
Minnesota (MDPS 2003)	Yes	NR
Missouri (Rojek, Rosenfeld, and Decker 2004)	Yes	NR
Nevada (McCorkle 2003)	Yes	Whites are less likely to be stopped for a nonmoving violation
New Jersey Turnpike (Lamberth 1994)	No	NA
New York, NY (Spitzer 1999)	No	NA
North Carolina (Zingraff et al. 2000)	No	NA
Overland Park, KS (Novak 2004)	Yes	Whites are more likely to be stopped for moving violations, unsafe driving, and speeding
Richmond, VA (Smith and Petrocelli 2001)	Yes	No
Sacramento, CA (Greenwald 2003)	Yes	Black drivers are more likely to be stopped for nonhazardous violations
San Antonio, TX (Lamberth 2003a)	No	NA
San Diego, CA (Cordner, Williams, and Zuniga 2000)	Yes	No
San Diego, CA (Cordner, Williams, and Zuniga 2002)	Yes	No
San Jose, CA (Landsdowne 2002)	No	NA
Sedgwick County, KS (Withrow 2003)	Yes	No
Texas (TDPS 2000)	No	NA
Washington (WSP 2001)	Yes	No
Wichita, KS (Withrow 2002)	Yes	Blacks are more likely to be stopped if officer has high level of discretion

[a]NA, not applicable; NR, not reported; No, no difference found.

Are Minorities Searched More Frequently?

Although not all researchers ask this question, those who do consistently find that racial and ethnic minorities are searched more frequently than nonminorities during traffic and pedestrian stops. The one exception is in Richmond, Virginia, where Smith and Petrocelli (2001) found that overall, Black drivers are no more likely to be searched than White drivers. In fact, White drivers in Richmond are more often the subjects of consent searches than Black drivers (see Table 2.5).

Studies that differentiate between the type or justification for searches reveal more about the searching patterns of police officers and are more instructive to our understanding of racial profiling and the dynamics of traffic stops. Generally, there are six types or justification for searches. These include consent, inventory, stop and frisk, warrant, incident to arrest, and plain view. Searches incident to an arrest, inventory searches, and searches conducted on the basis of a warrant, while an important part of police procedures, are of limited value to our understanding of racial profiling. These searches are either required by law, required by department policy, or authorized by an impartial magistrate after the officer establishes probable cause. In other words, the officer's discretion is limited. Furthermore, if minorities are arrested at disproportionately higher rates than nonminorities, then minorities will also be overrepresented in searches incident to arrest and inventory searches. Unfortunately, most racial profiling data cannot establish the temporal order of arrests and searches. In most cases it is unclear whether the findings of the search resulted in the arrest or whether an arrest created the need for the search. Plain view searches occur when a police officer approaches an individual and perceives evidence of criminal activity. For example, when a police officer approaches a motorist stopped for a violation of the traffic code and notices a container of marijuana on the dash board, the officer has an absolute right to arrest and charge the individual. As a result, plain view searches reveal little about the potential for abuse of police power within the context of the racial profiling controversy.

Consent and stop and frisk searches are the most critical types of searches to our understanding of racial profiling. During these instances the police officer has an extremely high level of discretion. Stop and frisk searches are a common form of warrantless searches, but they are limited in scope. In 1968, the United States Supreme Court authorized the police practice of stopping and searching individuals without establishing probable cause for the narrow purpose of determining whether or not the individual has a weapon. The officer must be able to articulate a reasonable suspicion that the individual has a weapon. The Court recognized the officers' legitimate need to conduct cursory "pat down" searches in situations that are perceived to be threatening for the sole purpose of identifying a weapon that could be used to harm the officer if the officer has reasonable suspicion that the individual possess a weapon (*Terry v. Ohio* 1968). The Court has limited the scope of these searches to a level of invasiveness necessary to insure officer safety (*Minnesota v. Dickerson* 1993).

David Harris (2002), however, argues that the totality of the Court's decisions since *Terry* in stop and frisk cases have expanded the police authority to the point that nearly any individual is subject to a cursory search regardless of whether the officer has reasonable suspicion. Similarly, police officers enjoy a very high level of discretion to conduct consent searches. Consent searches require no reasonable suspicion. Literally, an officer can ask anyone, anytime, for any reason, or for no reason at all, for permission to conduct a search as long as the search is voluntary (*Ohio v. Robinette* 1996). As discussed in the previous chapter, most people comply. Because stop and frisk and consent searches are highly discretionary and difficult to control, they deserve the most attention from racial profiling researchers, yet only a handful of researchers evaluate these types of searches separately and comprehensively (DPD 2002; Smith and Petrocelli 2001; Withrow 2002).

Of the twenty-four studies included in this portion of the analysis, sixteen asked whether minorities are searched more frequently than nonminorities. Of these, all but one (Smith and Petrocelli 2001) found that minorities are more likely to be searched (Cordner, Williams, and Zuniga 2000, 2002; Cox et al. 2001; DPD 2002; Farrell et al. 2004; Greenwald 2003; Lamberth 1996, 2003a; McCorkle 2003; MDPS 2003; Rojek, Rosenfeld, and Decker 2004; Smith and Petrocelli 2002; WSP 2001; Withrow 2002, 2003; Zingraff et al. 2000).

An important corollary to this research question is whether police officers are more likely to find minorities in possession of contraband. If so, then one can legitimately argue that differential searching rates (by race) are somewhat justified. This is, however, not the case. Of the nine studies that considered this question all but two (DPD 2002; Greenwald 2003) found that searches involving minorities or vehicles operated by minorities are less likely to produce contraband. In Denver, Colorado, the researcher reports that the hit rates are the same for Blacks and Whites and lower for Hispanics (DPD 2002). In Sacramento, California, and in Maryland hit rates are equal across all racial groups (Greenwald 2003; Lamberth 1996). In Wichita, Kansas, the researcher found that hit rates are higher for Blacks than for Whites and lower for Hispanics (Withrow 2002). Beyond these exceptions, the most consistent findings do not justify the more frequent searching of minorities based on an increased probability of finding contraband.

Are Stops Involving Minorities More Punitive?

Of the twenty-four studies included in this analysis, thirteen address this research question, and all of those report differences in the dispositions of stops with respect to the race or ethnicity of the individual stopped. Two report that Blacks and Hispanics are more likely than Whites to receive a citation pursuant to a traffic stop (Cox et al. 2001; Farrell et al. 2004). Nine report that minorities are more likely to be arrested than nonminorities (Cordner, Williams, and Zuniga 2000; Cox et al. 2001; DPD 2002; Rojek, Rosenfeld, and Decker 2004; McCorkle 2003; Spitzer 1999; WSP 2001; Withrow 2002, 2003). Two studies report that Black drivers are less likely to receive a citation and more likely to be arrested than drivers of other races or ethnicities (DPD 2002; McCorkle 2003).

The Sedgwick County, Kansas, study (Withrow 2003) found that while Blacks and Hispanics are arrested at disproportionately higher rates than Whites, a significant portion of these arrests are nondiscretionary. Blacks represent 7.6 percent of all stops, 23.6 percent of all arrests, 11.9 percent of all misdemeanor warrant arrests, and 23.6 percent of all felony warrant arrests. Hispanics represent 6.7 percent of all stops, 13.4 percent of all arrests, 14.0 percent of all misdemeanor warrant arrests, and 11.7 percent of all felony warrant arrests. It is not likely the deputies knew of an active warrant prior to the stop.

The overall trend is rather consistent. Stops involving minorities appear more likely to result in more formal or punitive

TABLE 2.5 Are Minorities Searched More Frequently?

Study	Difference Reported?	Are Hit Rates Higher for Minorities?
Anonymous (Meehan and Ponder 2002)	NR	NA
California (CHP 2000)	NR	NA
Connecticut (Cox et al. 2001)	Blacks and Hispanics slightly more likely to be searched	NR
Denver, CO (DPD 2002)	Overall Blacks and Hispanics searched at higher rates during traffic stops; Blacks had highest percentage of incident to arrest searches; Blacks and Hispanics had highest percentage of cursory and incident to arrest stops involving pedestrians	Same for Blacks and Whites, lower for Hispanics
Kansas (Police Foundation 2003)	NR	NA
Maryland (Lamberth 1996)	Blacks more likely to be searched during traffic stops	Same for Blacks and Whites
Massachusetts (Farrell et al. 2004)	Minority drivers are more likely to be searched during a traffic stop	NR
Minnesota (MDPS 2003)	Blacks and Hispanics are more likely to be searched during a traffic stop	Searches of minorities are less likely to produce contraband

Missouri (Rojek, Rosenfeld, and Decker 2004)	Blacks and Hispanics are roughly twice as likely to be searched as Whites	NR
Nevada (McCorkle 2003)	Blacks searched at more than twice the rate of White drivers	Hit rate for Blacks and Hispanics are lower than for Whites and Asians
New Jersey Turnpike (Lamberth 1994)	NR	NA
New York, NY (Spitzer 1999)	NR	NA
North Carolina (Zingraff et al. 2000)	Blacks more likely to be searched than Whites	Contraband is less likely to be found in searches of vehicles operated by Black drivers
Overland Park, KS (Novak 2004)	NR	NA
Richmond, VA (Smith and Petrocelli 2001)	Blacks No more likely to be searched; Whites more likely subjected to consent-type searches	NR
Sacramento, CA (Greenwald 2003)	Blacks and Hispanics are more likely to be searched than Whites	Hit rates are equal across race and ethnic categories
San Antonio, TX (Lamberth 2003a)	Black and Hispanic drivers are more likely to be searched than White or Asian drivers	Hit rates are consistently lower for minority drivers

Continued

NA, not applicable; NR, not reported

59

TABLE 2.5 Continued

STUDY	DIFFERENCE REPORTED?	ARE HIT RATES HIGHER FOR MINORITIES?
San Diego, CA (Cordner, Williams, and Zuniga 2000)	NR	NA
San Diego, CA (Cordner, Williams, and Zuniga 2002)	Blacks and Hispanics are overrepresented in all types of searches	Hit rates are generally lower for Hispanic drivers and highest for searches involving White or Black drivers
San Jose, CA (Landsdowne 2002)	NR	NA
Sedgwick County, KS (Withrow 2003)	Blacks and Hispanics are searched at disproportionately higher rates	NR
Texas (TDPS 2000)	Blacks and Hispanics are searched at disproportionately higher rates	NR
Washington (WSP 2001)	Minorities (non-white) searched at disproportionately higher rates	Rate of contraband seizures is higher for Whites than non-Whites
Wichita, KS (Withrow 2002)	Blacks and Hispanics are more likely to be searched	Hit rates are generally higher for Blacks and lower for Hispanics

NA, not applicable; NR, not reported

sanctions. Nothing in the literature, however, suggests that these arrests are arbitrary. None of the researchers report that arrests involving minorities are more likely to result in claims of false arrests or releases without prosecution. In short, it appears that arrests involving minorities are just as valid as arrests involving nonminorities. At least one researcher (MacDonald 2003) interprets these findings as proof that the police are accurately targeting the offending population.

Three studies report that minorities are less likely to receive a citation or be arrested than nonminorities (Novak 2004; Smith and Petrocelli 2001; Zingraff et al. 2000). Zingraff et al. (2000) reports that overall, Blacks are less likely to be cited than Whites, but within some age categories the opposite is true. Similarly, Withrow (2003) found that in Sedgwick County, Kansas, age is a stronger predictor of an arrest than race or ethnicity. The Overland Park, Kansas (Novak 2004), and Richmond, Virginia (Smith and Petrocelli 2001), studies appear to capture the essence of the racial profiling controversy, that is, the use of pretextual stops. Both of these studies report that Blacks are less likely to receive a formal citation or be arrested pursuant to a stop.

While it may seem at first glance that the police are less punitive to minorities or more willing to give them a break, some would argue that this finding suggests the police use traffic stops as a pretext to conduct more extensive searches of minorities without probable cause. When no evidence of criminal activity is found, the drivers are simply allowed to leave without a formal sanction. In the absence of a formal citation, and usually a formal record of the contact, there is very little that the complainant can do to convince authorities that the stop was not justified. There is some evidence that minorities view these results differently than nonminorities (Fridell et al. 2001; Withrow and Jackson 2002). The anecdotal evidence consistently reveals that minorities question the validity of a stop when a formal sanction (i.e., a citation) does not occur. Some consider the absence of a formal sanction as evidence of racial profiling. "If it was important enough for the officer to stop me, then why did I not receive a ticket?" is the typical response. Both Novak (2004) and Smith and Petrocelli (2001) concluded that their findings may be interpreted as evidence of the police use of minor traffic violations as pretexts to initiate traffic stops for the purpose of conducting a more extensive search (see Table 2.6).

TABLE 2.6 Are Stops Involving Minorities More Punitive?

STUDY	DISPOSITION DIFFERENCES BY RACE?
Anonymous (Meehan and Ponder 2002)	NR
California (CHP 2000)	NR
Connecticut (Cox et al. 2001)	Blacks and Hispanics are more likely to be arrested or ticketed rather than warned
Denver, CO (DPD 2002)	Blacks most likely to experience a field interview. Hispanics and Whites more likely to receive a citation. Blacks and Hispanics are more likely than Whites to be arrested
Kansas (Police Foundation 2003)	NR
Maryland (Lamberth 1996)	NR
Massachusetts (Farrell et al. 2004)	Non-white drivers are more likely to receive a citation than White drivers
Minnesota (MDPS 2003)	NR
Missouri (Rojek, Rosenfeld, and Decker 2004)	Blacks and Hispanics are roughly twice as likely to be arrested
Nevada (McCorkle 2003)	Black drivers are less likely to receive a citation but more likely to be arrested than drivers of other races or ethnicities
New Jersey Turnpike (Lamberth 1994)	NR
New York, NY (Spitzer 1999)	Higher proportions of Blacks and Hispanics are arrested pursuant to a stop than Whites
North Carolina (Zingraff et al. 2000)	Overall, Blacks are less likely to be cited, but this varies between age and gender categories
Overland Park, KS (Novak 2004)	Minorities are less likely to receive formal sanction (citation), suggesting possibility of pretextual stops
Richmond, VA (Smith and Petrocelli 2001)	Whites are more likely to be ticketed and arrested than Blacks
Sacramento, CA (Greenwald 2003)	NR

TABLE 2.6   Continued

Study	Disposition Differences by Race?
San Antonio, TX (Lamberth 2003a)	NR
San Diego, CA (Cordner, Williams, and Zuniga 2000)	Black and Hispanic drivers are more likely to be arrested than White or Asian drivers
San Diego, CA (Cordner, Williams, and Zuniga 2002)	NR
San Jose, CA (Landsdowne 2002)	NR
Sedgwick County, KS (Withrow 2003)	Black and Hispanic drivers are arrested at disproportionately higher rates. Age is a more accurate predictor
Texas (TDPS 2000)	NR
Washington (WSP 2001)	Non-whites appear slightly more likely to be arrested than Whites
Wichita, KS (Withrow 2002)	Stops involving Blacks and Hispanics are more likely to result in an arrest

NR, not reported.

Are Minorities Detained Longer During Stops?

Of the twenty-four studies outlined here, only three address this question. The Denver, Colorado, study (DPD, 2000) found that minorities are not detained longer than nonminorities. In the Sedgwick County, Kansas, study there is some evidence that minorities are detained longer than nonminorities. In this study the average length of traffic stops is slightly less than twelve minutes. Whites are detained an average of eleven and a half minutes. Blacks are detained an average of fifteen minutes. Hispanics are detained an average of seventeen minutes. Administrators from this department argue that the longer duration of stops involving Hispanics is likely due to the communication difficulties related to language experienced by nonbilingual deputies. In addition, the findings of this study do not consider how the outcome of the stop affects its duration. One would expect that stops involving searches or arrests would last longer than stops that do not include these features and outcomes. Therefore, as in this study, if minorities are arrested more frequently than nonminorities, one would anticipate that minorities would be detained longer (Withrow 2003). The Wichita, Kansas, study is more instructive. In Wichita most stops (51.3 percent) last from five to fifteen minutes. This finding is consistent for every racial and ethnic group. A logistic regression reveals that the race of the driver tends to reduce the duration of the stop. Stops involving Black drivers tend to be briefer, but the effect (of the driver's race) is quite minimal. Predictably, stops involving searches, more than one officer, arrests, and large numbers of occupants in the vehicle tend to last longer than stops that do not (Withrow 2002). From these findings one can logically conclude that race and ethnicity are, by themselves, not likely valid predictors of the duration of a stop (see Table 2.7).

Are Incidents Involving Physical Resistance and Confrontation More Frequent?

Two of the twenty-four studies considered here address this issue. In both of them the researchers concluded that stops involving minorities are more likely to involve incidents of physical resistance or confrontation. In Sedgwick County, Kansas, Withrow (2003) found that incidents of physical resistance are more frequent during stops involving racial and ethnic minorities. Overall only 0.2 percent of all stops involve physical resistance. White drivers represent 89.4 percent of all stops and 66.7 percent of all incidents of physical resistance. Black drivers represent 7.6 percent of all stops and 33.3 percent of all incidents involving physical resistance. Similarly, Hispanic drivers represent 6.7 percent of all stops and 12.5 percent of all stops involving physical resistance. In this study the researcher did not consider whether or not the outcome of the stop (e.g., an arrest versus a citation) affects the differential pattern of physical resistance by race.

In the Wichita, Kansas, study Withrow (2002) also found that very few (0.9 percent) of the stops involve physical resistance. Only 0.6 percent of all stops involving White drivers result in physical confrontation. Alternatively, 1.7 percent and 1.2 percent of all stops involving Black and Hispanic drivers, respectively, result in physical resistance. The researcher developed a logistic regression model to identify the factors that might predict physical resistance

TABLE 2.7   Are Minorities Detained Longer During Stops?

STUDY	DETAINED LONGER?
Anonymous (Meehan and Ponder 2002)	NR
California (CHP 2000)	NR
Connecticut (Cox et al. 2001)	NR
Denver, CO (DPD 2002)	No
Kansas (Police Foundation 2003)	NR
Maryland (Lamberth 1996)	NR
Massachusetts (Farrell et al. 2004)	NR
Minnesota (MDPS 2003)	NR
Missouri (Rojek, Rosenfeld, and Decker 2004)	NR
Nevada (McCorkle 2003)	NR
New Jersey Turnpike (Lamberth 1994)	NR
New York, NY (Spitzer 1999)	NR
North Carolina (Zingraff et al. 2000)	NR
Overland Park, KS (Novak 2004)	NR
Richmond, VA (Smith and Petrocelli 2001)	NR
Sacramento, CA (Greenwald 2003)	NR
San Antonio, TX (Lamberth 2003a)	NR
San Diego, CA (Cordner, Williams, and Zuniga 2000)	NR
San Diego, CA (Cordner, Williams, and Zuniga 2002)	NR
San Jose, CA (Landsdowne 2002)	NR
Sedgwick County, KS (Withrow 2003)	Yes
Texas (TDPS 2000)	NR
Washington (WSP 2001)	NR
Wichita, KS (Withrow 2002)	No

NR, not reported.

during a stop. Stops resulting in an arrest or involving a search appear to strongly predict the incidence of physical resistance. Stops involving Black drivers appear slightly more likely to result in physical resistance. Ethnicity alone does not appear to increase the probability of physical resistance.

While these studies indicate that incidents of physical resistance are more frequent during stops involving minorities, this is not definitive evidence that the police are consistently more brutal toward minorities in general. None of the available studies are able to establish the temporal order of a search, an arrest, and an incident of physical confrontation. It is not clear whether the physical confrontation is the cause or the result of an arrest or a search (see Table 2.8).

Do Officer Characteristics Matter?

Four of the twenty-four studies included here consider the effect of officer characteristics on traffic stopping behaviors (see Table 2.9). These studies consistently report that officer characteristics have no effect on traffic stopping behaviors. White officers are no more likely to stop, search, or arrest minority drivers (Smith and Petrocelli 2001). Officer characteristics are unrelated to the race of the individual stopped for a traffic violation (Novak 2004). Similarly, Greenwald (2003) and Withrow (2002) found no differences with respect to officer characteristics in stopping behaviors or outcomes. In Wichita, Kansas, the researcher considered the officer's race, age, gender, and years of service. None of these factors affect the overall findings of the research. In a separate study, using the same data set, Withrow (2004a) found that the racial composition of an officer's beat assignment is more important than the race of the officer at predicting the racial or ethnic composition of drivers stopped by the officer (see Table 2.9).

Overall Limitations of the Research

Undoubtedly, the number of racial profiling studies will increase significantly over the next decade. Police administrators recognize that resistance to conducting such studies becomes in itself a political issue. Few are willing to resist public calls for inquiries, nor should they. Each time a racial profiling study is completed we learn more about how officers conduct routine traffic stops, the effect of departmental deployment strategies, the efficiency of searches, and many other important aspects of a critically important police function. In addition, the racial profiling controversy has attracted the attention of the scholarly community. It has developed into a distinct and multidimensional research agenda relevant to a wide range of academic and scholarly specialists. It is therefore important to pause and review a few of the overall limitations of the

TABLE 2.8   Are Incidents of Physical Resistance and Confrontation More Frequent?

STUDY	MORE PHYSICAL RESISTANCE AND CONFRONTATION?
Anonymous (Meehan and Ponder 2002)	NR
California (CHP 2000)	NR
Connecticut (Cox et al. 2001)	NR
Denver, CO (DPD 2002)	NR
Kansas (Police Foundation 2003)	NR
Maryland (Lamberth 1996)	NR
Massachusetts (Farrell et al. 2004)	NR
Minnesota (MDPS 2003)	NR
Missouri (Rojek, Rosenfeld, and Decker 2004)	NR
Nevada (McCorkle 2003)	NR
New Jersey Turnpike (Lamberth 1994)	NR
New York, NY (Spitzer 1999)	NR
North Carolina (Zingraff et al. 2000)	NR
Overland Park, KS (Novak 2004)	NR
Richmond, VA (Smith and Petrocelli 2001)	NR
Sacramento, CA (Greenwald 2003)	NR
San Antonio, TX (Lamberth 2003a)	NR
San Diego, CA (Cordner, Williams, and Zuniga 2000)	NR
San Diego, CA (Cordner, Williams, and Zuniga 2002)	NR
San Jose, CA (Landsdowne 2002)	NR
Sedgwick County, KS (Withrow 2003)	Incidents of physical resistance are more prevalent when the individuals stopped are either Black or Hispanic
Texas (TDPS 2000)	NR
Washington (WSP 2001)	NR
Wichita, KS (Withrow 2002)	Stops involving Blacks and Hispanics are more likely to include physical resistance

NR, not reported

TABLE 2.9 Do the Officers' Characteristics Matter?

STUDY	DIFFERENCE WITH RESPECT TO OFFICER CHARACTERISTICS?
Anonymous (Meehan and Ponder 2002)	NR
California (CHP 2000)	NR
Connecticut (Cox et al. 2001)	NR
Denver, CO (DPD 2002)	NR
Kansas (Police Foundation 2003)	NR
Maryland (Lamberth 1996)	NR
Massachusetts (Farrell et al. 2004)	NR
Minnesota (MDPS 2003)	NR
Missouri (Rojek, Rosenfeld, and Decker 2004)	NR
Nevada (McCorkle 2003)	NR
New Jersey Turnpike (Lamberth 1994)	NR
New York, NY (Spitzer 1999)	NR
North Carolina (Zingraff et al. 2000)	NR
Overland Park, KS (Novak 2004)	Officer characteristics are unrelated to the race of the individual for traffic violations
Richmond, VA (Smith and Petrocelli 2001)	White officers are no more likely to stop, search, or arrest minority drivers
Sacramento, CA (Greenwald 2003)	No consistent pattern of stops by race or ethnicity with respect to the officer's race or ethnicity
San Antonio, TX (Lamberth 2003a)	NR
San Diego, CA (Cordner, Williams, and Zuniga 2000)	NR
San Diego, CA (Cordner, Williams, and Zuniga 2002)	NR
San Jose, CA (Landsdowne 2002)	NR
Sedgwick County, KS (Withrow 2003)	NR
Texas (TDPS 2000)	NR
Washington (WSP 2001)	NR
Wichita, KS (Withrow 2002)	No differences in stops with respect to the race or ethnicity of individuals and officer characteristics

NR, not reported.

current research. A more thorough discussion of the methodological challenges is the subject of Chapter 3.

Most researchers define racial profiling within the context of the police decision making process. For them, racial profiling occurs when the police use race or ethnicity inappropriately as an indicator of current or future criminal behavior. Unfortunately, none of the research projects to date make any attempt to actually measure, or at least document, how police officers make enforcement decisions. Instead they use a disparity in aggregate numbers as *prima facie* and conclusive evidence of racial profiling. Unless and until researchers are able to measure the actual influence of race on police decision making, the racial profiling controversy will suffer with this analytical challenge. "The problem with interpreting these findings is that the mere presence of disparity in the aggregate rate of stops does not, in itself, demonstrate racial prejudice, any more than racial disparity in prison populations demonstrates racial prejudices by sentencing judges" (Engel, Calnon, and Bernard 2002, 250).

The appropriateness of the benchmark or baseline data used to estimate the racial proportions of individuals exposed to routine police observation is a raging debate among racial profiling researchers. Each of the benchmarks have advantages and disadvantages and none are universally acceptable for every enforcement context. For the most part, researchers do an adequate job of recognizing the limitations of their benchmarks. More often than not, however, the decision of which benchmark to use is based on the overall limitations of the resources available to the researcher. There is an emerging body of literature that attempts to compare different benchmarks. One such study was conducted in the city of Wichita, Kansas. Police stop data collected in 2001 is compared to three independent collected benchmarks: field observations, population, and traffic accidents. The researcher reports that while the results vary slightly, the overall findings, that is, the racial and ethnic disparity evident in traffic stops, were not affected (Withrow 2004b). Undoubtedly, similar studies will be conducted in the coming years in other sites. Whether or not these studies will yield an appropriate and universally acceptable benchmark is unclear. It is more likely that researchers will continue to qualify their findings with respect to the limitations of their benchmarks.

Currently, the findings relating to the differential severity of dispositions subsequent to a traffic stop are of limited value without additional contextual information about the severity of the reason for the stop. When measured at all, the reason for the stop is measured nominally. This level of measurement, by definition, does not allow the analyst to draw a statistical correlation between the severity of the reason for the stop and the severity of the disposition. This forces the researcher to use rather imprecise nominal statistical tests (e.g., Chi square) that provide little insight into the causal relationship between the reasons for and outcomes of stops. Rather than simply indicating a general reason for the stop, it would be more helpful for the officer to indicate the relative severity of the driver's behavior on at least an ordinal scale based on some indicator of flagrance or threat to public safety.

The statistical tests used by racial profiling analysts are rudimentary at best (Lundman and Kaufman 2003). Most findings are based on simple correlations that cannot adequately determine a causal relationship between variables. With the exception of four studies (Novak 2004; Smith and Petrocelli 2001; Withrow 2002, 2003), most researchers do not employ more rigorous multivariate statistical tests. These statistical models would enable researchers to determine (predict) the relative effects of various factors on the police decision making process. In addition, these tests allow researchers to rule out alternative explanations of behavior (Engel, Calnon, and Bernard 2002), a necessary element of causality.

It is important to pause here and suggest that studies that rely exclusively on statistical analyses may lose some of the human richness of the racial profiling controversy. No statistical analysis can comprehensively account for the dynamic nature of routine enforcement. Traffic stops have an individual effect on both the driver and the officer. The research has yet to fully capitalize on the qualitative nature of racial profiling and its effect on individuals. Research based on field observations, ethnographic studies, and victim surveys is noticeably absent in the literature, and the controversy would surely benefit from such inquiries.

With the exception of those using existing data, racial profiling studies depend on stop data collected by the officers who are being evaluated. There is some evidence that the imposition of a racial profiling study, that is, the requirement for officers to complete another form for that specific purpose, may inappropriately interrupt the patrol function. Some argue that the police will report data incorrectly or incompletely because they are afraid of the consequence of a study finding racial disparity in traffic stops. While this accusation is logical, no researcher has yet definitively proven systematic, active, and sustained disengagement wholly related to the racial profiling data collection process. This is likely to be the case for some time. In most departments there is no single and definitive place where all police-citizen contacts are recorded. Most departments collect information from citations, case reports, and radio communications. Few, however, record information from warnings and unofficial police-citizen contacts. In short, there is an overall lack of baseline data on comprehensive police activity with which to conduct an audit of racial profiling police in stop data.

The current racial profiling research is limited in scope. Most research occurs in well-defined jurisdictions and is not likely generalizable beyond the community in which it is conducted (Lundman and Kaufman 2003). The findings in one community, or even in one part of a community, may not be relevant to another. The Kansas study (Police Foundation 2003) is illustrative of this limitation. In this study the researcher found evidence of racial profiling in some, but not all, of the observation sites. It is not possible to lump the findings from all observation sites into a single overall finding for the entire state. As a result, the researchers are forced to base their findings on inconsistent results. Furthermore, there is a general lack of agreement among researchers on exactly how much disparity is necessary for one to conclude that racial profiling is occurring (Engel, Calnon, and Bernard 2002).

The current research is also limited in its context. Most of what we know about racial profiling comes from research conducted by and for municipal and state police agencies and focuses on traffic enforcement and drug interdiction activities. Very little is known about how race affects officers who observe pedestrian traffic, how security guards observe shoppers, or how airport screeners select travelers for additional searches.

The studies are somewhat lacking in their ability to identify the effects of various other factors on the incidence and outcome of traffic stops. For example, individual factors like the the gender, age, and socio-economic status of a driver may affect an officer's decision to stop, conduct a search, or initiate an arrest. Contextual factors, like the time of day, predominant race of the neighborhood, and crime rate may also have a profound effect on the dynamics of a routine enforcement program.

Finally, very few racial profiling studies undergo rigorous peer review by objective evaluators. Most are written by police department specialists or independent analysts to be consumed by the general public. While it is important for the community to participate in and learn about racial profiling, the advancement of science demands that results be evaluated by independent and scholarly analysts, preferably blindly. The peer review process effectively ferrets out analytical inconsistencies, methodological violations, and logical errors. In doing so, it vastly improves the quality of the research.

SUMMARY

The number of racial profiling studies has grown exponentially during the past decade. More than 400 agencies have conducted racial profiling studies with varying levels of detail and comprehensiveness. Few studies have been attempted at the national level. Most are conducted at the state or local levels.

Racial profiling is defined in one of two ways. First, racial profiling is defined as the inappropriate use of race or ethnicity in the police decision making process. Using this definition, the police would be guilty of racial profiling if they summarily considered racial minorities as more likely to be involved in criminal activity. The use of race within the context of a description of a known suspect would not, using this definition, be considered racial profiling. Second, racial profiling is sometimes defined as a disparity between the proportional racial representation of a community (residents, licensed drivers, actual drivers, etc.) and the proportional racial representation of individuals stopped by the police. In this instance, any statistically significant disparity would indicate the existence of ongoing racial profiling.

Racial profiling research relies on two principal measures. First, stop data, normally collected by street level police officers, provides information on who actually gets stopped and, in most cases, what happens to them once they are stopped. Generally, this information is collected via machine-readable paper forms by the officers in the departments that are being studied. In some cases researchers use mobile display terminals, laptops, or pocket computers. In a few cases the researchers use existing data from police department information systems. Second, a benchmark that accurately indicates the proportional representation of individuals available to be stopped is necessary to determine if disparate patterns exist in stopping behavior. Most benchmarks are based on populations like licensed drivers, individuals over a certain age, or census tracts. The early benchmarks were based on actual field observations of drivers within selected intersections or stretches of highway. An emerging benchmark is based on information from not-at-fault drivers in two-vehicle accidents. Each benchmark has its relative advantages and disadvantages and none are universally acceptable.

There are two general analytical components of racial profiling research. The first attempts to determine whether an overall disparity exists, with respect to race or ethnicity, between the proportional racial representations of who could be stopped (based on the benchmark) and who is actually stopped (based on the police stop data). It is upon these analyses that most researchers determine whether racial profiling is occurring. Nearly all of the available research indicates that racial and ethnic minorities are stopped at higher levels (proportionately) than they are represented within the benchmark.

The second analytical components are more insightful. These analyses focus on what happens to individuals once they are stopped. Normally, the focus of these analyses is on differential treatment with respect to the race or ethnicity of the individual. While some differences exist with respect to race in the reported reason for the stop, there appears to be no consistent pattern. The research appears to indicate that race cannot accurately predict the reason for the stop. With rare exceptions, racial profiling studies indicate that minorities are searched more frequently than nonminorities. This disparity is especially evident in discretionary or consent searches, which are arguably more important to the racial profiling controversy than inventory or incident to arrest searches. Of more concern is that hit rates do not justify the more frequent searching of minorities. Consistently, minorities are less likely to be in possession of contraband. Stops involving racial minorities are more likely to result in formal or more punitive dispositions than stops involving nonminorities. While this may be consistent with the historical record of police brutality in the minority community, it is only partially relevant to the racial profiling controversy. A few researchers find that racial minorities are more likely to receive informal sanctions, like a verbal warning.

While it may appear to most that the police are giving the minorities a break, some researchers consider this further evidence of racial profiling. The police, they allege, use relatively minor infractions of the traffic code as mere pretexts to stop racial minorities in the hope that drivers will consent to more thorough searches. The results of the available research are mixed with respect to whether racial minorities are detained for longer periods during stops than nonminorities. Most researchers found that stops are longer if a search is conducted or an arrest is made. A few studies found that incidents of physical resistance are more frequent during stops involving racial minorities. Here again, stops involving searches and resulting in an arrest are more likely predictors of physical resistance. Furthermore, the available research cannot establish the temporal order of physical resistance, a search, and an arrest. Finally, none of the available research found substantial differences with respect to officer characteristics (age, gender, experience, etc.) and the racial representation of individuals stopped or what happens to individuals once they are stopped.

It is likely that racial profiling research will continue at the same rate for the foreseeable future. Therefore, more attention should be placed on improving the quality of the research. This includes developing an objectively measurable definition of racial profiling, establishing a universally acceptable benchmark, measuring the severity of the reasons for the stop, developing rigorous statistical models that provide more accurate insight into the intricacies of police stops, and subjecting racial profiling research to the scrutiny of peer review.

DISCUSSION QUESTIONS

1. What are the inherent problems or opportunities associated with the two general types of racial profiling definitions presented in this chapter?
2. Which of the seven salient research questions outlined in this chapter appear to be sufficiently answered? Which are not?
3. Among the limitations of the research outlined in this chapter what is the most threatening to the advancement of our knowledge of racial profiling, and why?

4. Would racial profiling research in shopping centers or airports produce results similar to those found in traffic enforcement contexts? Why or why not?

5. How does the overreliance on quantitative research affect our understanding of racial profiling?

6. Develop and defend a definition of racial profiling. Provide examples.

CASE STUDIES

1. A researcher provides the following definition:

   ...any police-initiated action that relies on the race, ethnicity, or national origin rather than the behavior of an individual or information that leads the police to a particular individual who has been identified as being, or having been, engaged in criminal activity. (Ramirez, McDevitt, and Farrell 2000, 3)

   Which of the following scenarios, using this definition, constitute racial profiling? Explain your response.

   Scenario A   A police officer stops a young Black man in a predominately White neighborhood because he does not "fit in."

   Scenario B   A police officer, in response to valid intelligence information that a predominantly Hispanic gang is planning a drive-by shooting, pays particular attention to vehicles operated by Hispanic youths in her beat.

   Scenario C   A police officer receives a report that a convenience store has been robbed. The description of the robber is a Black man in his early twenties wearing a white t-shirt and blue jeans. The officer observes a man meeting this description near the location of the robbery. He stops and questions the man.

2. Representatives from a local police officers' union have threatened to file a lawsuit if the city insists that officers record their identification numbers on racial profiling reporting sheets. It is likely that the union would win such a lawsuit.

How would the exclusion of the officers' identification numbers affect the outcome of the research?

3. You have been appointed by a federal court to conduct a racial profiling study in a local police department. The department refuses to allow you access to records that could be used to verify the accuracy and completeness of the stop data their officers collected anonymously. Discuss how you would go about verifying the accuracy and completeness of the police stop data within this environment.

chapter **3**

CRITICAL
METHODOLOGICAL ISSUES

OBJECTIVE

To outline the critical methodological issues relating to racial profiling research.

INTRODUCTION

Racial profiling research commands a great deal of public attention and generates an even greater amount of public debate. Interest in racial profiling research within the minority community is understandable. Concerned parents of newly licensed-to-drive teenagers typically restrict their sons' and daughters' driving exposure. It is not unusual for parents to prohibit their teenagers from driving at night or in high traffic locations, at least until the new driver gets some experience. Parents of young Black teenagers are, of course, equally concerned about their children's safety, but their concern goes beyond the inexperience of their young drivers. Many are worried about how racial profiling may affect their children's safety and report spending considerable time counseling their children on how to avoid being a victim of racial profiling (Meeks 2000). The interest in racial profiling research, however, is not limited to the minority community. Political leaders, the police, the media, and even individuals with little to no risk of being a victim are legitimately concerned about racial profiling. They all want to know whether their police departments are fair and just. Because of the intensity of the attention racial profiling attracts, the research demands accuracy. This means paying attention to important methodological concerns. How we know what we know is just as important as what we know. When racial profiling research finds disparity in the routine enforcement patterns of the police department, it effectively taints the image of the police. Overwhelmingly, police officers are dedicated public servants. They deserve the researchers' attention to detail and adherence to legitimate methodological procedures.

The purpose of this chapter is to discuss the critical methodological concerns within the racial profiling controversy. Developing an acceptable definition of racial profiling is an important first step. Equally important is designing a data collection strategy that is responsive to the definition. Establishing an acceptable benchmark that accurately estimates the racial and ethnic proportions of individuals exposed to routine police observation would be the most important contribution to the validity of racial profiling research. This chapter includes an extensive discussion of how benchmarks are developed by contemporary racial profiling researchers, as well as their relative advantages and disadvantages. Measuring who gets stopped is a relatively easy data collection exercise. It is, however, potentially reactive and subject to the predictable inaccuracies of social data. Finally, it is important to review the rules of causality. Racial profiling research is somewhat hampered by its inability to either establish the temporal order of events or eliminate plausible alternative explanations, two key rules of causality.

DEFINING RACIAL PROFILING

Finding an acceptable definition of racial profiling has plagued racial profiling researchers since the beginning of the controversy. Generally there are two key issues. The first is a lack of agreement on how to define, either conceptually or operationally, the term *racial profiling*. There is even some disagreement on exactly what term to use. This lack of consensus is so pervasive that a fair portion of researchers do not even bother developing a definition. The second issue is more critical. More often than not, the data collection strategy and its resulting analyses are disconnected from the definition. Racial profiling is defined in one way and measured in another. The variables chosen are often not responsive to the salient research questions. Racial profiling is often defined as the use of race in police decision making, but few researchers pay any attention at all to the police decision making process. Instead, the disparate effect of an enforcement program is considered *prima facie* and conclusive evidence of racial profiling (McMahon et al. 2002). We are, in effect, weighing apples to determine the average weight of oranges.

Conceptual and Operational Definitions

Most researchers use the term *racial profiling*. It is the most commonly used term and communicates a specific social phenomenon: the inappropriate use of race as an indicator of potential criminal behavior. David Harris (2002), more than anyone else, has popularized the term *driving while Black*. This term, Harris suggests, commutates a distinct meaning that blackness coupled with driving has for all practical purposes become a violation of the law warranting the attention of police officers. After all, the term *driving while Black* is quite similar to *driving while intoxicated*. Some researchers prefer to use broader terms like *race-based policing* (Cordner, Williams, and Zuniga 2000, 2002; Withrow 2002). Their use of this term attempts to extend the controversy beyond police stops and allow consideration of a broader range of police operations and procedures. For example, this term would be applicable in a study of how race or ethnicity affects the decision making process of police detectives or police department administrators. In an extensive study of racial profiling written primarily for police administrators, Fridell, et al. (2001) uses the term *race-biased policing*. She argues that the term *racial profiling* is too narrow and does not fully communicate the breadth of the issue. Race, she argues, potentially affects a broad range of police decisions, including deployment, hiring, recruiting, promotion, and resource allocation.

While defining racial profiling, it is helpful to recognize that the relative influence of an individual's race or ethnicity in police decision making may vary (depending on the enforcement context) and in some cases may be appropriate. Two researchers have attempted to define racial profiling with respect to its relative importance in police decision making. Cleary (2000) and MacDonald (2003) argue that in some instances the use of race in police decision making is likely appropriate. For example, the police routinely receive notices to be on the lookout for a known suspect. Normally, these notices include various physical descriptors like gender, age, height, weight, color of hair and eyes, and of course race or ethnicity. These physical descriptions constitute a profile and often include certain behavioral characteristics consistent with the *modus operandi* of the suspected offender. If an officer, during a routine tour of duty, encounters an individual meeting most of these criteria, then he is likely to initiate a contact. MacDonald

(2003) labels this *soft* profiling, and Cleary (2000) labels this *broad* profiling. Even the most ardent critics of the police, they argue, would not characterize the use of race in this context as racial profiling. On the other end of the spectrum is what MacDonald (2003) calls *hard* profiling and Cleary (2000) refers to as *narrow* profiling. Both of these terms describe a practice whereby the police use race as either the primary or sole factor in decision making. For example, if a police officer believes minority youths are more likely to possess drugs, he may, in response to this prejudicial attitude, stop and search a disproportionately higher percentage of young Black males. These authors argue that it is the routine use of race, ethnicity, and national origin as a general indicator of criminal suspiciousness that crosses the threshold into racial profiling.

At the conceptual level, racial profiling definitions focus on the extent to which race and ethnicity influence routine police decision making. More specifically, racial profiling is generally defined as police officers' use race or ethnicity as a general indicator of criminal suspiciousness. Overwhelmingly, the scope of the research is limited to individual street level decision making. Almost no attention is placed on how race may play a role in administrative decision making or overall resource allocation. A definition developed by Ramirez, McDevitt, and Farrell (2000) is typical of most conceptual definitions. They define racial profiling as "... any police-initiated action that relies on the race, ethnicity, or national origin rather than the behavior of an individual or information that leads the police to a particular individual who has been identified as being, or having been, engaged in criminal activity" (p. 3). Among the conceptual definitions, two common themes are evident. First, these definitions either state or imply that racial profiling occurs when the police focus on individuals' race or ethnicity rather than their behavior when deciding whether to initiate a contact. Second, most conceptual definitions specifically state that racial profiling is a proactive rather than a reactive process. The term *police-initiated activity* is commonly used. This implies that citizen-initiated contacts, such as calls for service, could not be considered racial profiling.

Operational level definitions are more analytically parsimonious. They focus exclusively on the overall disparate effect by race of a traffic enforcement program and seldom pay attention to the reasons for the disparity. The Police Foundation's (2003) multi-jurisdictional study in Kansas is an example of an operational definition.

The researchers in this study propose that racial profiling occurs when minorities are stopped at disproportionately higher rates than they are represented within the benchmark that indicates the proportional racial representation of actual roadway users. Researchers who use operational definitions are not at all concerned about whether an officer is inappropriately influenced by the race of the driver. For them, the proof is in the aggregate outcome of an enforcement program. The process by which the outcome occurs is largely irrelevant.

Among the twenty-four studies outlined here, nine neither state nor imply a definition of racial profiling (Cordner, Williams, and Zuniga 2000, 2002; DPD 2002; Farrell et al. 2004; Rojek, Rosenfeld, and Decker 2004; Smith and Petrocelli 2001; TDPS 2000; WSP 2001; Zingraff et al. 2000). In five of these nine studies, the researchers were simply tasked with reporting the findings from a data collection exercise required by state statute (Farrell et al. 2004; Rojek, Rosenfeld, and Decker 2004; TDPS 2000; WSP 2001; Zingraff et al. 2000). None of these nine studies report that the data support a conclusion of racial profiling.

Ten of the twenty-four studies analyzed here used a conceptual definition of racial profiling that focuses on how race or ethnicity affect police decision making (CHP 2000; Cox et al. 2001; Greenwald 2003; Landsdowne 2002; McCorkle 2003; Meehan and Ponder 2002; MDPS 2000; Novak 2004; Withrow 2002, 2003). Three of these ten used the conceptual definition developed by Ramirez, McDevitt, and Farrell (2000) (Novak 2004; Meehan and Ponder 2002; MDPS 2000). In another two of these ten studies racial profiling is defined by state statute (Cox et al. 2001; McCorkle 2003). The researchers in eight of these ten studies report that minorities are overrepresented in police stops (Cox et al. 2001; Greenwald 2003; Landsdowne 2002; McCorkle 2003; Meehan and Ponder,2002; MDPS 2000; Novak 2004; Withrow 2002). Based on this evidence alone, only two of these eight studies conclude that racial profiling, as defined in their conceptual definition, is occurring (Meehan and Ponder 2002; MDPS 2000). Interestingly, none of these studies collect data that would describe or document the police decision making process in general, and in particular how race or ethnicity affects it.

Five of the twenty-four studies analyzed here either state or imply an operational definition of racial profiling that focuses on the disparate effect of police enforcement activities (Police Foundation

2003; Lamberth 1994, 1996, 2003a; Spitzer 1999). Again, the principal analytical component of these studies is a comparison of the proportional racial representation of individuals stopped, with a benchmark that estimates the proportional racial representation of individuals exposed to routine police observation. There is, however, a level of consistency among these researchers between their definitions, the data they collect, and their analytical conclusions. Four of the five studies using an operational definition report that minorities are overrepresented in police stops. All four of these conclude that racial profiling is occurring (Police Foundation 2003; Lamberth 1994, 1996; Spitzer 1999). One of these studies reports that minorities are not overrepresented in traffic stops and justifiably concludes that racial profiling is not occurring (Lamberth 2003a) (see Table 3.1)

TABLE 3.1   Summary of Effect of Type of Definition Used on Analytical Outcomes or Conclusions of Racial Profiling Research

STUDY AND DEFINITION USED	DISPARITY FOUND?	PROFILING?
No Definition Stated or Implied		
Denver, CO (DPD 2002)	Not reported	No
Massachusetts (Farrell et al. 2004)	Yes	No
Missouri (Rojek, Rosenfeld, and Decker 2004)	Yes	No
North Carolina (Zingraff et al. 2000)	Yes	No
Richmond, VA (Smith and Petrocelli 2001)	Yes	No
San Diego, CA (Cordner, Williams, and Zuniga 2000)	Yes	No
San Diego, CA (Cordner, Williams, and Zuniga 2002)	Yes	No
Texas (TDPS 2000)	No	No
Washington (WSP 2001)	No	No

Continued

TABLE 3.1 *Continued*

STUDY AND DEFINITION USED	DISPARITY FOUND?	PROFILING?
Conceptual Definition		
California (CHP 2000) " ... when a police officer initiates a traffic or investigatory stop based primarily on the race or ethnicity of the individual" (p. 1)	No	No
Connecticut (Cox, et al., 2001) " ... the detention, interdiction or other disparate treatment of an individual solely on the basis of the racial or ethnic status of such individual." (p.1); defined by statute	Yes	No
Sacramento, CA (Greenwald 2003) "Any police-initiated activity that relies on the race, ethnicity or national origin of an individual rather than the behavior of an individual or information that leads the police to a particular individual who has been identified as being or having been engaged in criminal activity. Race, ethnicity, or national origin can be used only as a descriptive factor along with others, but cannot be given undue weight." (p. 3)	Yes	No
San Jose, CA (Landsdowne, 2002) " ... a practice in which a police officer initiates a vehicle stop on a motorist based solely upon the race or ethnicity of the vehicle's driver." (p. 2)	Yes	No
Nevada (McCorkle, 2003) " ... reliance by a police officer upon the race, ethnicity, or national origin of a person as a factor in initiating action when the race, ethnicity, or national origin of the person is not	Yes	No

Continued

TABLE 3.1 *Continued*

Study and Definition Used	Disparity Found?	Profiling?
part of an identifying description of a specific suspect for a specific crime." (p. iii); defined by statute		
Anonymous (Meehan and Ponder 2002) " ... any police-initiated action that relies on the race, ethnicity, or national origin rather than the behavior of an individual or information that leads the police to a particular individual who has been identified as being, or having been, engaged in criminal activity." (Ramirez, McDevitt, and Farrell 2000, 3)	Yes	Yes
Minnesota (MDPS, 2003) " ... any police-initiated action that relies on the race, ethnicity, or national origin rather than the behavior of an individual or information that leads the police to a particular individual who has been identified as being, or having been, engaged in criminal activity." (Ramirez, McDevitt, and Farrell 2000, 3)	Yes	YeS
Overland Park, KS (Novak 2004) " ... any police-initiated action that relies on the race, ethnicity, or national origin rather than the behavior of an individual or information that leads the police to a particular individual who has been identified as being, or having been, engaged in criminal activity." (Ramirez, McDevitt, and Farrell 2000, 3).	Yes	No
Wichita, KS (Withrow 2002) " ... a practice whereby a police officer routinely makes law enforcement decisions ... solely on the basis of a citizen's race or ethnicity." (p. 4)	Yes	No

Continued

TABLE 3.1 *Continued*

Study and Definition Used	Disparity Found?	Profiling?
Sedgwick County, KS (Withrow 2003) "...a practice whereby a police officer routinely makes law enforcement decisions ... solely on the basis of a citizen's race or ethnicity." (p. 2)	No	No
Operational Definition		
Kansas (Police Foundation 2003) Implied as when minorities are stopped at disproportionately higher rates than they are represented within the benchmark that indicates the proportional racial representation of actual roadway users	Yes	Yes
New Jersey Turnpike (Lamberth 1994) Implied as when minorities are stopped at disproportionately higher rates than they are represented within the benchmark that indicates the proportional racial representation of actual roadway users	Yes	Yes
San Antonio, TX (Lamberth 2003a) Implied as when minorities are stopped at disproportionately higher rates than they are represented within the benchmark that indicates the proportional racial representation of actual roadway users	No	No
Maryland (Lamberth 1996) Implied as when minorities are stopped and frisked at disproportionately higher rates than they are represented within the benchmark that indicates the proportional racial representation of the population of pedestrians	Yes	Yes
New York, NY (Spitzer 1999) Implied as when minorities are stopped and frisked at disproportionately higher rates than they are represented within the benchmark that indicates the proportional racial representation of the population of pedestrians	Yes	Yes

Validity

In research design the term *validity* "refers to a match between a construct, or the way a researcher conceptualizes the idea in a conceptual definition, and a measure" (Neuman 2004, 112). Stated another way, validity "refers to the extent to which an empirical measure adequately reflects the real meaning of the concept under consideration" (Babbie 1999, 113). In other words, the data collected should produce variables that actually measure what they purport to measure. Unlike reliability, which refers to the consistency or predictability of a particular measure, it is difficult to empirically measure validity.

In reality, very few measures of social phenomenon are completely valid. For example, how does one measure crime? One way is to use the Uniform Crime Report (UCR) published annually by the Federal Bureau of Investigation. The UCR tabulates a national crime rate (called a crime index) based on the number of crimes reported to police departments per 100,000 residents. Nearly all police departments submit quarterly and annual reports. In 2002, the UCR represented 93.4 percent of the total United States population. At first glance the UCR Crime Index may appear to be a valid measure of crime and a useful measure of crime trends over time, but it is not completely valid. The UCR Crime Index only measures a selected group of seven crimes (Part I): murder, aggravated assault, rape, robbery, larceny-theft, burglary, and, more recently, hate crimes. Drug crimes (reported in Part II) are noticeably absent in the UCR Crime Index. These types of crimes represent a substantial portion of criminal behavior and are directly responsible for the recent increase in prison populations throughout the nation. This explains why the prison population has increased over the past decade while the UCR Crime Index has decreased. In addition, the UCR Crime Index only reports crimes that are reported to the police. Not all crimes are reported and not all crimes are reported with equal frequency. For example, it is likely that murders, motor vehicle thefts, and aggravated assaults will be reported. For a number of sociological and psychological reasons, sexual assaults may not be reported as frequently. Thus, as a comprehensive measure of crime, the UCR Crime Index is somewhat invalid.

Social science research does not require absolute validity, and very few researchers are able to find measures of social phenomena or behaviors that are completely valid. It is, however, absolutely necessary that researchers recognize, attempt to mitigate, and ultimately report the potential threats to the validity of their research. In particular, researchers are required to collect data that actually measures what the research purports to measure, as represented in their conceptual definition. If the researcher states that racial profiling occurs when a police officer proactively uses an individual's race rather than behavior as an indicator of potential criminal behavior and then, in compliance with this belief, initiates an official contact, then the researcher must actually measure the extent to which an individual's race affects a police officers decision making. A simple finding of disparity with respect to race or ethnicity in an enforcement program is not a valid measure of the police decision making process. On the other hand, if racial profiling is defined as a disparate effect with respect to race or ethnicity in an enforcement program (as in the cases of the operational definitions described above), then a measure of disparity would be a valid indicator of racial profiling.

Admittedly, this is a narrow point, but for two reasons it is critically important to the racial profiling controversy. First, savvy consumers of racial profiling research, including most police administrators, are normally quick to see the incongruence between definitions and the measures. After all, the police are specifically trained to evaluate measures (which they call evidence) against a definition (which they call a statute). A well-informed police officer may observe, "Nothing in this report actually measures how race influences a police officer's decisions." Second, disparity by itself is easily explained away. That same officer may observe, "None of these people would have been stopped had they not committed a real violation of the law. We don't have time to just hassle people. We are busy. And, if we are prejudiced and only stop people because of their race, then where are all the false arrest lawsuits?" In this context all of our sophisticated discussions of the dynamics of traffic stops and their potential for abuse normally fall on deaf ears. The bottom line is this: the legitimacy of research is directly related to the extent to which the researcher adheres to well-established methodological procedures. These include developing measures that are valid indicators of the phenomenon under investigation.

THE DENOMINATOR PROBLEM

Unquestionably, the most important methodological issue facing racial profiling researchers is finding an appropriate method to estimate the population of individuals who are exposed to routine police observation. Nearly every researcher and commentator active in racial profiling research recognizes the importance and limitations of the commonly used benchmarks (see Cordner, Williams, and Zuniga, 2000, 2002; Cox et al. 2001; DPD 2002; Engel, Calnon, and Bernard 2002; Farrell et al. 2004; Fridell et al. 2001; Greenwald 2003; U.S. GAO 2000; Harris 1999a,b, 2002; Lamberth 1994, 1996, 2003a; MacDonald 2003; McMahon et al. 2002; Novak 2004; O'Reilly 2002; Police Foundation 2003; Ramirez, McDevitt, and Farrell 2000; Rojek, Rosenfeld, and Decker 2004; Smith and Petrocelli 2001; Walker 2001, 2003; WSP 2001; Withrow 2002, 2003; Zingraff et al. 2000). Gathering data on police stops is of little value unless it can be compared against a valid measure of individuals, by race and ethnicity, who are exposed to the police. O'Reilly (2002) observed that racial profiling research is strong in the numerator (police stop data) and weak in the denominator (benchmark). State legislatures that impose detailed data collection requirements on police departments never provide any direction on which benchmark to use for comparative purposes. Without a reliable base rate, conclusions of racial prejudice are premature (Engel, Calnon, and Bernard 2002), not likely sufficient during a legal challenge (STATS 1999), and may generate inappropriate corrective measures (McMahon et al. 2002). "Until someone devises an adequately sophisticated benchmark that takes into account population patterns on the roads, degrees of law breaking, police deployment patterns, and the nuances of police decision making, stop data are as meaningless as they are politically explosive" (MacDonald 2003, 22).

Walker (2003) proposes that an effective benchmark must meet three basic criteria. First, the benchmark must be scientifically credible. It should be methodologically sound and able to withstand the rigors of peer review. Second, the benchmark should have practical utility. It should provide insight into the findings and illustrate a solution to the problem. Third, the benchmark must have political credibility. Racial profiling research never occurs in a vacuum. The benchmark must be recognized as valid by the stakeholders.

Smith and Alpert (2002) make an important distinction between benchmarks and baselines. They define benchmarks as previously collected data about a population, like census or department of motor vehicles data. Baselines refer to observations of populations conducted specifically for comparative purposes, such as a racial profiling inquiry. These researchers argue that baselines are more appropriate for racial profiling research. First, baselines can be designed to capture a specific population of interest, for instance, drivers. Second, using a baseline allows for the collection of information on the specific number of individuals available for stops. Third, baselines allow the researcher to count people at specific places or times. "The best approach in developing a reliable comparison population in research on racial profiling involving traffic stops is direct observation of the driving public" (p. 688).

Researchers typically rely on various proxies like population, licensed drivers, field observations, or traffic accident records to estimate the racial proportions of individuals available to be stopped by the police. In a few cases researchers have developed benchmarks from various sources. There have been a few attempts to differentiate between the violator and nonviolator populations within racial and ethnic classifications (Lamberth 1994; Lange, Blackman, and Johnson 2001). Two researchers have conducted racial profiling analyses using competing benchmarks (Engel and Calnon 2004b; Withrow 2004b).

The purpose of this section is to describe and critically analyze the benchmarks commonly used by racial profiling researchers. Because of the controversy, particularly among academic researchers, it is very likely that within the next several years the list of benchmarks developed for racial profiling research will grow substantially. None of the benchmarks considered here are universally adaptable to every racial profiling evaluation. Local variables, such as the proximity of the community to other population centers or international borders, the potential for the under- or overreporting of population statistics, commuter traffic to and from suburban and regional areas, the anticipated transient driving population, and seasonal driving patterns should be considered by the researcher while identifying an appropriate benchmark.

Types of Benchmarks

Benchmarks used in racial profiling research are usually based on one of three information sources. They are

- Population
- Field observations
- Accident records

Within these categories is an extensive array of variations that include using subpopulations (e.g., licensed drivers); sophisticated imputation procedures to account for migration; crime rates; citizen surveys; police deployment differences; and many others. In addition, at least one researcher argues for the efficacy of a system of internal benchmarks (Walker 2003).

Population

The most common benchmarks are based on the resident population of the community in which the racial profiling research is conducted. In some cases population benchmarks are based on the entire population (Withrow 2002, 2003). This is particularly important if the stop data set includes information on juveniles and non-drivers. Some researchers prefer to use only licensed or likely licensed drivers (Smith and Petrocelli 2002). At least one research project used a sophisticated spatial weighting technique to account for migration in traffic patterns (Rojek, Rosenfeld, and Decker 2004). Similarly, in Overland Park, Kansas, Novak (2004) considered the populations of various population centers in close proximity to his research site. In San Jose, California, the benchmark was developed from the resident population figures, crimes rates, and police deployment patterns (Walker 2001).

Regardless of the population estimate used or how it is amended to fit the researchers' particular needs, the validity of all population-based benchmarks is dependent on several assumptions. First, one must assume that the racial proportions of residents equal the racial proportions of drivers *and* traffic law violators. For example, if 20 percent of the resident population is minority, then 20 percent of the drivers and traffic law violators are minority. Second, one must assume that police resources (i.e., patrol) are equally distributed throughout the research site. For example, an individual's risk of being stopped for a traffic violation is essentially equal throughout the city. Third, regardless of their assignment and personal preferences, police officers are equally attentive to all potential law violations and apply consistent enforcement criteria. If an observed violation precipitates a stop and citation from one officer, then the same violation would produce a stop and citation from another officer. If we accept these assumptions, then we can conclude that if members of certain racial or ethnic groups are overrepresented in police stop data (when compared to the population-based benchmark), then an individual's race might play an important role in influencing a police officer's decision to initiate a traffic stop (Withrow 2004b).

The analysis of racial profiling data is relatively straightforward when a population-based benchmark is used. If a statistically significant higher proportion of minorities are stopped than represented in the benchmark, then the analyst may conclude, in the absence of alternative explanations to the contrary, that racial profiling is occurring.

Field Observation

The first racial profiling studies (see Lamberth 1994, 1996) used benchmarks based on the systematic field observation of actual roadway users. This researcher argues that there is no empirical connection between the resident and driving populations. In other words, the racial proportions of residents may not equal the racial proportions of drivers. For example, population-based benchmarks do not account for transient traffic, that is, people who drive through but do not live in a community (Police Foundation 2003).

This benchmark requires the systematic observation of actual drivers at randomly selected locations and times. In most cases observers attempt to classify drivers with respect to race, ethnicity, and approximate age. More sophisticated studies attempt to determine the percentage of drivers within each racial or ethnic classification that violate the traffic (speed) law (Lamberth 1994; Lange, Blackman, and Johnson 2001; Zingraff et al. 2000). To be sure that an adequate sample size will be collected, researches typically select high volume intersections and stretches of roadway. Field observers at stationary sites (intersections) observe single lanes of traffic and alternate between lanes during an observation period. On interstate highways or rural locations, field observers use rolling surveys. In these situations observers drive along a preselected route, usually between exits or interchanges, at a constant speed and record the pertinent information about drivers who pass them or who they pass (Withrow 2004b).

The analysis of this data requires an odds ratio whereupon the benchmarks are compared against the actual stop data provided by the police department for each observation site. It is not possible to merge the benchmarks from various locations throughout a city into a single estimate of the driving population for the entire city. An odds ratio of 1.0 indicates that the racial proportions of individuals stopped at a location equal the racial proportions of individuals observed at a location. Given the potential measurement error associated with both the police stop data and field observations, most researchers do not conclude racial disparity until the odds ratios exceed 1.5 for any one racial or ethnic group (see Police Foundation 2003).

Accident Records

Accident records have been used by traffic engineers for more than seventy years to estimate the qualitative features of roadway users and the relative risk factors among drivers (Alpert, Smith, and Dunham 2003). Using accident records to estimate the racial composition of roadway users was first introduced to the racial profiling research agenda by the Washington State Patrol in 2001 and later by Alpert, Smith, and Dunham in 2003.[1]

In 1967, Thorpe proposed a method, commonly referred to as induced or quasi-induced exposure analysis, for estimating the relative exposure of various classes of drivers and types of vehicles to accident involvement (Haight 1970). This process determines "the relative likelihood of driver involvement in an accident as the ratio of the number of involvements to the exposure" (Stamatiadis and Deacon 1997, 37). After developing a technique for reliably identifying the at fault-drivers in two-vehicle accidents, Carr (1969) abandoned Thorpe's initial assumption that at-fault and not-at-fault drivers in two-vehicle accidents are essentially the same population. Carr's relative risk (RR) statistic is computed by dividing the frequency of accident occurrence for selected types of at fault drivers (e.g., males) by the frequency of accident occurrence for the same types of not-at-fault drivers. Later, Lyles, Stamatiadis, and Lighthizer (1991) proposed an involvement ratio (IR) statistic. The IR statistic is calculated by dividing the marginal proportion of at-fault drivers by the marginal proportion of not-at-fault drivers for various types of drivers or classes of vehicles. If the proportion of at-fault male drivers is higher than the proportion of not-at-fault male drivers involved in two-vehicle accidents, then the researcher concludes that males are more likely to be involved in accidents (Withrow 2004b). "Underlying the quasi-induced exposure method

---

[1] The Washington State Patrol developed a benchmark based on all drivers involved in accidents. Alpert, Smith, and Dunham developed a benchmark consistent with the quasi-induced measures that only uses the not-at-fault drivers in two-vehicle accidents.

is the theoretical assumption that not-at-fault drivers in two vehicle crashes represent a random sample of the driving age population" (Alpert, Smith, and Dunham 2003, 11).

The application of this benchmark in racial profiling research uses the race or ethnicity of the not-at-fault drivers in two-vehicle accidents. Using this benchmark, the researchers compare the proportional representation of each group to the actual stop data provided by the police department. The analysis is very similar to those conducted by researchers using population-based benchmarks. For example, if White drivers represent 75 percent of the not-at-fault drivers in two-vehicle accidents, then the researchers will conclude that at any given time or day, 75 percent of all drivers are White (Withrow 2004b).

Internal Benchmarks

Samuel Walker (2003) proposes the use of an internal benchmark. Internal benchmarks compare individual officer performance against similarly situated officers. This benchmark may provide some insight into the racial profiling problem (Fridell et al. 2001) and may provide a better estimate of the population available for stops (Miller 2000). Since 1997, the Pittsburg, Pennsylvania, Police Department has been using an internal benchmark. They began actively evaluating officer performance in this way after they entered into a consent decree that arose from a pattern of excessive force incidents. The system, called The Police Assessment and Review System, includes data on twenty-four officer performance indicators. These include extensive information relating to the race of the individuals stopped and the conditions under which the stops were conducted. Officers are reviewed and compared with the performance of similarly assigned officers. For example, if 20 percent of the individuals stopped by officers assigned to a particular beat and shift are Black, then an officer assigned to that beat and shift would warrant the administration's attention if 40 percent of the individuals he stops are Black (Walker 2003).

Advantages and Disadvantages
of Benchmarks

Each of the benchmarks commonly used by racial profiling researchers have advantages and disadvantages. The appropriateness of a benchmark largely depends on the conditions associated with the research site. None of the benchmarks are universally adaptable. In the final analysis the researcher's judgment is the most important determining factor.

Population

The data used for population-based benchmarks are easy and inexpensive to obtain. Population estimates are available from various sources, the most common being the U.S. Census Bureau. Estimates from the Census Bureau are particularly useful because they can be disaggregated to smaller geographical units. This feature may assist researchers interested in smaller geographical areas within a large research location (Withrow 2002). Population-based benchmarks allow researchers to consider a wider range of enforcement contexts. For example, because population estimates include the entire population, the researcher can evaluate an enforcement program's effect on juveniles, pedestrians, and other nondrivers. Population estimates can (and should) guide researchers on how to collect police stop data. For example, if the estimate differentiates between race and ethnicity, then the police stop data should also make this distinction. The U.S. Census is nearly universally criticized because of its inability to estimate various portions of the nation's population. Hispanics are particularly at risk of being undercounted. Despite this problem, official population estimates are readily recognized as legitimate by the consumers of racial profiling research (Withrow 2004b).

Population-based benchmarks are routinely criticized by racial profiling researchers. Walker (2001) argues that population-based benchmarks are not accurate because they do not reflect the population at risk of being stopped. Alpert, Smith, and Dunham (2003) found that census data, "even if adjusted for the driving age population, do not provide a reliable benchmark against which the racial composition of motorists stopped by the police should be compared" (p. 5). Several researchers argue that population estimates measure only the static and not the transient population. Lamberth, the most vocal opponent of population-based benchmarks, cites the research he conducted for the *State of New Jersey v. Pedro Soto* (1996) and *Wilkins v. Maryland State Police* (1993) cases as evidence in support of his criticism. In both cases Lamberth demonstrated that the resident population estimates did not accurately predict the transient population of drivers in the research sites when compared to his field observations (Police Foundation 2003). Similarly, Greenwald (2003) reports differences in the race of drivers observed at major intersections when compared to census data surrounding the intersections. A British study found after comparing census data against video camera evidence that the population of individuals who are routinely present in pubic areas is different than the population proportions. Specifically, the study reports that minorities are represented in higher proportions as drivers than as residents (Miller 2000). In Denver, Colorado, less than half of the individuals stopped by the Denver Police Department from June 2001 through May 2002 are actually residents of Denver (DPD 2002).

Population-based benchmarks are not useful for research conducted in rural or highly transient areas, like interstate highways. Similarly, population-based benchmarks do not include individuals from other communities who routinely drive to or through the community under consideration (Withrow 2004b). This issue was particularly salient to Rojek, Rosenfeld, and Decker (2004) in their statewide study in Missouri. The researchers responded to this by using a sophisticated spatial weighting technique and mapping software to better estimate the racial composition of the driving population in various locations throughout the state. This method amended the population data by assigning greater weights to the racial proportions of residents of nearby and larger communities.

Benchmarks based on population estimates are regularly criticized because of the inability to measure all residents. For example, undocumented immigrants prefer not to report their presence to government authorities even on an anonymous survey like the U.S. Census (Withrow 2004b). Underreporting is even more relevant today because of the growth of the Hispanic population over the past two decades. Hispanics are the fastest growing segment of the population and are estimated to be one fourth of the United States population by 2050 (Walker, Spohn, and DeLone 2000).

After the 2000 U.S. Census it is less likely that traditional racial or ethnic categories will be as meaningful as they have been in the past. In 2000, the U.S. Census Bureau provided a "multiracial" category within the traditional attributes that describe an individual's race. Prior to this respondents were required to pick one and only one race category. Multiracial individuals self-identified themselves based on their personal preference. There is some evidence that the multiracial designation may have substantially encroached into the traditional racial categories. Clearly, it highlights the inadequacies of the census to accurately depict an individual's race and calls into question our traditional understanding of the social importance of racial categories (Navarro 2003).

The validity of population-based benchmarks is particularly challenged by evidence of differences in driving frequency and vehicle ownership between racial groups. Few studies have examined the potential for racial differences in driving and offending behavior. What is clear, however, is that there are substantial differences in driving frequency and vehicle ownership between racial groups. Blacks are six times more likely to use public transportation as their primary means of transportation and therefore may be less likely to operate private vehicles than Whites. Blacks own fewer vehicles per household and are less likely to have a driver's license than Whites (Engel and Calnon 2004a; Langan et al. 2001). The extent to which this might affect the validity of population-based benchmarks is unclear, and the data upon which these estimates are based may be dated given recent increases in middle-class Black families. They are, however, important findings and should be accounted for by the researcher. One would expect that, based on this evidence, minorities are less likely to be stopped by the police because they drive less. If Blacks use public transportation more often than Whites, then the fact that they are overrepresented in police stops of individual vehicles is an even greater concern.

Despite their disadvantages, population-based benchmarks can be used effectively. Fridell et al. (2001) suggest that with some modifications, the validity of population-based benchmarks can be improved. They recommend using the most current estimates, including a residency indicator on the police stop data form, counting only people of driving age, and adjusting the estimate with vehicle ownership data.

Field Observations

According to Smith and Alpert (2002), field observations may be the best way to estimate the population of drivers available to the police for a stop. If a benchmark is based on a sufficiently random series of field observations, then it can produce a relatively accurate estimate of the driving population. Population-based benchmarks erroneously assume that all residents drive the same number of average daily miles and are therefore equally exposed to police surveillance. To accept this assumption, one must accept the notion that a twenty-year-old resident drives as much, or as little, as an eighty-year-old resident. Field observation benchmarks are capable of accounting for the transient population as well as variations in driving exposure. In addition, unlike population-based benchmarks, field observation benchmarks are not adversely affected by underreporting.

Because field observation benchmarks are not dependent upon a resident population, they are particularly useful for highly transient and rural research contexts that are not proximal to a well-defined residential population. These benchmarks are equally useful on urban interstate highways where the racial proportions of drivers and nearby residents are not likely to be equivalent.

Field observation benchmarks provide the researcher with the opportunity to identify potential differential offending patterns with respect to race. Lamberth (1994) reports no difference in the offending behavior of individuals with respect to race. However, the threshold he used (one or more mile an hour over the speed limit) may be too strict. Few drivers can legitimately profess to drive at this level of compliance. Other researchers found statistically significant differences in offending behavior with respect to race (Lange, Blackman, and Johnson 2001). Researchers can overcome this controversy by collecting information relating to driver behavior, specifically offending, while collecting the baseline and developing an important analytical dimension not possible with population-based benchmarks. This may, however, be difficult given the complexity and diversity of traffic violations (Zingraff et al. 2000).

The costs, in terms of money and time, associated with collecting a field observation–based benchmark can be substantial (Engel and Calnon 2004b). Although field observers are paid a relatively low wage, they are required to work long hours to insure they collect an adequate sample size. There are also costs associated with training, lodging, travel, and meals. Because observers will sometimes be in remote locations at any hour of the day or night, the principal investigator must take additional precautions to insure their safety (Withrow 2004b).

There is some legitimate concern that the data upon which field observation benchmarks are based may be unreliable (Alpert, Smith, and Dunham 2003; Engel and Calnon 2004b; Greenwald

2003). It may be difficult for observers to differentiate between Hispanic and White or Black and Hispanic drivers. Routine inter-rater reliability tests, such as those conducted by Lamberth (Police Foundation 2003) can assess the reliability of the sample. Unfortunately, these additional assessments increase the personnel costs associated with collecting the sample. The validity of the sample is also questionable and may be adversely affected by darkness, speed, tinted windows, and traffic volume. To address these issues, one research team (Lange, Blackman, and Johnson 2001) installed digital cameras on the overpasses of an interstate highway and photographed drivers. They also recorded the vehicles' speeds. The researchers, using a three-person inter-rater reliability test, classified drivers by race and ethnicity. This data collection strategy overcame many of the methodological problems associated with this benchmark and provided the researchers with some insight into the potential for differential (by race or ethnicity) offending rates (Withrow 2004b).

Adequate sample size is critical to a field observation benchmark. Often researchers will choose high volume intersections or stretches of highway to ensure they get an acceptable sample in the least amount of time. Sometimes the researcher may choose a site because of prior allegations of racial profiling among frequent drivers at this location. Unfortunately, selecting observation sites this way may bias the sample and adversely affect the accuracy of the benchmark. Furthermore, it is not possible to merge a series of field observations collected throughout a city into a single estimate of the driving population for the entire community. Racial profiling studies that use field observation benchmarks are limited in scope to the actual observation sites.

The researcher's conclusion of whether or not racial profiling is occurring depends on a comparison (odds ratio) between the benchmark and the records of stops (reported by the police department) occurring within the observation site(s). Unfortunately, a number of factors could adversely affect the validity of the stop data provided by the police department. The final location of the stop may not be the same location where the violation took place, or, more importantly, the place where the motorist came to the attention of the officer. Additionally, for safety reasons, officers are reluctant to initiate traffic stops at or near the high volume intersections typically chosen as observation sites (Withrow 2004b).

Accident Records

Accident records, upon which to base racial profiling benchmarks, are normally easy and inexpensive to obtain. Usually differentiating between the at-fault and not-at-fault drivers is relatively easy if officers are required to designate between them on the reporting forms. If not, the researcher can obtain access to the officers' narrative descriptions of the accidents to determine which of the drivers are not (or least) at fault. It is also possible for the researcher to verify the race or ethnicity of the drivers if the state driver licensing databases include this information. Unfortunately, most do not. Benchmarks based on accident records are particularly useful for racial profiling evaluations because they account for differential exposure rates among various classes of drivers. They account for drivers who are not included in the population estimates but drive in a community and individuals who are included in the population estimates but either do not drive or limit their driving. Accident record–based benchmarks are more flexible than the other types of benchmarks. If the accident data is sufficiently detailed, then the researcher can develop a benchmark for an entire city or just a portion of it. Because rural and interstate highways often do not have an associated resident population, these types of benchmarks are particularly useful in these locations.

Unfortunately, there is a lack of empirical studies that can verify the accuracy of accident records as an approximate measure of the driving population (DeYoung, Peck, and Helander 1997; Lyles, Stamatiadis, and Lighthizer 1991; Stamatiadis and Deacon 1997). Additional research utilizing detailed driver trip logs and field observations is necessary to evaluate the validity of this benchmark. Determining who is at fault in a two-vehicle accident may not be easy in all cases, and seldom is one driver totally at fault. The legal distinction of fault, used by a lawyer, may be different than the theoretical definition of fault used by a social science researcher (Withrow 2004b). Table 3.2 summarizes the key advantages and disadvantages of the three principal benchmarks used in racial profiling research

Does it Really Make a Difference?

At a recent (2003) meeting of the Academy of Criminal Justice Sciences, Matthew Zingraff questioned whether finding an acceptable benchmark is really that important. He argued that as long as

TABLE 3.2 Summary of Advantages and Disadvantages of Benchmarks

BENCHMARK	ADVANTAGES	DISADVANTAGES
Population	• Readily available • Inexpensive • Can be used for entire jurisdiction or disaggregated into smaller units (e.g., patrol districts or beats) • Estimates total population, not just driving or adult population	• Does not include transient population • Does not account for differential exposure to police observation • Historical underreporting problems, specifically for ethnic minorities (e.g., Hispanics)
Field observations	• Accounts for transient population • Accounts for differential levels of exposure to police observation • Can be applied to situations without proximal residential populations (e.g., rural areas) • Can estimate differential rates of offending	• Very expensive • Time consuming • Potentially unreliable in low light, high volume, or high speed locations • Limited in scope to observation site • Difficult to associate with relevant portions of stop data
Not-at-fault drivers	• Readily available in most jurisdictions • Inexpensive • Accounts for transient population • Accounts for differential levels of exposure to police observation • Can be used for entire jurisdiction or	• Lack of empirical studies on the validity of the measure • May be difficult to differentiate between at-fault and not-at-fault drivers

Continued

TABLE 3.2 *Continued*

Benchmark	Advantages	Disadvantages
	disaggregated into smaller units (e.g., patrol districts or beats) • Can be applied to nearly every research context (e.g., urban or rural areas, highways or city streets)	

researchers, and the consumers of the research, are aware of the relative limitations of the benchmarks they use, then we should be willing to accept some measurement error. Whether or not the consumers of the research, usually the general public, are willing or able to recognize these limitations is not clear. There is, however, some evidence that the benchmark may make little difference in the ultimate findings of the research. In 2004, I conducted a comparative analysis of the Wichita Stop Study data using three separate benchmarks: population, field observations, and accident records. Wichita, Kansas, is one of only a few jurisdictions where all three of these benchmarks are available for comparative analysis. The purpose of this analysis was to compare the results of three independent racial profiling studies that were conducted in the same community, with the same police-officer collected stop data, and at essentially the same time but utilizing three different benchmarks. The objective of this analysis was to determine whether this methodological difference affects the outcome of the research.

It appears that Professor Zingraff may be correct. The overrepresentation of Black drivers is essentially the same (2:1) when using either the population or accident record benchmarks. Comparisons based on the population and field observation benchmarks both found the same levels of disparity with respect to Black and Hispanic drivers. None of the researchers in the two independent studies (Police Foundation 2003; Withrow 2002) concluded that racial profiling was occurring on the basis of these comparisons alone. It is likely that a third researcher comparing this police stop data against an accident-based benchmark would come to the same conclusion (Withrow 2004b).

Measuring Who Gets Stopped

Early on in the racial profiling controversy, the police vehemently denied the accusations of racial profiling leveled against them. They argued that there was no evidence of racial disparity, much less racial profiling, and they were right. Until the mid-1990s very few departments routinely collected data relating to vehicle stops, in particular the race or ethnicity of the drivers they stopped. Prior to the passage of statutes requiring the collection of racial profiling data, only three state police organizations were required to record the race and ethnicity of the individuals they stopped for routine traffic violations. In most departments officers were required to record the race of the driver only if the stop resulted in an arrest. Even in these situations the data were not stored electronically, making meaningful analysis difficult (Cleary 2000).

With the exception of a few state level or narrowly focused projects that used existing stop data (CHP 2000; Lamberth 1994, 1996; TDPS 2000; WSP 2001), police stop data is collected for the sole purpose of racial profiling analysis. Normally these data are recorded on specially designed paper forms, often called contact cards (DPD 2002; Withrow 2002, 2003). In some cases the data fields one would normally see on a paper form are available to officers via their mobile display terminals, laptops, or pocket computers (Cox et al. 2001; Landsdowne 2002; MDPS 2003; Smith and Petrocelli 2001). In one case the data were recorded by dispatchers based on information radioed by officers in the field (Meehan and Ponder 2002).

Rather than amend their current information or data gathering system, most departments, unless they are using existing statistics, impose an additional requirement on police officers to collect racial profiling data. This means that in addition to completing the routine paperwork required by the department (e.g., tickets, case reports, accident forms, vehicle inventory reports, etc.), the officers must complete a form to record the data necessary to conduct the racial profiling analysis. This introduces three important methodological issues that may threaten the quality of the data.

Accuracy

The accuracy of any data is potentially adversely affected anytime an interruption occurs during the collection process. Data is more accurate at the point at which it occurs. When data is collected by police officers in the field via paper forms it must be transferred to an electronic format for analysis. This transfer process may, especially if dependent upon stand-alone data entry, degrade the accuracy of the data. This potential is mitigated by using machine-readable "bubble" forms that do not (with the possible exception of the comments section) require the intervention of an independent data entry process.

Likely, one of the most common threats to the validity of police stop data is a simple, and sometimes understandable, misinterpretation of an individual's race or ethnicity. For many reasons, police officers and administrators are reluctant to ask citizens for this information, not the least of which is that the mere asking of this question may unnecessarily insult a driver or taint the contact with an air of racial tension (Fridell et al. 2001). As a result, most departments allow the officers to make this determination. Although race is obvious in most situations, the officer may guess incorrectly. This may be particularly true for multiracial individuals.

Beyond this administrative issue a more insidious threat lies. Most departments, in preparation for a racial profiling study, initiated a policy requiring officers to complete reporting forms. An administrative rule is however no guarantee of compliance (Alpert, 1997; Fyfe, 1979; Geller and Scott, 1992; Leo and Thomas, 1998; Oakes, 1970). Within this context the most severe threat to the accuracy of police stop data is outright deception whereupon the officer intentionally misrepresents the race or ethnicity of the individual in order to avoid potential administrative attention or sanction. Most stop data collection forms do not include other information about the drivers (e.g., a driver's license or vehicle registration number) with which to conduct an internal review for accuracy. Another type of deception that would affect the accuracy of stop data is known as "ghosting." Ghosting occurs when officers enter vehicle registration numbers from cars owned by White drivers on the forms they fill out pursuant to a stop involving a Black driver. This practice was documented in 1994 during the data collection process in the New Jersey study (Meeks 2000).

Completeness

The completeness of stop data is adversely affected by officers who either chose not to record or report certain stops, in particular those involving minority drivers or establish personal stopping quotas based on race. Police officers are, for the most part, aware of the proportional racial representation of their beats. After reviewing their work over routines tour of duty, it is conceivable, although we like to think highly unlikely, that officers would realize they had stopped a disproportionately high number of minorities. In this case an unscrupulous officer might discard the data forms from some of the minority stops (particularly those resulting in unofficial dispositions like nonwritten warnings or undocumented field interviews) or simply decide not to record information relating to an appropriate number of stops involving minorities. In either case the data are incomplete. To achieve the same thing, officers might establish informal quotas based on the proportional racial representations of their beat assignments. Using these quotas they may either stop certain individuals for relatively minor violations just to fill in their quotas for that particular racial or ethnic group. Conversely, to avoid stopping too many minorities an officer may ignore flagrant violations, unless, of course, there are witnesses. This process has come to be labeled "balancing." Because much of police work is conducted far away from active supervision, it is highly unlikely, in the absence of an internal audit system, that officers behaving in this manner would be detected. With few exceptions (see Lamberth 1994), there is little evidence of balancing within the racial profiling literature. Furthermore, it appears that behavioral changes such as these are temporary and easily overcome with routine supervision and training (Farrell et al. 2004).

Reactivity

Sometimes referred to as the Hawthorne effect, reactivity is a threat to the external validity of experimental results. It occurs when research subjects alter their behavior because they are aware of being studied or measured. This issue is particularly salient within the racial profiling controversy. In most cases the issue is merely self-consciousness on the part of the subject and dissipates over time. In more extreme cases it involves active and ongoing deception involving a number of coconspirators. The pattern in racial profiling research appears more likely to be the former. The mere "implementation of a racial profiling study is likely to heighten police awareness of their stop patterns" (Cleary 2000, 19).

Changes in police behavior, including a reduction in the overall number of stops and searches, are well documented in the literature (Cleary 2000; Donohue 2000; Farrell 2003; Meeks 2000; Withrow 2002). Researches in Great Britain report that, in addition to overall reductions in productivity, officers experience lower morale when racial profiling studies are implemented (Ramirez, McDevitt, and Farrell 2000). At some level, a reduction of productivity is predictable. After all, the officers are required to complete an additional form, and while doing so they are not on routine patrol and making stops. At the individual level, the time necessary to complete a form is miniscule. Collectively, however, it can result in a considerable amount of patrol time.

The data collection phase of a racial profiling study may last from six months to several years. During the course of that time any number of events can occur that might result in overall reductions of productivity. For example, during the data collection phase of the Wichita, Kansas, study, overall traffic stops decreased by 30 percent. Police departments in similarly sized communities in the region not collecting similar data do not report decreases in overall traffic stops during the same period. At first the researcher thought the reduction was directly related to the data collection process. A more careful review of the administrative and policy changes that occurred prior to and during the data collection phase revealed an alternative explanation. Immediately prior to the data collection phase the department decentralized its traffic enforcement function. During the data collection phase the department eliminated its motorcycle unit and reassigned those officers to routine patrol in automobiles. Previously, the traffic enforcement and motorcycle units accounted for the majority of the traffic stops conducted in the city. The decentralization and redeployment effectively interrupted the production of traffic stops, but only for a time. After the affected officers settled into their new assignments and patrol officers were provided additional traffic enforcement training, the number of stops returned to previous levels (Withrow 2002).

CAUSALITY: CORRELATION IS NOT CAUSE

To establish a causal relationship between variables, scientist must satisfy three rules. The first is temporal order. The cause must occur prior, preferably immediately prior, to the effect. Furthermore, every time the cause occurs, so must the effect. Second, there must be a correlation between the cause and the effect. If the correlation is positive, then an increase in the level of magnitude of the cause, or independent variable, must result in an increase in the level of magnitude of the effect, or dependent variable. If the correlation is negative, then an increase in the cause must result in a decrease in the effect. Preferably this relationship should be, absent intervening variables, consistent. Third once temporal order and correlation are established, the scientist must eliminate alternative plausible explanations.

An interesting phenomenon occurs on public beaches at the end of each spring. Following steady increases in the temperature of the water, the number of drowning victims increases. When the temperature of the water decreases, the number of drowning victims decreases. One might conclude from this that there is a causal relationship between water temperature and drowning. Both temporal order and correlation have been established, but what about alternative explanations? Could the number of drowning victims be related to the overall number of individuals who swim during the summer, when the water is warmer, versus the number of individuals who swim during the winter, when the water is cooler? Of course it could. This example demonstrates the necessity for science to validate each of the three causal rules before alleging a causal relationship between variables.

To the extent that benchmarks and stop data are accurate, racial profiling researchers have established correlation. Minorities are consistently found to be overrepresented among individuals stopped when compared to a benchmark that indicates their representation within the general population or among actual drivers. To some extent, temporal order has also been established. An individual's race or ethnicity is established long before becoming available to routine police observation. Officers, if they are prejudiced, likely develop those attitudes long before they enter the academy and certainly before the stops are made. What racial profiling research has failed to do is eliminate alternative explanations.

Upon finding evidence of disparity, the easy thing to do is allege that the police are racists and use race as a general indicator of criminal suspiciousness. To do so, however, violates the rules of causality and potentially limits the advancement of this research agenda. Racial profiling research has not yet matured to the level where alternative plausible explanations to what appears obvious to some can be discounted. For example, we really do not know whether minorities are more likely than nonminorities to drive aggressively or violate the law. We do not know the effects of deployment or if minorities are inadvertently subjected to higher levels of police observation. Until we are able to respond to these questions, and many more, science is not prepared to definitively state that an individual's race affects a police officer's decision to initiate a traffic stop.

SUMMARY

Because of the attention given to racial profiling studies, researchers have a special responsibility to be accurate and adhere to proven scientific procedures and techniques. The first step is to develop an acceptable definition of racial profiling. Most researchers use a conceptual definition that focuses on how race affects a police officer's decision making process. Unfortunately, the data these researchers collect do not produce the variables necessary to measure the police decision making process. As a result, despite the fact that nearly every researcher using this definition finds evidence of disparity with respect to race in routine enforcement programs, few are convinced that racial profiling is occurring. Other researchers advocate for a more operational approach that defines racial profiling as a disparate effect evident in an enforcement program. In these situations evidence of disparity is a valid indicator of racial profiling. As a result, researchers who use this definition conclude that racial profiling is occurring.

The most critical methodological issue within the racial profiling controversy is measuring the population of individuals exposed to police observation. The earliest research developed benchmarks based on field observations of drivers. Most researchers now design benchmarks based on population data. An emerging benchmark, borrowed from the traffic engineering field, is based on demographic data from not-at-fault drivers in two-vehicle traffic accidents. At least one researcher advocates the use of internal benchmarks wherein an officer's stopping behavior is compared against similarly situated officers from the same department. Within these broad categories a number of important variations exist. Each has advantages and disadvantages and none are universally acceptable in every research context.

Stop data, the numerator in racial profiling research, is more often than not collected by police officers. Data collection is often temporary and conducted in addition to other routine data gathering or reporting requirements. Because of the nature of the racial profiling controversy, there is some concern that the data may be either inaccurate or incomplete. In addition, the data collection process, because it relies on police officer compliance, may be reactive.

Finally, the rules of causality require researchers to establish temporal order, correlation, and a lack of plausible alternative explanations. Racial profiling research has for the most part established temporal order and correlation. It has not yet eliminated all plausible alternative explanations of why disparity exists.

DISCUSSION QUESTIONS

1. How should validity problems associated with racial profiling definitions be appropriately addressed?
2. What problems do the two types of racial profiling definitions pose for the analyst?
3. Is the attention placed on the accuracy of benchmarks warranted?
4. Compare and contrast the benchmarks discussed in this chapter. Which of them would be the most generally accurate?
5. Does an overrepresentation of minorities in traffic stops provide sufficient proof of the discriminatory intent of police officers? Why or why not?
6. Explain how an internal benchmark would be an appropriate (or inappropriate) method to evaluate the potential for discriminatory behavior of officers.

CASE STUDIES

1. A police chief is planning to use a population-based benchmark in a racial profiling study in her department. However, she thinks the benchmark would underestimate the number of Blacks at risk of being stopped. The university professor supervising the research suggests that the population estimates be amended to account for higher arrest statistics involving Blacks. This will increase the estimated proportion

of Blacks at risk of being stopped. Advise the chief on the feasibility of making this change.

2. Using the following conceptual definition of racial profiling, develop a way to measure how race affects a police officer's decision to stop a vehicle. Your measure should account for the anecdotal evidence that officers are seldom aware of an individual's race prior to the stop.

> ...any police-initiated action that relies on the race, ethnicity, or national origin rather than the behavior of an individual or information that leads the police to a particular individual who has been identified as being, or having been, engaged in criminal activity." (Ramirez, McDevitt, and Farrell 2000, 3).

3. The local newspaper reports that traffic stops within predominately minority neighborhoods have declined 75 percent since the beginning of a racial profiling study three months ago. In addition, it appears that calls for service (police assistance) in these same neighborhoods have increased more than 50 percent during the same time frame. You, a crime analyst, verify that the newspaper story is correct. How should the chief of police respond to this news?

EXPLAINING THE DISPARITY

To identify and critically analyze the various explanations for the overrepresentation of minorities among individuals stopped by the police.

INTRODUCTION

Theory provides a systematic explanation of the relationship between social events. Explanatory theory enables us to determine exactly why events happen or fail to happen. It has three basic functions in research. First, theory prevents us from being tricked by coincidence. Second, theories enable us to recognize patterns, and in doing so allow us to either prevent undesirable or encourage desirable outcomes in the future. Third, theories "shape and direct research efforts, pointing toward likely discoveries through empirical observation" (Babbie 1999, 29).

Despite the intense public, political, and legal attention given to racial profiling, the current research has taken us only slightly further in our understanding of routine patrol procedures than we were in the early 1970s. Data collection to date has largely ignored the need to explain why officers make a decision to stop (Engel, Calnon, and Bernard 2002). The intensity of media attention has not been matched by an acceptable level of conceptualization of the issues, a sophistication of analytical techniques, or the development of explanatory theory (Tomaskovic-Devey, Mason, and Zingraff 2004). According to Engel, Calnon, and Bernard (2002), the inability of the current research to advance our knowledge of racial profiling is directly related to an overall lack of explanatory theory. The lack of explicitly stated theories that could explain racial disparity in enforcement programs results in confusion and hampers our ability to develop corrective policy. In short, there is more rhetoric than reason.

To demonstrate the importance of theory in research, consider our recent experience with police pursuit policy. During the 1990s considerable attention was given to police department policies relating to high speed vehicular pursuits. In 2000, the Police Executive Research Forum published a comprehensive study of police pursuit practices. The research was funded by the National Institute of Justice and looked at police pursuits from various perspectives. The most interesting findings came from the interviews with offenders. The researchers asked offenders a series of questions including why they ran, and, more importantly, why they stopped. Most offenders indicated that they ran because they were driving a stolen car, had a suspended driver's license, were escaping a crime scene, were under the influence of alcohol or drugs, or were afraid the police would beat them. Although offensive, these are plausible explanations of behavior. The researchers then asked the offenders what would have made them slow down during a chase. Seventy-five percent of the respondents indicated that they would have slowed down when they felt safe. "The suspects reported, on average, that to feel safe, they had to be free from seeing emergency lights or hearing sirens for approximately two blocks in town, between two and 2.2 miles on the highway, and 2.5 miles on the freeway" (Alpert et al. 2000, 123). In other words, regardless of their reasons for running, offenders will likely stop if they do not perceive they are being chased. This theoretical statement explains why individuals do not stop when chased by the police. More importantly, the research findings indicate a potential solution to the high speed pursuit problem that can be adapted in nearly every policing context.

The purpose of this chapter is to identify and critically analyze the various theoretical explanations offered to explain the overrepresentation of minorities among individuals stopped by the police. A number of authors propose similar explanatory continuums, suggesting that the practice of racial profiling may exist at various levels of intensity within a department. Some authors attempt to identify potential theoretical explanations of racial profiling from the classic sociological and criminological literature. One author, after conducting a rigorous analysis of stop data at the beat level synthesizes an assortment of theoretical perspectives into an integrated theory.

EXPLANATORY CONTINUUMS

A number of researchers propose that the explanation for the overrepresentation of minorities in traffic stops may be explained along a continuum. Tomaskovic-Devey, Mason, and Zingraff (2004) offer four possible bias mechanisms as explanations for this disparity.

1. Because of their racial prejudice, police officers consciously target minorities and subject them to higher levels of scrutiny.
2. Because police officers have access to stereotypes developed and sustained within the police subculture that suggest minorities are more likely to engage in criminal activity, they stop minority drivers at higher rates. This culturally imposed bias may be present in both minority and nonminority officers.
3. Because police organizations encourage the use of race-inclusive profiles (particularly for drug couriers) and reward officers for drug arrests and seizures of drugs and assets, the officers proactively target minority drivers.
4. Because police departments deploy more officers to high crime rate areas that are also predominately populated by minorities, police officers inadvertently subject minorities to higher levels of observation and therefore stop a higher percentage of minority drivers.

Carter and Katz-Banister (2004) offer a similar set of propositions that define how police officers use race. The use of race in enforcement decisions ranges as follows:

1. No intentional use of race or racial profiling
2. Race and ethnicity used objectively as part of a description of a known suspect or offender
3. Race and ethnicity used subjectively in combination with other factors to initiate pretextual stops
4. Intentional and insidious use of race and racial profiling

To date, no researcher has directly empirically tested these propositions. There is no evidence that police officers are either more or less racially prejudiced than other professionals. For example

Norris et al. (1992) report that, contrary to public opinion, police prejudice does not significantly lead to disparate treatment. Furthermore, they found that once the stop is underway, Blacks are not treated less respectfully.

We do know that the police officer subculture, like subcultures in other professions, is quite pervasive and does explain some police behavior. However, we do not know the extent, if any, to which the police subculture sustains racial stereotypes and the extent to which this results in disparate treatment.

There is some evidence that police departments encourage the use of profiles, some of which include race or ethnicity as indicators of probable criminal behavior. Furthermore, as discussed in Chapter One, there is some evidence that police officers are encouraged through their department's merit and promotion system to actively seek drug couriers and to seize large amounts of contraband and assets. Court documents from the Maryland study reveal that the police were encouraged by their department to actively seek drug couriers, who are predominately Black males and females. The ACLU (1999) reports that the Eagle County, Colorado, Sheriff's Department provided its offices with a list of indicators of potential drug couriers that included race.

There may also be some merit to the deployment explanation. Withrow (2004a) reports that deployment, as measured by the number of stops, is higher in patrol beats that experience higher crime rates and calls for service. In this local study, most of these beats, but not all, are also populated primarily by racial minorities. In a separate study Withrow and Jackson (2002) also found that disparity may be the result of deploying officers to higher crime areas that are heavily populated by racial minorities. Citing evidence of higher rates of drug-related crime involving Black victims, MacDonald (2003) argues that police resources are justifiably deployed to predominantly Black neighborhoods. After all, she asks, shouldn't the police go to where the crime happens?

DO DIFFERENTIAL OFFENDING RATES EXPLAIN THE DISPARITY?

One of the most provocative explanations for the overrepresentation of racial and ethnic minorities in traffic stops is based on the proposition that minorities commit higher levels of crime and traffic law infractions. If minorities as a group drive more aggressively and violate the traffic law at higher rates, then a disparity would be likely. Disproportionately higher rates of offending are well established for gender and age groups. Males, and particularly young males, are as a group more aggressive drivers. As a result, they are overrepresented in police traffic stops. Is the same true for racial minorities? The results of prior research are inconclusive and constitute a substantial threat to the advancement of research in this area. "The ultimate question in the profiling controversy is whether the disproportionate involvement of Blacks and Hispanics with law enforcement reflects police racism or the consequences of disproportionate minority crime" (MacDonald 2001, 1). Similarly, a United States Government Accounting Office report found a "key limitation of the available analyses [is that it could not determine] whether different groups may have been at different levels of risk for being stopped because they differed in their rates and/or severity of committing traffic violations" (U.S. GAO 2000, 1).

Covington (2001) and Lamberth (1994) found that racial minorities are no more likely to speed than nonminorities. Lamberth's research, however, has been criticized as having an overly broad measure of violation in which speeding is defined as one or mile an hour over the speed limit. Harris (2002) urges caution in using offending or arrest rates as evidence of criminality. Arrest rates, he argues, do not accurately measure criminality. Instead, they measure the performance of the police.

Recognizing the inadequacies of available research to determine if differential offending rates can explain the disparity in police stops with respect to race, MacDonald (2001, 2003) makes the following observations. Black drivers represent 10 percent of all drivers, yet they account for 16 and 13 percent of the drivers involved in accidents resulting in injury and death, respectively. While this may appear to indicate that Blacks are more likely aggressive or prone to take risks while driving, she cautions us to consider the impact of differential rates of compliance with seat belt laws among racial minorities as a possible explanation of increased fatality rates among Black drivers.

At least two racial profiling researchers have addressed the question of differential (by race) offending rates. Neither of these researchers found substantial differences in offending rates (of the traffic law) between racial or ethnic groups (Lamberth 1996; Zingraff et al. 2000). One of the most comprehensive studies of differential offending rates was conducted on the New Jersey Turnpike. Lange, Blackman, and Johnson (2001) used digital cameras to capture images of drivers at several locations along the turnpike. The devices also recorded the speeds of the vehicles. The images were then classified by race, ethnicity, gender, age, and speed. The researchers used a rigorous cross verification technique wherein images were removed from the analysis unless three reviewers agreed on the demographic features of the drivers (i.e., race, ethnicity, age, and gender). The study reports "significant and substantial differences in the rates of speeders among some racial groups in some areas" (p. 18). Specifically, the researchers observed that White drivers are significantly underrepresented among speeders in all 65-mile per hour zones of the turnpike. Conversely, Black drivers are significantly overrepresented among speeders in the same areas. The age and gender of the drivers do not fully account for the racial differences observed.

POTENTIAL THEORETICAL EXPLANATIONS

Bernard and Engel (2001) propose that criminal justice theory should be organized with respect to its dependent variable. Specifically, and with respect to this particular research agenda, explanations of the disparity with respect to race in police stops should be organized into the following categories:

1. The behavior of individual criminal justice actors
2. The behavior of criminal justice agencies
3. The behavior of the entire criminal justice system and its component parts

A year later, using this typology, they offered several alternative theoretical explanations of racial profiling (Engel, Calnon, and Bernard 2002).

The Behavior of Individual Criminal Justice Actors

This perspective argues that racial profiling is caused by the prejudice of individual officers. Although not explicitly stated, it is the most prominent explanation implied by contemporary racial profiling researchers. Within this category there are three plausible theories (Engel, Calnon, and Bernard 2002).

Theory of Reasoned Action

This theory (Ajzen and Fishbein 1977, 1980) proposes that attitudes held by police officers (e.g., racial prejudice) affect their behavior. Importantly, these theorists found strong relationships between attitudes and behavior. In effect, these theorists allege that racial profiling is caused by endemic racial prejudice among police officers. Unfortunately, there is no definitive evidence that police officers, as a whole, are any more or less racially biased than other people. Furthermore, accurately measuring racial bias has so far eluded science.

Theory of Coercive Action

This theory (Tedeschi and Felson 1994) alleges that the police make certain decisions to achieve certain goals. Specifically, the police use coercion to control the behavior of others, restore justice, and protect their authority. One of the most potentially coercive actions a police officer can take is a traffic stop. During a traffic stop the police officer has near unfettered authority. The mere presence of a police officer likely produces voluntary compliance. This theory alleges that police use coercion to control individuals (e.g., minorities) who threaten the status quo.

Expectancy Theory

This theory (Mitchell 1974; Campbell and Pritchard 1976) attempts to explain worker output as a function of what supervisors expect of subordinates. A police officer's work product is dependent upon what is expected. More specifically, a police officer will do what is required to be measured as a productivity indicator. This theory may explain officer aggression in drug interdiction enforcement. Given the emphasis placed on drug interdiction by police administrators, as well as their political leaders, this theory does indeed seem to be a plausible explanation. If so, then one might expect a reduction of the disparity in stops if a department abandons, or at least deemphasizes, the war on drugs.

The Behavior of Criminal Justice Agencies

This perspective argues that racial profiling is the result of behavior institutionalized into criminal justice agencies (Engel, Calnon, and Bernard 2002). These theories are popular among researchers proposing that guidance (e.g., intelligence reports indicating a high probability that drug couriers are racial or ethnic minorities) from knowledgeable and influential police agencies (e.g., the United States Drug Enforcement Agency) ultimately affects the behavior of individual officers.

Institutional Expectations and Bargaining

This theory (Wilson 1968; Van Maanan 1983, 1984) proposes that the expectations of the department affect the behavior of individual officers. It is similar to expectancy theory, yet distinguishable because it emphasizes the importance of bargaining between officers and supervisors. Proponents of this theory argue that officers bargain with supervisors to receive favorable treatment from them. It is plausible that part of this bargaining may involve the creation of formal or informal standards of behavior or productivity. Officers who meet certain production quotas (e.g., drug seizures) expect favorable treatment from their departments.

Institutional Perspectives

This theory (Crank and Langworth 1992; DeJong, Mastrofski, and Parks 2001; Mastrofski, Ritti, and Snipes 1994) alleges that "powerful myths" within the police organization add legitimacy and stability to the police organization and encourage individual officer behaviors (Engel, Calnon, and Bernard 2002, 266) For example, if police officers believe that racial profiles are an effective tool for identifying criminal suspects, then they will more frequently stop and question individuals of the suspected racial category. The myth will be perpetuated by demonstrations of its effectiveness. The myth therefore becomes a self-fulfilling prophesy (Harris 2002).

In a later article Engel and Calnon (2004a) argue that the institutionalization of the war on drugs into police departments explains much of the racial disparity in enforcement. Their evaluation, within the context of Crank and Langworth's (1992) institutional perspectives theory "clearly indicates that the incorporation of aggressive profiling strategies into the activities and structure of police organizations (resulting from the politicization of the war on drugs) provided police departments with stability, legitimacy, and additional resources" (p. 53). They further argue that influential police administrators perpetuated these myths by creating reward systems favoring officers who seize large amounts of drugs and assets. The officers in turn initiated aggressive policing strategies and actively sought ways to improve their productivity. More specifically, they looked for ways to improve their hit rates in searches. It is understandable that when intelligence information in the early 1990s began to suggest that drug couriers are more likely to be racial and ethnic minorities, police officers would use this information to improve their productivity and hence receive positive reinforcement. Support for this argument comes from Harris' (2002) observation that both Black and White officers appear to stop racial minorities at the same disproportionately high rates. It would indeed be difficult to allege racism among Black officers. This theory alleges that organizational pressures have an affect on individual officer behavior, regardless of the officer's personal feelings.

The Behavior of the Entire Criminal Justice System and its Component Parts

This collection of theories suggests that racial profiling may be the result of interaction between components of the criminal justice system or the larger society. This interaction is usually in the form of conflict (Engel, Calnon, and Bernard 2002).

Theory of Norm Resistance

This perspective (Lanza-Kaduce and Greenleaf 1994; Turk 1969) is based on conflict theory. It proposes that racial profiling may be the result of conflict between the norms or desired outcomes of competing groups. The norm of the dominant group is domination of the subordinate groups. This is necessary for them to maintain their dominant position. The norm of the subordinate group is deference to authority. When these norms conflict, incongruence occurs. Normally, the dominant group wins, especially if supported by formal social control mechanisms like the police. This theory would also be of some value in explaining why minorities view traffic stops differently than nonminorities.

Theory of Law

This theory (Black 1976) argues that as society becomes more complex, it creates more levels of social stratification. This ultimately results in a greater quantity of law. This law (in the form of additional laws and increased sophistication of legal systems) is then used by the dominant subculture to impose restrictions (i.e., control) on the subordinate classes. Ultimately, this leads to disparity between groups.

Conflict Theory

Most sociological theories are based on an assumption of consensus within society. Using this approach, law and the administration of justice arise from the common norms that represent society's collective feelings of what is just and right. Within this paradigm, we all believe laws are necessary to insure social order. A crime, therefore, is considered a violation of the collective norms of society. Beginning in the 1970s, some criminologists began to investigate a collection of perspectives that eventually became known as conflict theories. Conflict theorists view social interaction quite differently. According to a conflict theorist, law is the result of conflict between the dominant and subordinate classes. Ultimately, the dominant class wins, but not without making some limited concessions. The result is a series of laws and a law enforcement program that favor the dominant class. (See Chambliss 1994 and Chambliss and Seidman 1971 for a comprehensive discussion of conflict theory.)

Conflict theory is a macro-level theory. Its focus is on how social institutions and the groups within them interrelate. Therefore, it does explain behavior at the individual level. For example, conflict theory cannot explain why an individual officer decides to stop an individual or whether race influenced the officer's decision. It is, however, instructive as an explanation of how the dominant culture might exercise its control over the subordinate classes (i.e., minorities) through the authority of the law and the power of the police department.

At least one group of researchers has attempted to use conflict theory as an explanation for racial profiling. Using the data from the Richmond, Virginia study, Petrocelli, Piquero, and Smith (2003) report a number of findings consistent with conflict theory. In a beat level analysis of this data they found that the total number of stops is best explained by the crime rate, rather than the predominant race of the individuals who reside in the beat. This supports the notion that patrol resources are allocated to patrol beats on the basis of demand, rather than the race of its residents. Additionally, the proportion of Black residents and the crime rate within a beat tend to decrease the percentage of stops ending in an arrest. These finding do not support a conflict theory explanation. Alternatively, they report that the percentage of stops resulting in a search is best predicted by the proportion of Blacks living in the beat. In beats populated primarily by Blacks, searches are more likely. This finding may support a conflict theory explanation. The authors ultimately determine that their results are inconclusive. While some of the findings tend to support a conflict theory explanation, others do not. They suggest further analysis using multivariate techniques that can isolate the relative effects of various factors on police decision making.

The Theory of Contextual Attentiveness

A beat level analysis of police stops, like the one conducted by Petrocelli, Piquero, and Smith (2003) provides important insight into the racial profiling controversy and may produce explanatory theory. Using the stop data from the Wichita, Kansas, study Withrow (2004a) attempted to determine whether the demographic features of smaller geographical areas (i.e., patrol beats) influence the enforcement behavior of police officers. Most racial profiling studies compare stop data and benchmarks that represent an entire community or state. At this level, the data cannot determine whether the specific context of a particular beat affects enforcement patterns. For example, is a White driver in a neighborhood populated predominately by Black residents as likely to be stopped and searched as a Black driver in a neighborhood populated predominately by White residents? Second, broad analyses cannot determine whether officer deployment patterns affect disparity in stops with respect to race or ethnicity. A beat level analysis can determine whether racial and ethnic groups are stopped at disproportionately higher rates because the police deploy a larger proportion of officers in neighborhoods that are predominately populated by racial and ethnic minorities.

Does Context Matter?

A person walking alone at 10:00 P.M. on a Saturday night near a popular restaurant might not seem particularly suspicious. However, that same person walking alone at 1:00 A.M. near the same restaurant on a Wednesday might appear more suspicious, unless of course he was wearing a waiter's uniform. Drivers and their passengers with inconsistent stories about where they are going or where they have been, juveniles out at night in a commercial area or during school hours in a residential neighborhood, and even loud noises in normally quiet neighborhoods are contextual inconsistencies that tend to attract the attention of even the most inexperienced officers. Police officers learn, either through experience or interaction with other officers, that responding to these inconsistencies often results in an arrest, the acquisition of important criminal intelligence, or the interruption of potential criminal activities. Any of these results are considered good police work by the department's administration.

For more than three decades policing scholars have attempted to identify the factors that explain how and why police officers make enforcement decisions. The early studies suggested that police officers develop alternative approaches to their routine tasks based on various situational, organizational, and individual characteristics (Black 1971; Black, and Reiss 1970; Powell 1981; Smith and Visher 1981; Smith, Visher, and Davidson 1984; Wilson 1968). However as late as 1980, Black argued that "little scientific theory has been developed to predict and explain how policing varies from one setting to another" (p. 1). Since then, the research has matured and clearly indicates that neighborhood contexts affect police officer behavior. Race may play a role, but not necessarily by itself (Alpert and Dunham 1988; Klinger 1994, 1997; Sacks 1972; Smith, Graham, and Adams 1991; Weitzer 1999, 2000). Furthermore, while officers' interpretations of observed events are heavily influenced by the demands of their agency, their professional attitudes, and their experiences (Alpert and Dunham 1988; Brown 1981; Gieryn 2000; Manning 1997, Van Maanen 1974, 1978), they appear also to be influenced by the attitudes (including prejudices) of the community in which they are assigned to work (Banton 1964; Bittner 1970, 1979; Brown 1981; Muir 1977; Wilson 1968). The police use their knowledge of an area (Bittner 1970) or territory (Brown 1981; Rubinstein 1973) as a behavioral cue. For example, Sherman (1989) found that the police behave quite differently in known high crime areas or in areas where they perceive a threat. Skolnik (1994) reports that a police officer's behavior, particularly at the individual level, is highly influenced by an officer's experience working with people. The police tend to classify people or events and regard as suspicious anyone or anything that does not fit into the dominant theme of an area. The police develop profiles of "symbolic assailants" based on experience. They learn to recognized gestures, language, and attire as "preludes to violence" (p. 45). The use of these profiles is an "integral part of a policeman's work" and may include an ethnic dimension (p. 83).

Powell (1981) found significant differences among agencies in the use of discretion and found that these differences are influenced by the racial mix of both the community and the department. The police in predominantly Black urban centers have the highest overall use of personal discretion and were slightly more punitive to White offenders than Black offenders. The police in predominantly White urban centers and suburbs are considerably more punitive toward Black offenders than White offenders. Powell concluded from this that the police are less punitive toward Blacks in Black communities because of more frequent association with them. Smith and Alpert (2002) report that as the racial composition changes between areas of the city, the racial proportions of individuals stopped changes. Specifically, it appears that within a specific geographic area, as the proportion of Black residents increases, the proportion of stops involving Whites increases, and visa versa. Likewise, Meehan and Ponder (2002) proposed an ecological dimension to racial profiling. In their study Blacks appear to be stopped at proportionately higher rates when driving through predominately White neighborhoods, and in particular the White neighborhoods farther away from predominately Black neighborhoods. Unfortunately, their analysis did not provide any insight into the possibility that the opposite may be true.

The findings of this body of literature provide some insight into how various factors affect an officer's behavior after a stop has been initiated. Unfortunately for racial profiling researchers, little is known about how these factors affect a police officer's decision to initiate an arrest. Previous researchers interested in identifying the factors that affect a police officer's enforcement decision with respect to an individual within a well-defined and quantifiable situation have a substantial advantage over those attempting to identify the factors that determine why a police officer focuses his or her attention upon a particular individual in the first place or independent of a potential criminal event. In almost every police-citizen contact in which an arrest is possible, an official record is created and in most cases is available to the researcher. This record (intended to document the officer's official involvement in a situation) includes many of the extra-legal factors necessary to differentiate between those arrested, warned, cited, or released. From this information, researchers are able to determine the differences between and the similarities among groups and ultimately infer the salient factors that might predict an officer's enforcement decision. Researchers interested in identifying the factors that affect a police officer's decision to focus upon a particular individual are not so fortunate. There are no accurate records kept on citizens accessible to but not noticed by the police. Furthermore, this research tends to focus on what the suspect *is* and how that affects a police officer's decision. The process of police officer decision making may be better understood if the focus of scholarly attention is on what the suspect *is not* within the context of a situation and how that might affect an officer's attentiveness.

A Look Inside the Beats

Using data from the 2000 U.S. Census, Withrow (2004a) developed beat profiles for each of the city's patrol beats, representing their proportional racial and ethnic group representation. The data reveal a racially segregated pattern of settlement. Only four of the 36 patrol beats are populated primarily by Black residents. Two patrol beats are populated by a diverse mixture of racial and ethnic groups. The remaining thirty beats are populated primarily by White residents.

The analysis reveals that the race of individuals stopped within a patrol beat is highly numerically related to the predominant race of the residents who live there. As the number of Black residents increases within a patrol beat, the number of stops involving Black drivers also increases. The same is true for White drivers in beats populated primarily by White residents. More importantly, the cross-correlations (White drivers in Black beats and Black drivers in White beats) are negative. As the number of Black residents increases within a patrol beat the number of stops involving White drivers decreases, and visa versa.

Does Deployment Explain the Disparity?

The differential deployment of patrol resources is often considered an explanation for the overrepresentation of minorities in police stops. Demand for patrol resources is not evenly distributed. As a result, most departments allocate patrol resources to beats based on the population, distribution of living structures, size of the beat, crime rate, and calls for service. Beats with denser populations, more calls for service, and higher rates of reported crime and victimization tend to be smaller or assigned more patrol resources. These beats may also be populated by racial and ethnic minorities. Because more police officers working in a beat may result in more stops, the racial and ethnic minority residents who live in these beats are more at risk of being stopped than the residents of other portions of the city.

While it is not possible to accurately determine the level of patrol resources routinely assigned to a particular beat (because of occasional inter-beat dispatching), the only available reliable indicator of patrol deployment is the number of stops that occur within a beat. The results (based on a multiple regression) indicate that the only important predictors of stops (the dependent variable) within a beat are the population of the beat and the number of reported crimes per 1,000 residents. Beats with larger populations and higher rates of crime receive the most police attention. The race of the individuals who live in the beat does not appear to affect the number of stops within the beat. From this one should conclude that race does not appear to influence patrol deployment and that deployment may be a plausible alternative explanation for the overrepresentation of minorities in traffic stops (see Table 4.1).

Driving While *not* Black

A subsequent analysis of the beat level statistics reveals a remarkable enforcement pattern within the most racially segregated beats. Within the predominantly White beats, Black drivers are consistently overrepresented in terms of their proportional representation. Conversely, within the predominantly Black beats, White drivers are

TABLE 4.1 Regression Model Predicting the Number of Stops (as a Measure of Deployment) Within a Patrol Beat in Wichita, Kansas

VARIABLES	BETA COEFFICIENTS	SIGNIFICANCE
Beat population	.689	.000
Reported crimes per 1,000 residents	.437	.008
Proportion of Black residents[a]	.067	.670

R square = .388; constant = 654.874 (unstandardized); dependent variable: number of stops within the beat.
[a]Not included in the resulting model.

TABLE 4.2 Proportion of Residents and Stops by Type (Defined by Racial Proportional Representation) in a Patrol Beat in Wichita, Kansas[a]

TYPE OF BEAT	MEAN PROPORTION OF NON-BLACK RESIDENTS	MEAN PROPORTION OF NON-BLACKS STOPPED	MEAN PROPORTION OF BLACK RESIDENTS	MEAN PROPORTION OF BLACKS STOPPED
Non-Black[b]	92.72	85.02	7.38	14.70
Mixed[c]	60.15	46.46	39.85	53.55
Black[d]	23.34	33.33	76.66	66.68

[a]Percentages may not sum to 100% due to rounding error.
[b]Seventy percent or more non-Black residents, N = 30.
[c]From 50 percent to 70 percent non-Black residents, N = 2.
[d]Less than 50 percent non-Black, N = 4.

consistently overrepresented in terms of their proportional representation (see Table 4.2).

It would appear that race, within the context of the beat, does affect the racial proportions of individuals stopped. More specifically, it appears that the race an individual *is not* is at least as important as the race an individual *is*, within the racial context of the beat. From this one could conclude that a White motorist driving in a beat populated primarily by Black residents is just as likely to be stopped as a Black motorist driving in a beat populated primarily by White residents.

The theory of contextual attentiveness expands our understanding of police officer decision making and focuses the research on the factors that influence a discretionary police-citizen contact. This theory attempts to explain why police officers focus their discretionary attention. The theory proposes that

1. Police officers use the circumstances associated with a distinct episode or location to define what is usual, customary, or expected within that particular context.
2. Police officers are differentially attentive toward individuals or behaviors that appear inconsistent with predetermined conceptualizations of what is usual, customary, or expected within a particular context.

3. Once an individual or behavior is defined by the police officer as inconsistent with what has been previously determined to be usual, customary, or expected within a particular context the police officer may seek a pretext to justify an official encounter (Withrow, 2004a).

This may explain why a Black citizen in a White neighborhood attracts the attention and suspicion of a police officer and why a White citizen in a Black neighborhood attracts the attention and suspicion of a police officer. Both situations are equally inconsistent within the contexts of their locations. The theory may be particularly relevant to our understanding of racial profiling, especially when one considers how effective, and potentially abusive, traffic stops and consent searches are within enforcement programs.

Testing this theory may be difficult for two reasons. First, it is immensely difficult to determine the proportional representation of drivers by race subject to police observation, even within a well-defined geographical area. Benchmarks based on population are unable to measure transient populations. Benchmarks based on field observations tend to be limited to single intersections and stretches of road and cannot be generalized to neighborhoods or beats. Benchmarks based on accident rates may be useful, but they lack sufficient confirmation of their validity. Second, conducting a controlled experiment is potentially harmful to human subjects. It might be possible to station White individuals in Black neighborhoods and vice versa and measure the number of times they are contacted by the police. It is, however, highly unlikely that an institutional review board or police department would allow a researcher to place individuals at this level of risk.

Certain officers seem to be quite skilled at detecting and apprehending drug couriers, while similarly situated officers are not. In the early days of highway drug interdiction, police administrators conducted extensive observations and interviews with their most prolific officers. These officers were asked dozens of questions about the indicators they use to determine which drivers might be transporting contraband. Many of the early drug courier profiles were developed in this manner. The results of these observations, when aggregated, provided an empirically based drug courier profile. A similar method could be initiated to test the theory of contextual attentiveness.

SUMMARY

The importance of theory in developing effective enforcement programs cannot be understated. Unfortunately, the racial profiling controversy is nearly devoid of a theoretical base. Some experts suggest that the overrepresentation of minorities in police stops is the result of a range of possibilities from outright discrimination to deployment strategies that inadvertently concentrate police observation on minority citizens. Theories relating to the behavior of individual officers, the impact of institutional demands upon officers, and the interaction of social institutions may produce an acceptable theoretical explanation. The theoretical basis for racial profiling may already exist within existing sociological or criminological theory. While the results are inconclusive, it appears that control theory may provide some insight into why racial minorities are stopped, searched, and arrested more frequently. Stop data, particularly at the beat level where contextual differences between neighborhoods are more visible, provide important insight into the effect of race on police officer decision making. It may be that race matters, but it appears that the context in which race is perceived may matter more.

DISCUSSION QUESTIONS

1. Discuss the importance of theory for identifying a solution to social problems.
2. Among the theories presented in this chapter, which appears the most plausible, and why?
3. To what extent should context matter to a police officer's enforcement attention, and what are the larger social issues associated with this?
4. Does control theory offer a plausible theoretical explanation of racial profiling? Why or why not?
5. Is racial profiling a unique problem or an extension of what appears to be an overall racial bias throughout the criminal justice process?
6. Other than race or ethnicity, what factors could explain the overrepresentation of minorities in the criminal justice process?

CASE STUDIES

1. A group of older White citizens has approached you (the police chief), alleging that they are stopped frequently when they travel through predominantly minority neighborhoods to a popular bingo hall. How would you verify the validity of their allegations?

2. Using the institutional expectations theory, how would you evaluate whether or not your police department's emphasis on drug interdiction produces an overrepresentation of minorities in police stops?

3. The crime analyst and patrol captain of your department has proposed a reformatting of your city's patrol beats so that each of them is racially mixed. How would this affect your desire to implement a routine internal benchmark system to identify potentially racist officers?

THE POLITICAL AND LEGAL RESPONSE

INTRODUCTION

The racial profiling controversy offends one of the most important values of the American culture: fundamental fairness. Due process and equal protection are important to Americans and have been since the very beginning of the Republic. One could argue that it was the lack of due process and equal protection that led to both the Revolutionary and Civil Wars. We are especially offended when representatives of our government specifically charged with enforcing the law exercise their authority in an unjust manner. Even if we are not directly affected, most Americans recognize the inherent threat in the intersection between racial bias and unchecked power.

Despite the attention they receive, the results of racial profiling studies seldom change minds. A finding of racial disparity in an enforcement program is for one person evidence of profiling and for another, evidence of differential offending rates. People who generally support the police prior to a racial profiling study tend to do so after the findings are reported, regardless of what the researchers find. Debates rage within the academic community on how to measure the population of individuals exposed to police observation, collect police stop data accurately and completely, and develop a theoretical explanation for the overrepresentation of minorities in police stops. These debates will likely continue well into the future. After all, in more than a century of criminological research we have yet to agree on why people commit crimes. What matters most at this stage of the controversy is how political leaders and courts will respond to racial profiling research.

Police administrators no longer have the option of standing at the side of this issue. Nearly every major city in the nation has either faced a lawsuit or an investigation into racial profiling (Garrett 2000). The intensity of media interest in the controversy has attracted the attention of more than a few public officials. Many of these public officials have direct oversight of police departments. Even if they may be generally supportive of the police, they are seldom willing to ignore the controversy. Legal remedies for the practice of racial profiling have yet to fully mature. It is unclear which legal avenue holds the most promise for plaintiffs. Even though a few plaintiffs have been successful at causing police departments to accept comprehensive consent decrees, the long-term effectiveness of these legal decisions is unclear.

The purpose of this chapter is to outline and discuss the political and legal ramifications of the racial profiling controversy. In doing so, it is the author's intention to address the informational needs of a broad range of individuals. This book does not profess to provide legal advice. Individuals interested in knowing their legal options should consult the services of a competent attorney.

THE POLITICAL RESPONSE

The political response to the racial profiling controversy has been swift and consistent. Forty-one state legislatures and the United States Congress have either considered or passed laws prohibiting racial profiling and requiring the collection of statistical information. The initial legislative response to racial profiling at the federal level came from a bill filed by Representative John Conyers of Michigan in 1997. This bill, the Traffic Stops Statistics Act of 1997 would have required the United States Department of Justice to collect data and conduct a nationwide study of racial profiling. The act was proposed when there was intense interest in racial profiling among elected officials throughout the nation and was passed unanimously by the United States House of Representatives. Almost immediately many of the nation's police organizations voiced their opposition. The National Association of Police Organizations, representing thousands of police organizations, registered strong opposition to the act. According to these organizations, the collection of data required by this bill would be onerous for most police officers. Their opposition was effective. The bill received no serious consideration by the United States Senate and eventually faded away after the adjournment of the 105th Congress (Harris 2002).

The second federal attempt to address racial profiling came on June 17, 2003, when the United States Department of Justice issued a report titled *Guidance Regarding the Use of Race by Federal Law Enforcement Agencies*. This document was intended to provide direction to federal law enforcement authorities on the role race should, or should not, play in routine enforcement decisions. While its definition of racial profiling is consistent with that proposed by various human and civil rights organizations, some have criticized it for not going far enough. For example, the guidance

- Does not cover profiling based on religion, religious appearance, or national origin
- Does not apply to state or local law enforcement agencies
- Does not include any enforcement (corrective) mechanism
- Does not require data collection
- Does not specify any punishment for federal officers who disregard it
- Contains a blanket exception for cases involving a threat to national security, catastrophic events, and enforcing laws protecting the integrity of the Nation's borders (AIUSA 2004, 31)

In 1999, North Carolina was the first state to require its state police to collect racial profiling data. The state of Connecticut was a close second. By 2000, thirteen states had passed statutes requiring the collection of racial profiling statistics, and three adopted policies prohibiting racial profiling. By August 2004, twenty-nine states had passed racial profiling statutes and, of these, twenty-three specifically prohibit the practice of racial profiling. Of the twenty-three prohibitive statutes, eleven are considered, by virtue of how they define racial profiling, largely unenforceable. Only four prohibit profiling on the basis of religion or religious appearance. Two prohibit the use of pretextual stops. Two provide actual criminal penalties for officers who engage in racial profiling, and two provide a mechanism for individuals victimized by racial profiling to seek relief in a court. At least thirty-seven municipalities have voluntarily adopted ordinances requiring data collection, and five more have accepted external racial profiling reviews as part of a consent decree with the United States Department of Justice (AIUSA 2004; Buerger and Farrell 2002). More than 400 agencies nationwide have voluntarily conducted racial profiling studies (McMahon et al. 2002). Racial profiling has caught the attention of a broad range of police agencies, their administrators, and, more importantly, their governing bodies (Cleary 2000).

Even so, many government officials dismiss the controversy and in particular comments from minorities about their experiences with the police. Some even reject the personal experiences of minorities as being "anecdotal, uninformed, or overly sensitive." (Barlow and Barlow 2002, 335). They do so, however, at their own peril. It is not politically feasible to ignore the racial profiling controversy or even to question its scientific basis (MacDonald 2003). One recent event illustrates the political importance of the racial profiling controversy. Colonel Carl Williams, Superintendent of the New Jersey State Police, became a lightning rod in the racial profiling controversy when he publicly observed that the President of the United States had recently traveled to Mexico to talk to the President of that country about the drug problem in the United States. He further stated that the U.S. President did not have the same conversation with the prime ministers of Ireland or England. Colonel Williams was making a point, and a good one. Technically, it is true that the bulk of certain drug imports into the United States come from south of the border. For more than a decade the United States Drug Enforcement Agency has issued intelligence reports explicitly stating that likely drug couriers are nationals from various Central American, South American, and Caribbean nations. In saying so, however, Colonel Williams implied that Hispanics are more likely to be drug couriers and, more importantly, he appeared to support his troopers' use of ethnicity as a valid characteristic of drug couriers. He was fired by Governor Christine Whitman before the end of the following day. In her statement, Governor Whitman criticized Colonel Williams for being insensitive to the issue.

Despite the rather contentious nature of the racial profiling controversy, there are for political leaders at least three important opportunities. First, from a purely administrative perspective, racial profiling studies often produce important and detailed information about police patrol procedures. Well over half of the typical municipal police budget is allocated to the patrol function. It is an important part of a city's overall public safety program. Racial profiling studies provide public administrators with a great deal of insight into how these public resources are being consumed. For many administrators, it is likely their first tutorial into police patrol procedures.

Second, to the extent that racial profiling inquiries involve community stakeholders, there are real opportunities for engaging historically disenfranchised segments of the community in meaningful public involvement. Much of the rage existing in lower socioeconomic inner-city neighborhoods that sometimes escalates to violence is caused by feelings of frustration leading to despair with public services, particularly the police. The hopelessness of urban life can be overcome by providing individuals with a voice and an opportunity to participate in a process that could very well produce positive changes that will improve the quality of life for themselves and the communities they represent.

Third, contrary to what many think, there are solutions to the racial profiling controversy. These solutions appear to be relatively easy to implement administratively and can potentially address the racial profiling controversy in a positive way. Training has long been an effective change agent in American policing. Teaching officers how to conduct traffic stops is a relatively easy process. Developing in them an ability to understand how their behavior during a traffic stop may be perceived through another's cultural lens is more difficult, but not impossible. Effective cultural sensitivity training programs should permeate every aspect of an officer's pre- and in-service training. It is, in our multicultural world, very important. Controlling the practice of consensual search may be another important administrative remedy to the racial profiling controversy. The now familiar *Miranda* warnings were loudly criticized by police administrators during the late 1960s and well into the 1970s. Many thought that informing individuals of their right to remain silent would end all possibility for confessions, unnecessarily burdening the criminal investigation process. They were wrong. *Miranda* forced the policing profession to invest in professional development and supervisory control mechanisms. In the long term *Miranda* improved American policing. In the same way, requiring officers to inform citizens of their right to refuse to consent to a search would force officers to be selective about whom they search. In short, officers would be less inclined to use the consent search as a fishing expedition when they really have no reasonable suspicion to conduct a search. The potential for these solutions is discussed more thoroughly in Chapter Seven.

THE LEGAL RESPONSE

Racial profiling research and the courts are inextricably linked. Some of the first racial profiling studies (New Jersey, Maryland) arose from legal challenges of police enforcement practices. Other studies (Police Foundation 2003) have encouraged defendants to initiate legal challenges. The legal principle in all of these cases is whether the police administered the law "to the benefit of all members of society" or placed a portion of our society, namely racial minorities, at a "special disadvantage" (Tomaskovic-Devey, Mason, and Zingraff 2004, 4). The United States Constitution, specifically the Fourth, Fifth, and Fourteenth Amendments, provides a framework for establishing the balance between police practices and the rights of individuals (Fredrickson and Siljander 2002). The Fourth Amendment prohibits the police from conducting unreasonable searches and seizures. Normally, the police are required to establish probable cause and secure a warrant prior to conducting a search. In reality, however, most searches are conducted without a warrant through one of the several exceptions to this warrant rule. The Fifth and Fourteenth Amendments require the police to adhere to due process. This includes informing criminal suspects of their rights and adhering to formal prosecution procedures. The Fourteenth Amendment, passed after the Civil War, essentially acts as a conduit and is intended to ensure that all citizens enjoy the civil rights enumerated by the Bill of Rights regardless of the state in which they reside. The Fourteenth Amendment's promise of equal protection is a key issue in the racial profiling controversy.

Fredrickson and Siljander (2002) argue that racial profiling should not be considered a separate legal issue and that attempts to make it illegal are flawed. Instead, they argue that racial discrimination is already illegal under the U.S. Constitution and court challenges should rely on existing Constitutional law. Smith and Alpert (2002) agree. They argue that because there is no widespread agreement on what racial profiling is and what behaviors and practices in police departments constitute racial profiling, it is extremely difficult to prove its existence. The legal standard governing a police officer's decision to stop has "become so flexible and loosely-defined, that it is difficult to know whether, and to what extent, race influences the decision" (Davis 1997, 428). "From a legal point of view racial profiling is tricky because it can be difficult to prove" (Meeks 2000, 7). "With little empirical research to inform the legal debate over racial profiling and with an undeveloped national jurisprudence on the subject, courts are struggling to formulate a coherent strategy for addressing the use of race in law enforcement decision making" (Smith and Alpert 2002, 674). Furthermore, the courts have largely ignored the issue of race within the context of policing procedures (Heumann and Cassak 2003).

Court decisions relating to what we perceive to be the practice of racial profiling can be classified into one of three general categories (Smith and Alpert 2002). First, the courts have consistently ruled that the police may not stop individuals on the basis of race alone. In *United States v. Brignoni-Ponce* (1975) the Supreme Court ruled that Hispanic-looking men driving near the border does not by itself provide the legal grounds for a traffic stop by the United States Border Patrol. In *United States v. Jones* (2001) the Court ruled that the police do not have the legal grounds to stop a car occupied by four Black men on the basis of an anonymous tip that four Black men were drinking and acting disorderly in an area near where the stop occurred. Second, the courts generally allow officers to consider race if used in combination with other factors to establish probable cause for a stop. In *Brown v. City of Oneonta* (2000) and *United States v Martinez-Fuente* (1976) the Court ruled that the police may use race as one of several physical descriptors when searching for a suspect. In the absence of a known suspect, court decisions are mixed on whether race can be used as part of a series of probable indicators of criminal activity. In *United States v. Montero-Camaro* (2000) the Court upheld a stop involving Hispanics because they turned around to avoid a stationary United States Border Patrol check station. Finally, the police may not use race alone as a basis for conducting, or attempting to conduct, consensual interviews and searches. The courts have however allowed officers to consider race if other factors can be articulated to establish reasonable suspicion (*United States v. Travis* 1995).

The following sections include extensive discussions on the major sources of law relevant to the racial profiling controversy. These include the Fourth and Fourteenth Amendments as well as various statutory provisions. In addition, this chapter covers the key legal issues and definitions critical to the racial profiling controversy.

The Fourth Amendment: Unreasonable Search and Seizure

The Fourth Amendment of the United States Constitution prohibits unreasonable searches and seizures. The Amendment stipulates that "no Warrants shall issue, but on probable cause, supported by Oath or affirmation, and particularly describing the place to be searched, and the persons or things to be searched." The operative phrase in this Amendment is "probable cause." Probable cause is a level of proof higher than reasonable suspicion. It occurs when "facts and circumstances within the officers' knowledge and of which they have reasonably trustworthy information are sufficient in themselves to warrant a man of reasonable caution in the belief that an offense has been or is being committed" (del Carmen 1998, 73). Although the Constitution requires a warrant, most searches are conducted without one. There are six exceptions to the warrant rule: searches incident to a lawful arrest, consent searches, special needs beyond law enforcement (e.g., emergencies), exigent circumstances (e.g., evidence will be destroyed while the officer is getting the warrant), stop and frisk, and the motor vehicle exception. Of these, the consent search is the most commonly used exception and the most relevant to the racial profiling controversy. Plaintiffs alleging a violation of their Fourth Amendment rights must satisfy the court that the police conducted the search or seizure unreasonably or without probable cause.

There is some disagreement on whether the Fourth Amendment can be the legal remedy for racial profiling. Oliver (2000) argues that the Fourth Amendment could be appropriate for limiting suspicion-free searches if the courts required officers to (1) inform citizens of their right to refuse consent to conduct a search and (2) articulate their reasonable suspicion for requesting a consent search. The first requirement would function much as the *Miranda* warnings. The second requirement would effectively deter police officers' "fishing expeditions" predicated on the consent exception. So far no court has adopted such requirements.

Writing two years prior to the *Whren* decision, Magee (1994) noted the inadequacy of the Fourth Amendment and its corollary exclusionary rule to protect minorities against unreasonable searches. Briefly, the exclusionary rule "provides that any evidence obtained by the government in violation of the Fourth Amendment guarantee against unreasonable search and seizure is not admissible in a criminal prosecution to prove guilt" (del Carmen 1998, 81). This rule provides substantial motivation for police officers to adhere to the Constitution while conducting their business. Magee argues that the Supreme Court is deliberately blind to how race affects a police officer's motivation and is therefore not willing to expand the Fourth Amendment's protections to include searches based on race. The exclusionary rule is based on the premise of a good cop, but if the motivation of the officer (at least that portion based on race) cannot be addressed by the court, then we are less able to find the bad cops.

Trende (2003) proposes that the cost of ending racial profiling may outweigh the benefits in the current legal environment. He suggests that rather than creating new law (e.g., prohibitions against racial profiling), the courts should consider searches based even partly on the race of the individual as unreasonable under the Fourth Amendment.

The *Whren* decision effectively closed the door to a Fourth Amendment remedy for racial profiling victims. For review, here are the pertinent facts. On June 10, 1993, two plainclothes officers from the District of Columbia Metropolitan Police Department Vice Squad were patrolling a known "high drug crime area" in an unmarked car. These officers were not patrolling in the literal sense. More accurately, they were conducting surveillance on a suspected crack house. They became suspicious that the occupants (James L. Brown and Michael A. Whren) of a dark-colored truck were in possession of drugs. The truck had temporary license plates and remained stopped at an intersection for what seemed an unusually long amount of time, about twenty seconds. The officers turned around and headed for the truck to investigate. Upon observing the officers, the driver, without signaling, turned right and sped off at what the officers determined was an "unreasonable" speed. The officers followed the vehicle. When the vehicle stopped at a red light the officers pulled up alongside it, whereupon one of the officers (Ephraim Soto) exited his vehicle and approached the driver's door on foot. After identifying himself, Officer Soto directed the driver (Brown) to park the vehicle. While doing so, Officer Soto noticed in plain view two large plastic bags of what appeared to be crack cocaine in the passenger's (Whren) hands. Both occupants were arrested and the drugs were seized.

The defendants were charged with four counts of violating various federal drug laws. At a pretrial suppression hearing they challenged the legality of the stop and the resulting seizure. The basis of their argument was that the officers did not have the probable cause or even the reasonable suspicion to stop them for the drug violations. Furthermore, the defendants alleged that Officer Soto's stop based on an alleged traffic violation was merely pretextual, meaning that had the defendants not committed a traffic violation, the officers would have had no legal justification for stopping them in the first place. The stop, and subsequent seizure, therefore violated the Fourth Amendment's prohibition against unreasonable searches and seizures. The trial court was not convinced, and the defendants were convicted. The officers did not deny that they suspected the occupants of the vehicle were in possession of drugs and that they followed the vehicle with an intention to stop it when it committed a traffic violation.

The Court of Appeals affirmed the convictions and issued a direct response to the legal issues surrounding the suppression hearing. Specifically, the court ruled that "regardless of whether a police officer subjectively believes that the occupants of an automobile may be engaging in some other illegal behavior, a traffic stop is permissible as long as a reasonable officer in the same circumstances could have stopped the car for the suspected traffic violation." The Court of Appeals was not persuaded by the petitioners' argument that the officers, by virtue of their assignment to the vice squad, do not normally stop people for traffic violations. The United States Supreme Court granted the petitioners' request for certiorari.

The Supreme Court held that the temporary detention of a motorist based on an officer's probable cause to believe that the motorist violated the traffic law does not violate the Fourth Amendment's prohibition against unreasonable searches and seizures, even if a reasonable officer would not have stopped the motorist in the absence of an additional law enforcement objective. In effect, the Court applied an objective test and ruled that as long as the officer has an objective and bona fide reason to stop a motorist, even if the reason is a pretext, then any subsequent search or seizure does not violate the Fourth Amendment, assuming of course the officer does not offend the Constitution in some other way subsequent to the initial contact. It doesn't make any difference whether the officers, by virtue of their assignment, would have, might have, or should have stopped the motorist; the fact is that they could have. An ulterior motive for the stop does not make it illegal under the Fourth Amendment.

The Court's application of an objective or reasonable officer standard is critical to the racial profiling controversy. When applying this test, the Court needed only to establish whether the officers had the legal justification to stop the car. In this case they did because the driver violated two traffic laws: speeding and failing to signal. The stop therefore was legal. This test was first applied in *United States v. Smith* (1986). The use of the objective standard is quite advantageous to police officers. Because traffic laws are so numerous and frequently violated, a potential legal justification for a stop is as broad and varied as the traffic code (Bast 1997). Second, the level of coercion used by officers during a stop to conduct a more thorough search is not relevant when the objective standard is applied. This may effectively negate the Fourth Amendment protection, particularly for minorities, because the test does not account for the different perceptions of the police between racial groups (Cole 1999).

This potential for abuse is illustrated by *Wilson v. Tinicum Township* (1993). In this case the plaintiff was stopped by the police for a traffic violation. Specifically, he had obstructed the view through his windshield with a string that had previously held an air freshener on the rear view mirror. When the driver asked why he had been stopped, the officers responded that he was stopped because he is a young Black male, in a high crime area, and driving a good car. They further added that he would have to receive a warning for obstructing his windshield; otherwise, as the officers explained, the stop would not be legitimate. The court did not object, because it is against the law to obstruct a windshield. The plaintiff should have argued that the string could not have appreciably obstructed his view, and even if it did, the officer could not have seen it, because the stop was conducted at night (Bast 1997). Eventually, the plaintiffs settled for approximately $250,000 and a three year consent decree under which all records generated from police stops were made available to them.

The Supreme Court in *Whren* could have applied a subjective test to determine the legality of the stop and subsequent search. Using this test, the court would have more comprehensively questioned the officers' motives. For example, using this test, the Court would have asked the officers why they, as vice officers, felt it was so necessary to conduct a traffic stop. Had the Court applied a subjective test, it is likely that it would have ruled in favor of the plaintiffs (O'Reilly 2002). Unfortunately, there is really no way to know. Furthermore, it may very well be true that the totality of events surrounding a police-citizen contact have a way of sharpening an officer's ability to articulate reasonable suspicion and probable cause. In other words, the court's ability to separate what the officer was thinking prior to the stop from what the officer may have learned during the stop may often be limited.

While the *Whren* decision may have removed the possibility of a Fourth Amendment challenge to pretextual stops, Thompson (1999) argues that it may be too soon to dismiss it as a source of relief for racially motivated searches and seizures. In *Whren* the Court declared that the racial motivation of an officer is "categorically irrelevant to Fourth Amendment analysis" (p. 981), effectively preventing a future court from considering how an officer's racial bias affects his perception of an individual's tendency for criminal behavior. Thompson argues that this decision ignores the social science evidence suggesting that police officers perceive race differently and that racial stereotypes are deeply ingrained in the police subculture.

The Fourteenth Amendment: Equal Protection

The Equal Protection Clause of Fourteenth Amendment may be the most likely foundation for a legal remedy to racial profiling (Garrett 2000; Kennedy 1999). This Amendment states,

> All persons born or naturalized in the United States and subject to the jurisdiction thereof, are citizens of the United States and of the State wherein they reside. No State shall make or enforce any law which shall abridge the privileges or immunities of citizens of the United States; nor shall any State deprive any person of life, liberty, or property, without due process of law; nor deny to any person within its jurisdiction the equal protection of the laws.

This Amendment was ratified after the Civil War. It was designed to thwart any attempt by state or local authorities to deny civil rights and protections to recently freed slaves. Today, the Amendment acts as a conduit through which the civil protections enumerated in the Bill of Rights of the United States Constitution are enjoyed equally by all residents of the nation, regardless of the state in which they happen to reside.

The Fourteenth Amendment prohibits any state action (e.g., a police stop, search, or arrest) that discriminates against an individual or group on the basis of race. Police stops that are based solely on race are subject to the strict scrutiny of the court. To survive this scrutiny, the state must demonstrate that the use of race to decide whom to stop serves a compelling state interest. Furthermore, the state must show that the practice is narrowly tailored to advance that objective (Kennedy 1999; Susskind 1994).

While the Court in *Whren* effectively slammed the door on a racial profiling challenge based on the Fourth Amendment, in nearly the same breath it raised the hopes of many that it would consider a challenge to the practice of racial profiling based on the Equal Protection Clause of the Fourteenth Amendment. To be successful in a challenge of this sort, the defendant must demonstrate the discriminatory effect of a practice as well as its discriminatory intent. This is not an easy threshold to cross. The legal standard was established in *United States v. Armstrong* (1966). In *Armstrong*, a selective prosecution case, the Court ruled that the defendant has to prove that similarly situated individuals of another race could have been prosecuted but were not. In a racial profiling case the defendant would likely be able to demonstrate the discriminatory effect of police stops based on a comparison between police stop data and an acceptable benchmark. Police stop data, despite its potential for inaccuracy and incompleteness, may be the most accurate measure of who gets stopped, but unless and until the research can accurately measure who doesn't get stopped, an Equal Protection cause will not likely be successful. The current status of the research simply cannot measure the similarly situated individuals (Davis 1997; O'Reilly 2002; Smith and Alpert 2002; Susskind 1994).

The police are probably unwilling to admit that they intentionally target persons because of their race or nationality, and there is probably no formal written policy encouraging discrimination. As a result, plaintiffs must rely on circumstantial evidence, often in the form of statistical analyses, to prove their cases. In *McClesky v. Kemp* (1987) the Court considered the results of a logistical regression of 2000 Georgia death penalty cases finding that Black murderers are more likely to receive the death penalty when their victims are White. The Court, however, found the evidence insufficient to make a *prima facie* case for racial discrimination (Smith and Alpert 2002).

No court has yet considered whether or not a profile that includes race as an indicator of potential criminal activity warrants its strict scrutiny under the Equal Protection Clause (Banks 2001). Harris (1997) argues that the courts are typically hostile to the use of statistical analyses to demonstrate Constitutional violations. One case, however, came very close to meeting the legal and evidentiary requirements of the Equal Protection Clause. Operation Valkyrie was an effort by the Illinois State Police, funded by a federal grant, to identify and interdict drug couriers on the interstate highway system in Illinois. The program became quite effective, seizing large quantities of drugs and assets. In 1994, a class action suit was filed against the state police after the American Civil Liberties Union received numerous complaints from Black and Hispanic motorists alleging the Illinois State Police singled them out for enforcement primarily because of their race or ethnicity. The plaintiff's allegations were based in part on the fact that in Illinois, even though Hispanics represent only 8 percent of the population and only 3 percent of personal car trips, they represent 30 percent of the motorists stopped on the highways. Furthermore, the plaintiffs alleged that most of the stops were for minor violations like failing to signal lane changes and speeding from one to four miles over the limit. The plaintiffs alleged that troopers assigned to Operation Valkyrie were two to three times more likely to stop Hispanic motorists than other generally assigned troopers, even on the same highway (Oliver 2000).

The plaintiffs in *Chavez v. Illinois State Police* (2001) based their equal protection case on two primary databases maintained by the Illinois State Police. The first included information on citations and warnings, and the second included information from field reports completed by troopers (albeit inconsistently) pursuant to contraband seizures, custodial arrests, trooper injuries, and damage to department property. The second database included information on the race and ethnicity of individuals; the first did not. The proportion of Hispanics represented in the citations of warnings database was estimated by searching the name fields for Spanish surnames.

Ultimately, the court ruled that the statistical evidence was insufficient to support the first prong (discriminatory effect) of an equal protection case. The data in the citations and warnings database were found to be flawed in that they contained no reliable information on the race or ethnicity of similarly situated individuals. The court specifically discounted the accuracy of using Spanish surnames to estimate the proportion of Hispanic motorists in the database. The field report database didn't fair any better. The court found that because the reporting procedures were inconsistent, the field report database was not a representative sample. Even more damaging to this case, and others like it, the court found that the benchmark used to estimate the population of individuals subjected to police observation, that is, similarly situated individuals, was based on nearly a decade-old United States Census and amended using a broad-range study conducted several years earlier by the Federal Highway Administration.

Title 42, U.S.C., Section 14141: Pattern and Practice

The Crime Control Act of 1994 includes a provision making it

> unlawful for any governmental authority, or agent thereof, or any person acting on behalf of a governmental authority, to engage in a pattern or practice of conduct by law enforcement officers or by officials or employees of any governmental agency with responsibility for the administration of juvenile justice or the incarceration of juveniles that deprives persons of rights, privileges, or immunities secured or protected by the Constitution or laws of the United States.

The United States Attorney General has the exclusive authority, when given reasonable cause to believe a violation has occurred, to initiate a civil action against a police department to obtain appropriate equitable and declaratory relief to eliminate the pattern or practice that offends the Constitution. The types of activities actionable under this statute include, but are not limited to, excessive force, harassment, false arrest, coercive sexual conduct, and unlawful stops, searches, or arrests. Some legal experts propose that Section 14141 may be the most likely route to launching a successful legal challenge of racial profiling (Heumann and Cassak 2003; O'Reilly 2002). Unfortunately, the law is too new and there are too few cases upon which to predict litigation success.

Section 14141 cases are different from Section 1983 (discussed below) cases for several reasons. First, Section 14141 cases focus on the entire pattern and practice of an enforcement program and not a single event, as is the case in a Section 1983–based complaint. As a result, more attention is given to the disparate effects of department policy and procedures. Second, Section 14141 cases must be filed by the United States Department of Justice, thereby eliminating the need to find an individual defendant with an egregious complaint. Third, unlike a suit based on Section 1983, a suit based on Section 14141 can only result in equitable or declaratory relief. This means that actual damages, that is, cash awards, cannot be awarded to individuals who are harmed by the police department's behavior. Finally, Section 14141 cases are, by statute, heard before a single federal judge. Section 1983 cases can be heard by juries (O'Reilly 2002).

The authority to conduct Section 14141 cases resides in the Special Litigation Section of the United States Department of Justice. The statute authorizes the United States Department of Justice to initiate this civil litigation to remedy a measurable pattern of discrimination based on race, color, national origin, gender, or religious preference. Any law enforcement agency that receives financial assistance from the Department is subject to litigation under this section. According to the Department of Justice, recent settlements in Cincinnati, Steubenville (Ohio), Highland Park (Illinois), Washington, DC, Montgomery County (Maryland), and New Jersey have resulted in considerable improvements in police procedures. In most situations the cases are settled through a consent decree.

While it appears that Section 14141 may be the best option for a legal challenge of racial profiling, there are some lingering concerns. First, because of a lack of legislative intent and litigation history, questions exist concerning the exact meanings of some of the Section's terms. For example, it is unclear whether officers who use profiles based on personal experience are acting on behalf of their agencies. Second, the law specifically uses the plural term *officers*. It is not clear how many officers engaging in such acts would constitute a pattern or practice. For example, would a department be subjected to scrutiny under this act if a few rogue officers engaged in an illegal pattern or practice? How many officers constitute a pattern or practice? Third, and most importantly, it is not yet known how federal judges will interpret the section. Who has the burden of proof and what level of proof is required? More ominously, what evidence may be necessary to demonstrate the discriminatory intent of the pattern and practice? Unless and until these questions are resolved, the police "should be more alarmed by local media . . . than by the threat of an actual litigated 14141 case" (O'Reilly 2002, 103).

To date, the most extensive application of Section 14141 occurred in the mid-1990s in New Jersey. During the late 1980s and early 1990s minority drivers along the New Jersey Turnpike complained bitterly that they were subjected to more frequent stops, searches, and arrests than nonminority drivers. Criminal defense attorneys consistently complained that the actions of troopers assigned to the Turnpike appeared to be racially motivated. The term *racial profiling* had not yet entered the common language. By 1990, a group of these lawyers, representing seventeen defendants, initiated what was to become the most significant racial profiling case and effectively launched one of the most significant controversies facing American policing (Harris 2002). The New Jersey case "stands permanently on the books as the most important judicial decision to date on racial profiling" (MacDonald 2003, 26).

The plaintiffs' attorneys sought to dismiss drug trafficking charges based on the premise that their clients were improperly selected for enforcement on the basis of their race or ethnicity (*State of New Jersey v. Pedro Soto* 1996). The state trial judge agreed, finding that the state police had profiled minorities as probable couriers and therefore stopped a disproportionately higher number of minority motorists. He then summarily dismissed the charges. The state attorney general appealed the case. While the case was on appeal the United States Department of Justice found enough evidence to open an inquiry under Section 14141. Eventually the state withdrew its appeal, dismissed the charges, paid nearly $14,000,000 in damages, and accepted a massive consent decree that establishes an unprecedented level of external control over the state police.

For several reasons New Jersey was a prime target for racial profiling litigation. First, the New Jersey Turnpike is one of the most important conduits for drug trafficking between Washington, DC, and New York City. It is one of several primary fronts in the war on drugs. More than 250 troopers are assigned to patrol this stretch of highway. Most of them are specifically trained for and tasked with drug interdiction duties. It is likely these officers were heavily influenced by intelligence reports from the U.S. Drug Enforcement Agency indicating the increased probability that racial and ethnic minorities are drug couriers. Second, the political structure in New Jersey may have made administrative change within the State Police more difficult. In most states attorneys general are elected independently and the state police superintendents are appointed by independent boards or commissions. This effectively ensures that the attorney general, as the state's principal prosecutor, has some objectivity in prosecutorial decisions. In addition, state police superintendents in most states enjoy some independence from political influence. The New Jersey attorney general is appointed by the governor and has command and control over the state police. In short, this attorney general is both prosecutor and police. This potential conflict of interest became a reality during the *Soto* litigation. Third, the large minority populations centered around Newark, New Brunswick, Trenton, and Camden are politically active. There is a long history of contentious relations between the state police and this minority community (O'Reilly 2002).

The New Jersey litigation is an excellent example of how statistical information in conjunction with documentary evidence of institutional racism can combine to make an effective legal case. John Lamberth, a well respected professor at Temple University, was hired by the court to conduct what would become the nation's first bona fide racial profiling study. Regardless of the criticisms Lamberth's work has received from both the scholarly and practitioner communities, it was instrumental in developing an entirely new research agenda. After the Lamberth report the racial profiling controversy developed traction all over the nation. The judge's findings are particularly important to the racial profiling controversy because he considered the documentary and statistical information as evidence of the troopers' prejudicial motivation for initiating traffic stop. This, according to Heumann and Cassak (2003) is an important opportunity for plaintiffs. Unfortunately, to the disappointment of many, just a few weeks later the Supreme Court handed down the *Whren* decision, effectively slamming the door on the possibility of future courts considering an officer's motivation for initiating a traffic stop.

The consent decree signed by Attorney General Peter Verniero in 1999 included 124 unprecedented controls over the state police and is arguably "the most intrusive consent order in history of American policing" (O'Reilly 2002, 71). Among many other things, the state agreed to

- Develop race neutral criteria for deciding which traffic offenders to stop
- Document the process by which troopers decide who to stop
- Limit consent searches to situations in which officers have reasonable suspicion that the search will reveal evidence of a crime

- Inform motorists that they can refuse consent to search when initially asked and may revoke their consent at any time to limit the scope of the search
- Require a motorist's consent in writing,
- Allow federal lawyers to oversee training, supervision, performance evaluation, and the complaint process
- Expand the scope of internal affairs investigations beyond the instant issues
- Allow the use of circumstantial evidence in employee discipline matters
- Strengthen conflict of interest controls on those who participate in internal investigations
- Conduct internal investigations of officers who conduct frequent consent searches
- Maintain two independent monitors for a period of five years (at a cost of $500,000 each) to oversee compliance with the consent decree
- Publish quarterly progress reports (Oliver 2000; O'Reilly 2002)

Although it is too soon to fully determine the impact of this case, there is some evidence that the consent decree is having a profound effect on the New Jersey State Police. In the first year the number of searches fell to less than one-third of their pre-1999 levels. The consent decree effectively put the New Jersey State Police out of the drug interdiction business. It remains to be seen whether interdiction activities will return in the future. The department is experiencing a substantial growth of internal investigations. There does not, however, appear to be a substantial increase in the proportion of internal investigations that result in sustained allegations. Troopers report that the court actions and investigations have lowered overall morale (O'Reilly 2002). A portion of this consent decree is included at the end of this chapter.

It is more interesting to consider what has not changed. The requirements of the consent decree have clearly reduced the overall number of arrests and stops made by the New Jersey State Police. The proportion of arrests and stops for speeding involving minorities appears to be unaffected (MacDonald 2003). Here again, a cautionary statement is in order. It will take many years to fully evaluate the impact of the consent decree on the New Jersey State

Police. Any conclusions based on the data available to date are preliminary and may be misleading.

Stop and Frisk: The *Terry* Rule

In 1968, the Supreme Court provided the police with an important enforcement tool: the stop and frisk. Unfortunately, the use of stop and frisk procedures may add significantly to the perception of racial profiling. The leading case is *Terry v. Ohio* (1968). Here are the facts of this case. At 2:30 AM on October 31, 1963, a police detective noticed two men in downtown Cleveland who appeared to be "casing" a store. Several times, each of the two men independently looked into the store's window and returned to the corner to confer. The detective confronted the men and asked for identification. Receiving none, he conducted a cursory "pat-down" search, or frisk, whereupon he found both men to be carrying handguns illegally. The men were convicted on the weapons violations. On appeal, the defendants argued that the search was unreasonable under the Fourth Amendment. Specifically, they alleged that the detectives did not have probable cause to believe a crime had been or was about to occur. There was no way the detective could have suspected, much less had probable cause, that the men possessed weapons. The Court disagreed and ruled that an investigatory stop such as this is not equivalent to an arrest, that is, a seizure. Furthermore, the Court ruled that the police need only a reasonable suspicion of criminal activity to conduct a cursory search. Specifically, the Court allowed such searches during situations in which officers feel they are necessary to insure their safety (Davis 1997). This means the search must be limited to items that could threaten an officer's safety, like a handgun or knife.

In a later case the Court ruled against the police when their frisk went beyond that allowed by the *Terry* decision. In this case the officer conducted a pat-down search. The officer felt a small lump in the suspect's jacket, whereupon he thrust his hand into the pocket and seized a plastic bag containing cocaine. The court ruled the evidence inadmissible because the search went beyond the scope allowed in *Terry* (*Minnesota v. Dickerson* 1993).

While it may seem that the *Dickerson* decision effectively limited an officer's authority to search an individual, Harris (1994, 2002) argues that a long line of legal rulings have vastly expanded a police officer's authority to conduct searches without probable cause. The courts, he proposes, have "gradually required less and less evidence for a stop and frisk" (Harris 1994, 660). Harris is particularly critical of the use of factors relating to the location of the search and an officer's subjective perceptions of evasive behavior as justification for stop and frisk searches. The courts tend to defer to the judgment and experience of police officers and allow stop and frisk searches in historically high crime or violent locations. The Supreme Court has not specifically ruled on whether qualitative factors relating to the location of the search, by themselves, justify a *Terry* search. There are, however, numerous situations in which lower courts have allowed such searches based solely on the justification that they were conducted in high crime areas where the police have ample reason to fear for their safety. Second, the courts tend to defer to an officer's subjective perception that the suspect engaged in suspicious or evasive behaviors when he became aware of the police presence. At least four courts have ruled that merely avoiding the police is enough justification for a cursory search under the *Terry* rule (Harris 1994).

Given the apparent deference the courts tend to have for police officers in these cases, it does not appear that this particular body of law would be an appropriate basis for a legal challenge of racial profiling. There is a possibility that legally permissible stop and frisk procedures may be particularly harmful to minorities. First, *Terry* is most often used in pedestrian stops, a predominantly urban issue. Neighborhoods with high population densities within the urban core often have more foot traffic than sparsely populated areas or suburbs. The urban core is also more likely to be disproportionately populated by racial and ethnic minorities. As a result, minorities may be more at risk of being subjected to *Terry* stops. Second, many of the neighborhoods we characterize as "high crime" are populated primarily by minorities. The police are justifiably deployed in greater numbers in these communities and appear to have more reason to conduct routine stop and frisk searches to ensure their personal safety. As a result, residents of these neighborhoods are subjected to more intense police observation and ultimately are likely to be stopped and frisked more frequently (Harris 1994).Third, allowing the police to base a cursory search on a subjective perception of evasive behavior ignores the reality of the minority experience with the police. Because race is so pervasive an issue in the criminal justice system, minorities as a general rule are more fearful of the police and are more likely to avoid contact with them than nonminorities (Harris 1994;

Susskind 1994).Ultimately, the location and evasion standard results in the disproportionate application of stops and frisks and adversely affects the minority community. "This begins and perpetuates a cycle of mistrust and suspicion, a feeling that law enforcement harasses African-Americans and Hispanic-Americans with *Terry* stops as a way of controlling their communities" (Harris 1994, 660).

Pretextual Stops

A pretextual stop occurs when a police officer initiates a contact where the stated legal justification for the contact is merely an excuse for conducting a more invasive search of an individual. Usually, the police officer has absolutely no reasonable suspicion that the person is involved in any criminal activity beyond that which he alleges as justification for the stop. Furthermore, most states require individuals to identify themselves when asked to do so by a police officer. Failure to do so is a violation of the law (see *Hibel v. Sixth Judicial District Court of Nevada, Humboldt County* 2003). The process is relatively simple. A police officer observes an individual who, for whatever reason, he believes is suspicious. Suspicion in this context could simply be that the individual looks different than the predominant residents in the neighborhood. The police officer then observes the individual for a short time until a violation of the law is observed. This is usually a relatively minor violation of the traffic code like failing to signal a lane change or a dirty license plate. Then the officer initiates a traffic stop based on his observation of the traffic violation. During the traffic stop the officer engages in a friendly conversation with the driver. Eventually the officer asks, rather innocuously, "Do you mind if I search your car?" The vast majority of us will give our consent, and many of us do not even know we can refuse the officer's request. Most of us believe that our quick response will encourage the officer to believe that we have nothing to hide. Unfortunately, just the opposite is true and the officer initiates a completely suspicion-free search of our vehicles and personal effects.

Pretextual stops and consent searches are effective policing tools. Most experienced officers will tell you that even drug couriers, knowing they possess contraband or large sums of cash, will readily allow officers to conduct searches of their vehicles. Pretextual stops are a legally sanctioned means to effectively circumvent the Fourth Amendment prohibition against unreasonable searches and seizures. Furthermore, after *Whren* the courts are not likely to revisit the issue in the future (Davis 1997).

Admittedly, the courts are somewhat wary of suspicion-free stops and searches. As a result, police discretion has been limited in various types of regulatory stops, inventory searches, and sobriety checkpoints. However, limiting an officer to stopping only individuals who violate the traffic code "does not, as a practical matter, narrow the field of motorists he may seize" given the breadth of potential traffic violations and the inevitably of violation (Oliver 2000, 1419).

Pretextual stops are not even likely to be reviewed by a court if the individual is neither arrested nor charged. In most cases the officer will likely not bother to secure a warrant if the suspect does not consent to a search. More likely than not, the officer has no objective reason upon which to articulate probable cause for a search in the first place. Even so, the individual's privacy and freedom to travel have been violated (Davis 1997).

Title 42, U.S.C., Section 1983

The Civil Rights Act of 1871 was passed by the United States Congress after the Civil War to deter state sanctioned racial discrimination and abuse. It was passed during the same political climate that produced the Equal Protection Clause of the Fourteenth Amendment. The provisions of the act relevant to racial profiling are found in Title 42, Section 1983:

> Every person who, under color of any statute, ordinance, regulation, custom, or usage, of any State or Territory or the District of Columbia, subjects, or causes to be subjected, any citizen of the United States or other person within the jurisdiction thereof to the deprivation of any rights, privileges, or immunities secured by the Constitution and laws, shall be liable to the party injured in an action at law, suit in equity, or other proper proceeding for redress, except that in any action brought against a judicial officer for an act or omission taken in such officer's judicial capacity, injunctive relief shall not be granted unless a declaratory decree was violated or declaratory relief was unavailable. For the purposes of this section, any Act of Congress applicable exclusively to the District

of Columbia shall be considered to be a statute of the District of Columbia

Often referred to as Section 1983, the law provides a mechanism for aggrieved parties to receive compensation from state officials and agencies who, within their official capacity, violate the aggrieved parties' civil rights regardless of whether the actions are sanctioned by statute, policy, or custom. For example, a police officer may be held personally liable if he denies an individual his civil liberties even if he is required to do so in accordance with a bona fide statute or department policy.

This statute may be appropriate for a legal challenge of racial profiling. Plaintiffs could file a Section 1983 case alleging a violation of the Equal Protection Clause (Davis 1997) or on the basis of deliberate indifference, often used when departments fail to properly train officers (O'Reilly 2002). In this situation the plaintiff must prove that the actions of the police caused injury or damage. Certainly, a traffic stop predicated on nothing more than an officer's racial prejudice would be enough to prevail in an action of this sort. Unfortunately, even if the plaintiff prevailed, an appropriate compensation would be difficult to establish. The courts generally regard traffic stops as minor inconveniences and have yet to consider the cumulative effect of numerous or frequent stops. A judgment requiring a police officer to stop searching without probable cause would hardly be considered just compensation (Davis 1997). Even in cases where a police officer admits using race in a profile as an indicator of potential criminal behavior and will likely continue to do so, the courts may not necessarily be sympathetic to plaintiffs (Trende 2003).

Finally, it is unlikely that a police department will promulgate a written policy that explicitly encourages its officers to use race as an indicator of criminal suspiciousness. Instead, the incidence of profiling is more likely the result of informal policy, custom, or practice. In this case the importance of a well-executed and -interpreted racial profiling study cannot be overstated. Herein may lie the answer to why some police chiefs are resistant to voluntarily conducting studies within their jurisdictions. After all, why collect information that may be used one day against the department?

Other Key Legal Rulings

As a practical matter, racial profiling litigation, even if successful, is not likely to result in significant monetary awards for damages. Potential litigants are therefore reluctant (or unable) to commit the time and resources necessary to initiate a successful cause unless it is a class action. From a legal perspective, the onerous evidentiary standards as well as issues relating to standing are not likely to be easily addressed by litigants. Unless plaintiffs can definitively prove to the court that the actions of a police officer or police department caused them harm, it is exceedingly difficult for them to establish standing in civil suits relating to racial profiling. Civil remedies, even if significant, are not likely to be very effective at controlling the future behavior of the police. While news of substantial cash awards arising from civil lawsuits involving police department spreads very fast, it is often administratively difficult to establish a connection between the errant officer's behaviors and the future behaviors of other officers engaged in routine police operations. In spite of the legal and practical difficulties associated with legal challenges to racial profiling, a few plaintiffs have been quite successful. The most notable are the plaintiffs in New Jersey and Maryland.

As offensive as it may be to our social conscience, there are very few legal restrictions on the police use of race in decision making, even when the police admit that race plays a role in their enforcement decisions. As a whole, the courts tend to have considerable deference toward police officers. However, this does not mean that the police have carte blanche authority to be discriminatory. Over the past quarter century a number of important rulings have provided some restrictions on the police use of race as an indicator of potential criminal activity (see Table 5.1).

SUMMARY

The racial profiling controversy is one of the most contentious political and legal issues of our time. Attempts to control the practice of racial profiling statutorily at the federal, state, and local levels have not yet been successful. Although it passed unanimously in the United States House of Representatives, the most comprehensive proposal at the federal level failed to gain support in the United States Senate. An attempt to provide federal law

TABLE 5.1 Key Legal Rulings Relating to Profiling Practices

CASE	SYNOPSIS OF DECISION
United States v. Mendenhall 446 U.S. 544 (1980)	The first drug courier profile case. Court allowed stop based on drug courier profile and ruled search legal because subject had given consent.
Reid v. Georgia 448 U.S. 438 (1980)	Court ruled that the United States drug enforcement agent could not have known criminal activity was afoot on the basis of the four characteristic profiles.
United States v. Sokolow 490 U.S. 1 (1989)	Court approved the use of a profile but required officers to articulate the particular cause of their suspicion. Totality of circumstances should be considered on a case by case basis.
United States v. Brignoni-Ponce 422 U.S. 873, 95 S. Ct. 2574 (1975)	U.S. Border Patrol agents violated the Fourth Amendment when they stopped an individual on the basis of his apparent Mexican ancestry.
United States v. Montero-Camaro 208 F.3d 1122 (9th Cir. 2000)	Race is an impermissible basis for the U.S. Border Patrol agents to detain an individual.
United States v. Martinez-Fuente 428 U.S. 543 (1975)	Allowed U.S. Border Patrol agents to detain individuals at stationary border checkpoints (as opposed to roving patrols) on the basis of apparent Mexican ancestry.
Brown v. City of Oneonta 235 F.3d 769 (2d Cir. 2000)	The police did not violate the Equal Protection Clause of the Fourteenth Amendment when, using a description of a rape suspect that included race, they questioned many Black males.
Winfield v. Board of County Commissioners of Eagle County, Colorado 837 F. Supp. 338 (D. Colo. 1993)	Required sheriff's department to terminate use of race-based profile and demanded officers not stop, seize, or search unless they have reasonable articulable suspicion. Resulted in $800,000 settlement and dismissal of cases.

Continued

TABLE 5.1   *Continued*

Illinois v. Wardlow 528 U.S. 119, 120 S. Ct. 673 (2000)	An investigatory stop based on a defendant's attempt to evade police officers does not violate the Fourth Amendment.
United States v. Bautista 684 F.2d 1286 (9th Cir. 1982)	Race or color alone are not sufficient reasons for making an investigatory stop.
Florida v. Royer 460 U.S. 491, 103 S. Ct. 1319 (1983)	The police did not violate the Fourth Amendment when they approached an individual meeting a profile and asked his consent to voluntarily answer questions and submit to a search. The arrest in this case, however, was illegal and all evidence emanating from it was ruled inadmissible
Lyons v. City of Los Angeles 461 U.S. 95, 103 S. Ct. 1660 (1983)	Held plaintiffs do not have standing to seek injunctive relief against alleged police pattern and practice of illegal chokeholds.
Rodriquez v. California Highway Patrol 89 F. Supp. 2d 1131 (N.D. Cal. 2000)	Gave plaintiffs standing to seek injunction against racial profiling. Contrasts with *Lyons.*
Maryland State Conference of NAACP Branches v. Maryland Department of State Police 72 F. Supp. 2d 560 (D. Md. 1999)	Gave plaintiffs standing to seek injunction against racial profiling. Contrasts with *Lyons.*
Hughes v. State 269 Ga. 258 (1998)	Use of racial incongruity (e.g., Black man in a predominantly White neighborhood) as a basis for a stop and search violates the Fourth Amendment.
Ohio v. Robinette 519 U.S. 33 (1996)	Fourth Amendment does not require that a lawfully seized defendant be advised that he is "free to go" before his consent to search will be recognized as voluntary.

enforcement officers with guidance on racial profiling does not require data collection or provide a penalty for errant federal officers. Only about half of the state statutes are considered enforceable, and very few either prohibit other forms of profiling or provide penalties for officers and departments that engage in its practice.

Despite its contentious nature, the racial profiling controversy provides real opportunities for political leaders. An honest attempt to address the controversy provides an important context for a political leader to engage previously disenfranchised individuals in community problem solving. For many political leaders, racial profiling studies provide what may be their first comprehensive understanding of how the police department they oversee operates. Contrary to what many believe, there are many opportunities for public administrators to address the racial profiling controversy in a meaningful way.

There are many legal options available to plaintiffs. Even though the Supreme Court effectively, for now, slammed the door on a Fourth Amendment challenge to racial profiling, some experts believe these types of cases may be productive—that is, of course, if the Court could be persuaded to consider the use of race in police decision making unreasonable under the Fourth Amendment. The Equal Protection Clause of the Fourteenth Amendment seems to be tailor-made for a racial profiling legal challenge. Unfortunately, the evidentiary requirements for these cases are onerous and not likely to be met with the current sophistication of statistical information. A legal action based on the relatively new Title 42, U.S.C. 14141 may also produce positive results for plaintiffs. This statute appears to have an easier evidentiary threshold. Despite its effect in New Jersey, the statute is, however, too new and devoid of a litigation history to completely assess its potential as a legal remedy. What we do know is that in some situations, namely Maryland and New Jersey, successful court challenges have an effect on policing procedures. What remains unanswered is whether these changes will result in better policing and improvements in overall public safety.

DISCUSSION QUESTIONS

1. Discuss some of the strategies a political leader can use to appropriately address the racial profiling controversy.

2. Of the legal remedies discussed in this chapter, which is likely to have the most long-term impact on the racial profiling controversy, and why?

3. Discuss how researchers might sufficiently improve the accuracy of their data to make them acceptable in a court?

4. Should police officers be held civilly or criminally liable if they stop a disproportionately high number of minorities?

5. Why should a state pass a statute prohibiting racial profiling when, according to the Fourteenth Amendment to the United States Constitution, it is already illegal?

6. What effect would a statute prohibiting pretextual stops have on crime control strategies?

CASE STUDIES

1. In a case similar to *Whren* a new Supreme Court applied a subjective test and ruled that a stop based in part on the fact that the Black driver looked "out of place" in a White neighborhood was unconstitutional even though the driver committed a serious violation. What effect will this new ruling have on police procedures?

2. The mayor, involved in a close reelection campaign, has publicly accused the police department of "wholesale and systematic discrimination" after reading its recent racial profiling study. How would you, as police chief, respond to this accusation?

3. The state legislature is considering a bill that includes criminal penalties for officers who stop a disproportionately high number of minorities. You, as the president of the state's law enforcement organization, are assigned to testify in a public hearing on the bill. What would you say?

Summary of New Jersey State Police Consent Decree

In The United States District Court
for the District of New Jersey

UNITED STATES OF AMERICA,
PLAINTIFF,

v.

STATE OF NEW JERSEY

AND

DIVISION OF STATE POLICE OF THE NEW JERSEY DEPARTMENT
OF LAW AND PUBLIC SAFETY,
DEFENDANTS.
CIVIL NO. 99-5970(MLC)

Joint Application for Entry of Consent Decree

Plaintiff, the United States, and Defendants, the State of New Jersey and the Division of State Police of the New Jersey Department of Law and Public Safety, respectfully move this Court for entry of the attached Consent Decree.

The United States has simultaneously filed its Complaint against the Defendants alleging violations of 42 U.S.C. §14141 and 42 U.S.C. §3789d(c). The Complaint alleges a pattern or practice of conduct by troopers of the New Jersey State Police that deprives persons of rights, privileges, or immunities secured or protected by the Constitution and the laws of the United States. Defendants deny that the State Police has engaged in a pattern or practice of conduct that deprives persons of rights, privileges, or immunities secured or protected by the Constitution and laws of the United States.

The parties seek to enter into this Decree jointly for the purpose of avoiding the risks and burdens of litigation, and to support vigorous, lawful, and nondiscriminatory traffic enforcement that promotes traffic safety and assists law enforcement to interdict drugs and other contraband, arrest fugitives, and enforce firearms and other criminal statutes.

The United States and the State of New Jersey have agreed upon a proposed Consent Decree that would resolve all claims in the United States' Complaint. The proposed Decree would address the claims in the United States' Complaint by amending certain policies, practices, and procedures relating to the manner in which the State of New Jersey manages and operates the New Jersey State Police.

The proposed Decree addresses the following matters: policy requirements and limitations on the use of race in law enforcement activities and the procedures used for conducting motor vehicle searches; documentation of traffic stops including post-stop procedures and enforcement actions; supervisory measures to promote civil rights integrity; procedures for receiving, investigating, and resolving misconduct allegations; training; responsibilities of the Office of the New Jersey Attorney General concerning the New Jersey State Police; public reporting by the State Police about its law enforcement activities; and the establishment of an independent monitor to review and analyze implementation of the Decree by the State.

Specifically, the proposed Decree includes the following provisions:

1. *Policy Requirements* (¶¶26–28): State troopers may not rely to any degree on the race or national or ethnic origin of motorists in selecting vehicles for traffic stops and in deciding upon the scope and substance of post-stop actions, except where state troopers are on the look-out for a specific suspect who has been identified in part by his or her race or national or ethnic origin. The State Police shall continue to require that troopers make a request for consent to search only when they possess reasonable suspicion that a search will reveal evidence of a crime, and all consent searches must be based on the driver or passenger giving written consent prior to the initiation of the search.

2. *Traffic Stop Documentation* (¶¶29–34): State troopers engaged in patrol activities will document the race, ethnic origin, and gender of all motor vehicle drivers who are the subject of a traffic stop, and also will record information about the reason for each stop and any post-stop action that is taken (including the issuance of a ticket or warning, asking the vehicle occupants to exit the vehicle and frisking them, consensual and non-consensual vehicle searches, uses of force, and arrests).

3. *Supervisory Review of Individual Traffic Stops* (¶¶35–39): Supervisors regularly will review trooper reports concerning

post-stop enforcement actions and procedures, and patrol car video tapes of traffic stops, to ensure that troopers are employing appropriate practices and procedures. Where concerns arise, supervisors may require that the trooper be counseled, receive additional training, or that some other non-disciplinary action be taken. Supervisors also can refer specific incidents for further investigation, where appropriate.

4. *Supervisory Review of Patterns of Conduct* (¶¶40–56): The State will develop and implement an early warning system, called the "Management Awareness Program," that uses computerized information on traffic stops, misconduct investigations, and other matters to assist State Police supervisors to identify and modify potentially problematic behavior. At least quarterly, State Police supervisors will conduct reviews and analyses of computerized data and other information, including data on traffic stops and post-stop actions by race and ethnicity. These reviews and analyses, as appropriate, may result in supervisors implementing changes in traffic enforcement criteria, training, and practices, implementing non-disciplinary interventions for particular troopers (such as supervisory counseling or additional training), and/or requiring further assessment or investigation.

5. *Misconduct Allegations* (¶¶57–92): The State Police will make complaint forms and informational materials available at a variety of locations, will institute a 24-hour toll-free telephone hotline, and will publicize the State Police toll-free number at all State-operated rest stops located on limited access highways. The State also will institute procedures for ensuring that the State Police is notified of criminal cases and civil lawsuits alleging trooper misconduct. Allegations of discriminatory traffic stops, improper post-stop actions, and other significant misconduct allegations will be investigated by the Professional Standards Bureau inside the State Police or by the State Attorney General's Office. All investigations will be properly documented. Where a misconduct allegation is substantiated concerning prohibited discrimination or certain other serious misconduct, discipline shall be imposed. Where a misconduct allegation is not substantiated, the State Police will consider whether non-disciplinary supervisory steps are appropriate.

6. *Training* (¶¶93–109): The State Police will continue to implement measures to improve training for recruits and incumbent troopers. The training will address such matters as supervisory issues, communication skills, cultural diversity, and the nondiscrimination requirements of the Decree. The State Police also will take steps to continue to improve its trooper coach program for new troopers. The Independent Monitor selected by the parties will evaluate all training currently provided by the State Police regarding traffic stops, and will make recommendations for improvements.

7. *Auditing by the New Jersey Attorney General's Office* (¶¶110–113): The State Attorney General's Office will have special responsibility for ensuring implementation of the Decree. The Office will conduct various audits of State Police performance, which will include contacting samples of persons who were the subject of a State Police traffic stop to evaluate whether the stops were appropriately conducted and documented. The Office also will audit State Police implementation of the Management Awareness Program, and procedures used for receiving, investigating, and resolving misconduct allegations.

8. *State Police Public Reports* (¶114): The State Police will issue semiannual public reports containing aggregate statistics on certain law enforcement activities, including traffic stop statistics.

9. *Independent Monitor* (¶¶115–121): An Independent Monitor, who will be an agent of the court, will be selected by the United States and the State of New Jersey to monitor and report on the State's implementation of the Decree. The responsibilities of the Monitor will include evaluating samples of trooper incident reports, supervisory reviews of incidents, and misconduct investigations, supervisors' use of the Management Awareness Program, and the use of non-disciplinary procedures to address at-risk conduct.

10. *Decree Term* (¶131): The basic term of the Decree will be five years, however, based on the State's record of compliance, the United States and the Independent Monitor may agree to a request by the State to shorten the term of the Decree if the State has been in substantial compliance for at least two years.

Joint entry of this Decree is in the public interest since it provides for expeditious remedial activity and avoids the diversion of federal and State resources to adversarial actions by the parties. Additionally, the proposed Decree does not conflict with the collective bargaining agreements between the State Police and its troopers, as noted in the Decree at ¶128.

For the reasons discussed above, entry of the Decree is lawful and appropriate. Therefore, the United States and the State of New Jersey jointly move for entry of the Consent Decree.

Respectfully submitted:

FOR THE PLAINTIFF, THE UNITED STATES OF AMERICA:

ROBERT J. CLEARY
United States Attorney
District of New Jersey

BILL LANN LEE
Acting Assistant Attorney General
Civil Rights Division
U.S. Department of Justice

SUSAN C. CASSELL
Deputy Chief
Civil Division
United States Attorney
District of New Jersey
970 Broad Street, 7th Floor
Federal Building
Newark, New Jersey 07102
973/645-2700

STEVEN H. ROSENBAUM
Chief
MARK A. POSNER
KELLI M. EVANS
Trial Attorneys
Special Litigation Section
Civil Rights Division
U.S. Department of Justice
P.O. Box 66400
Washington, D.C. 20035-6400
202/307-1388

FOR THE DEFENDANTS, STATE OF NEW JERSEY, and DIVISION OF STATE POLICE, NEW JERSEY DEPARTMENT OF LAW AND PUBLIC SAFETY:
JOHN J. FARMER, JR.

Attorney General
State of New Jersey
Hughes Justice Complex, 8 West
25 Market Street
Post Office Box 081
Trenton, New Jersey 08625-0085
609/292-4925

CONDUCTING RACIAL PROFILING STUDIES (BEST PRACTICES)

OBJECTIVE

To outline and discuss the important steps for successfully conducting a racial profiling inquiry.

CHAPTER OUTLINE

Introduction
Precipitating Events
Common Obstacles
Critical Steps
   Enlisting the Help of Others
   Developing Salient Research Questions
   Data Collection Strategies
   Measurement: Variables and Attributes
     What to Collect and Why
      Information about the persons stopped
      Information about the stop itself
      Information about police officers

INTRODUCTION

From a purely scientific perspective, racial profiling research is deceptively simple. The challenges facing the researcher are usually overcome easily, and if not can be adequately mitigated. The measurement process is subject to the same kinds of error endemic to all social science research. The analytical components and statistical models are relatively straightforward and easily understood by most consumers of the research. So why dedicate an entire chapter of this book to the racial profiling research process? Racial profiling research seldom occurs wholly within the soft light of academia. It is an inherently public process that attracts the attention of a broad range of consumers. Seldom are the results conclusive and seldom do they effectively change minds.

Racial profiling researchers are characteristically creative. Many are successful at developing research plans that adhere to rigorous methodological demands in extremely difficult research contexts. We can and should use this body of research as a template for conducting future research. The purpose of this chapter is to outline the best, and a few of the worst, practices of racial profiling researchers. This chapter is intended to provide scholars and practitioners with guidance on how to conduct an effective racial profiling inquiry, and in doing so, make them more informed consumers of racial profiling research. It is, however, only a beginning. It is quite likely that within the next few years future researchers will develop techniques that advance the field substantially.

PRECIPITATING EVENTS

It is unlikely that a police chief will one day just decide to conduct a racial profiling inquiry. Most, given the potential danger to their department's public image, would rather not. A considerable number of racial profiling studies are required by a state law or municipal ordinance. In a few instances, namely New Jersey and Maryland, racial profiling inquiries were initiated within the context of a lawsuit. Most, however, are initiated in response to political pressure and after a series of very public precipitating events (Ramirez, McDevitt, and Farrell 2000) that serve to question the department's capacity to conduct its business fairly and equitably.

Nearly all voluntary racial profiling inquires are preceded by allegations of racial profiling from the minority community. Even though these complaints are rarely substantiated, the perception of racial profiling within the minority community is pervasive. In Wichita these complaints attracted the attention of the local media and resulted in a series of investigative reports. In North Carolina media attention led to the passage of the nation's first racial profiling data collection statute. In New Jersey complaints from minorities led to a comprehensive consent decree.

Anecdotal stories from citizens alleging to be victims of racial profiling are particularly effective at convincing police departments to conduct inquiries. In 1999, officers from the San Jose Police Department stopped a local Black minister named Michael McBride. The stop resulted in a search and an assault. McBride alleged publicly that he was the victim of racial profiling. The results of an internal affairs investigation were inconclusive. In 1997, officers from the San Diego Police Department stopped the driver of a Jeep Cherokee because, as they alleged, it fit the description of a stolen vehicle. The operator of the Cherokee was Shawn Lee, a San Diego Chargers football player. Lee alleged that he was stopped because of his race. A subsequent investigation revealed that the stolen vehicle was actually described as a Honda sedan (Ramirez, McDevitt, and Farrell 2000). When events like these occur there is very little a police department can do to restore its public image short of conducting a rigorous investigation into how race affects its enforcement programs.

COMMON OBSTACLES

In 1997, Representative John Conyers of Michigan introduced the Traffic Stops Statistics Act. This law would have required the United States Department of Justice to collect data and conduct a nationwide study of racial profiling. The proposal (H.R. 118) was offered when there was intense interest in racial profiling among elected officials throughout the nation. During this time at least fourteen states and nearly forty large municipalities had either passed or were seriously considering similar proposals. The bill was passed unanimously by the United States House of Representatives, indicating a high level of public interest in racial profiling. In contrast, the USA Patriot Act, passed hurriedly amid Congressional anger following the September 11, 2001, terrorist attacks on the United States, had one dissenting vote.

Almost immediately after the passage of the proposal in the House of Representatives many of the nation's police organizations voiced their opposition to it. Most notably, the National Association of Police Organizations, representing thousands of police organizations, registered strong opposition to the bill. According to these organizations, the collection of data required by this bill would be an onerous requirement for most police officers. Their opposition was effective. The bill received no serious consideration by the United States Senate and eventually faded away after the adjournment of the 105th Congress (Harris 2002).

Racial profiling research has contributed substantially to our understanding of police patrol procedures and how minorities are affected by them. It has identified dozens of issues and addressed many of the misconceptions about how police manage the patrol function (Farrell, McDevitt, and Buerger 2002). Even so, there is often strong opposition to conducting racial profiling research. Some of this opposition is purely political. Some people prefer not to explore what may become politically dangerous. Some of the opposition is based on the practical realities of field research. In most cases police administrators are wary of how the data collection process will affect the ability of their officers to maintain an effective enforcement program. The following issues appear consistently throughout the literature. They are summarized here and discussed more comprehensively throughout this chapter.

Police departments do not routinely collect the kind of information needed to conduct a racial profiling inquiry. Therefore, in most cases the data collection processes are imposed onto the administrative reporting procedures already in place in the department. In other words, officers are required to complete another paper form. Predictably, police administrators are wary to impose an additional reporting requirement on patrol officers. While not particularly time consuming at the individual level, collectively, the completion of these forms translates into a substantial commitment of time away from routine patrol duties. Some departments have mitigated this by developing mobile display terminal and laptop computer data entry screens with pull down menus.

Accurately determining an individual's race is not as simple as one might think. It is particularly difficult to determine for multiracial individuals. In some cities the officers were initially instructed to ask the citizens. Police officers, as well as their union representatives, recognized the potential volatility of this proposed practice and in many cases bitterly complained. Asking individuals their race, within the context of traffic stops where race is not supposed to matter, is unnecessarily intrusive and may imply a racial bias. As a result, most departments allow officers to classify the individuals they stop into racial or ethnic categories. This seems appropriate, especially when one recalls that an officer's perception of race is central to the racial profiling controversy.

Racial profiling research is dependent upon data from police stops. The best source of this information is the police officers themselves. Beyond the practical obstacles associated with collecting stop data, there are a few more menacing concerns. First, there is some concern that police officers, wary of how the information may be used, will report either incomplete or inaccurate data. Some police chiefs mitigate this by outlining how the data will be analyzed and reported and assuring the officers (and their union representatives) that the results will not be reported individually. Second, there is some concern that officers will simply disengage from routine enforcement during the data collection phase. There is some evidence of this in the literature (Farrell et al. 2004; Withrow 2002). The research also indicates, however, that over time officer productivity returns to normal levels. The disengagement may simply be caused by the additional paperwork requirements. What makes these obstacles so difficult to overcome is an inability to verify the accuracy and completeness of the stop data through an independent source of information. There are no central repositories of information in police departments that comprehensively record all police-citizens contacts. Normally there are databases that include citations, warnings, dispatch logs, and field interviews. These activities only represent a portion of the people a police officer contacts on a regular basis.

What appears important to the successful completion of a racial profiling inquiry is administrative consistency and leadership (Ramirez, McDevitt, and Farrell 2000; Schultz and Withrow 2004a). Many of the problems associated with racial profiling research can be overcome, but not without the guidance of a leader committed to the project. The following sections outline how various police administrators and researchers have addressed problems associated with racial profiling research.

CRITICAL STEPS

Throughout the literature there a few consistent practices that appear to improve the quality of racial profiling research. These practices are by no means the only ways to conduct racial profiling research. Indeed, within the next few years it is likely that many more techniques will be developed within this highly dynamic research agenda. What appears here are the best practices to date. Future researchers are encouraged to use these practices for guidance while conducting their own studies and, more importantly, for the critical analyzing of the work of others.

Enlisting the Help of Others

Racial profiling research provides an excellent opportunity to engage a broad spectrum of the community in a highly productive problem solving exercise. Enlisting the assistance of the community offers an opportunity for citizens and the police to discuss racial profiling and corollary issues in intelligent ways. Citizen task forces can become vehicles for solving intractable community problems (Cleary 2000; Farrell, McDevitt, and Buerger 2002). Fridell et al. (2001) recommend that effective approaches

- Encourage dialogue between the command staff and community stakeholders through frequent meetings
- Provide opportunities for community members to offer feedback
- Be highly visible to the broader community
- Enlist the assistance of representatives from immigrant populations through bilingual officers
- Encourage minority participation in substantive departmental decision making

An important part of this process is deciding who comes to the table. Internal stakeholders include the executive, administrative, and command staffs of the police department. In addition, representatives from patrol and special operations should be included. From time to time the expertise of other specialists (e.g., information technology) will also help the task force achieve its goals. That is the easy part. Identifying and enlisting the assistance of stakeholders external to the department demands a more cautious approach. Certainly representatives from the police labor organizations, if any, should be engaged early in the process. A labor dispute over the data collection process, or more likely over how the data will be used, is a potentially fatal threat to racial profiling research as well as the department's public image. Involving labor representatives early on appears to overcome many of the fears harbored by these advocates.

It seems to be a given that community task forces charged with implementing a racial profiling inquiry should include representatives from the minority communities. It is, however, important to note that not all minority groups are as representative of the minority community as they purport to be. There is considerable dissention within the minority community, just as there is in the nonminority community. The objective in forming a community task force is to include as many perspectives as possible, even if it hurts a little and appears to overly complicate the process. The general rule here is to err on the side of inclusion. To overcome this, some departments include representatives from neighborhood associations. Representatives from these communities provide a broader perspective and offer the department a great deal of feedback on how its enforcement program is perceived by its consumers.

Usually, representatives from the professional and business communities are overlooked as potential members. This oversight is likely due to the misperception that unless they are minority professionals or business owners, they do not have a personal stake in racial profiling research. This is not true. Increasingly, business leaders and professionals recognize how important the perception of community fairness is to their customers and employees. It is also important to recall that many of the major crime control strategies implemented in the twentieth century arose from local chambers of commerce. The most visible example of this occurred during the 1920s in Chicago. Business leaders, concerned about how organized crime was adversely affecting their community, organized a crime commission to address the city's increasing crime rate.

Once the membership of the task force has been established, it is important to develop a series of ground rules. Task force members must know the scope of their authority and responsibility. The first step is to establish the rules of engagement. Most task forces are purely advisory. Some departments allow task forces to actively manage the entire project. There are obvious advantages and disadvantages to either model. The key factor is communicating the exact role of the task force early on in the process. The next step is to determine who is in charge. In most cases the police department or a designated consultant will manage the project. In some communities it may be feasible for the group to designate its own leader.

It is likely that the first few meetings will be little more than gripe sessions. Although not likely productive at moving the project forward, these sessions are necessary in that they satisfy the members' legitimate needs to express their opinions and perspectives. Ultimately, it is critically important for the group to develop a sense of team prior to tackling any substantive issues (Farrell, McDevitt, and Buerger 2002).

Once established, the team should move onto setting realistic goals. Usually, goals are expressed in the form of analytical objectives for the racial profiling research. Ultimately, the goals will drive the data collection process. The experience in Seattle underscores the importance of setting goals early on in the process. Some of the stakeholders wanted the project to determine whether or not an officer's race, age, gender, or years of experience affected the selection of drivers to stop. To determine this, it was necessary to record the officers' identification numbers on the stop data reporting forms and append the stop database with demographic information about the officers from the personnel records. The police union representative strongly objected. The issue was resolved when a representative of the group, familiar with the literature, pointed out that no racial profiling study had ever found differences in the stopping behavior of officers with respect to these variables.

In the final analysis it really does not matter how accurate the data collection and analyses are if the community is not engaged in the process. Data collection and evaluation will not, by themselves, address or correct community frustrations (Cleary 2000; McMahon et al. 2002). In most situations prejudices are identified in both the police and minority communities (Carter and

Katz-Bannister 2004; Cleary 2000). Involving the community in the racial profiling research process provides the best, and maybe the only, opportunity a police department may have to proactively address community conflict (Fridell et al. 2001).

Finding a Research Partner

In the not so distant past, it was difficult to find someone working in a police department with the research and analytical skills normally developed through a university education. That has changed dramatically. Police leaders, cognizant of the value of crime analysis and program evaluation skills, are more receptive to hiring academically trained specialists. As a result, most departments have the in-house expertise to conduct racial profiling research. More than half of the racial profiling studies, and some of the most well-crafted projects, have been conducted by police department employees.

Even if a department has in-house analytical expertise, there is a clear need for an agency to establish a partnership with an independent evaluator at some stage during the process. This relationship should be established early on during the design phases of the project (McMahon et al. 2002; Ramirez, McDevitt, and Farrell 2000). An independent research partner can provide important operational and analytical expertise to the project (McMahon et al. 2002). Beyond this, an independent research partner ensures objectivity and, in some situations, legitimacy to the research process (Cleary 2000; Fridell et al. 2001).

It is usually not terribly difficult to find someone to assist the department in this capacity, despite the controversial nature of the topic. Most police departments already have informal relationships with university faculty who are qualified to conduct these analyses, and most would welcome the opportunity. If not, there are about a dozen stand alone consultants who specialize in these types of studies.

Developing Salient Research Questions

The most important task of any researcher is to develop a series of initial research questions. A sense of what one hopes to learn from the project drives many of the operational decisions relating to the project. In addition, the data should be collected at an appropriate level of measurement. For example, if the researcher wants to know if a relationship exists between the severity of the reason for the stop and the punitiveness of its outcome, then the data collection strategy should be responsive to this. This type of analysis requires data collected at the ordinal, internal, or ratio levels. Most racial profiling researchers collect this data, if at all, at the nominal level. This severely restricts the range of statistical models that can be used to respond to the research questions. This issue is discussed more comprehensively in "Measurement: Variables and Attributes." It is likely that as the project progresses, additional questions will arise. Most good research produces more questions than answers. The following are the most consistently asked research questions:

- Are racial and ethnic minorities stopped more frequently (or disproportionately) than nonminority citizens?
- Are there differences in the reasons for stops with respect to race or ethnicity?
- Are racial and ethnic minorities searched more frequently than nonminorities?
- Does the disposition of the stop differ with respect to the race or ethnicity of the individual stopped?
- Are racial and ethnic minorities detained longer during a stop than nonminorities?
- Are incidents involving physical resistance and confrontation more frequent during stops involving racial or ethnic minorities, and if so, why?
- What effect do officer characteristics have on the representation of minorities in traffic stops?

Data Collection Strategies

Racial profiling studies are seldom welcomed by police officers. For several reasons police officers tend to oppose collecting stop data. First, the collection of racial profiling data infers that all officers profile minorities. The logical end of this is the inference that police officers are prejudiced. Second, many police officers distrust statistical analysis (Carter and Katz-Bannister 2004). It is likely that much of this mistrust is due to the difficulties many have understanding the nuances associated with statistical analyses. Sometimes officers believe the data will be used to harm them or the police department. Unfortunately, in some cases their fears have been realized. Data collection has been blamed for sharp reductions in officer productivity and morale while at the same time increasing workload. Finally, racial profiling studies usually fail to produce sufficient information on the nature and extent of racially biased policing (Fridell et al. 2001). As a result, some officers fail to recognize the value of participating in a racial profiling inquiry.

Fortunately, there are considerably more advantages to data collection. The most obvious advantage to conducting a racial profiling study is that it helps an agency determine whether racially biased policing is a problem in their community (Fridell et al. 2001). Even if the inquiry does not produce conclusive data, it may provide insight into the causes for the community perception that racial profiling is systematic (Lamberth 2003b; Ramirez, McDevitt, and Farrell 2000). Second, the mere fact that an agency is proactively conducting a racial profiling study conveys a message of a commitment to unbiased policing and the value of equal protection (Fridell et al. 2001; Ramirez, McDevitt, and Farrell 2000). Third, a comprehensive racial profiling study can identify inefficiencies within the patrol function of the department and thereby enable the department to better allocate resources to address community concerns (Fridell et al. 2001; Lamberth 2003b; Ramirez, McDevitt, and Farrell 2000). Fourth, data from racial profiling studies is far more valuable than anecdotal stories of alleged racially motivated stops. Findings based on empirical data are considerably more useful to the policy process (McMahon et al. 2002). Finally, if the racial profiling inquiry is conducted by a broad range of community stakeholders, the process supports the community policing philosophy. It serves as a basis upon which a sense of trust and respect can be forged between the police and the community (Ramirez, McDevitt, and Farrell 2000). These benefits are of course predicated on the legitimacy of the department's attempt to address the racial profiling controversy in a meaningful way.

There are three general methods for collecting police stop data. Each method has its advantages and disadvantages, and within each method there are a few variations. The most common method for collecting stop data is the paper form. Normally, officers are directed to complete a form after each stop or police-citizen contact. In most situations these forms are machine readable, thereby eliminating the need for, and possibility of error associated with, subsequent data entry (see Figure 6.1). The most obvious

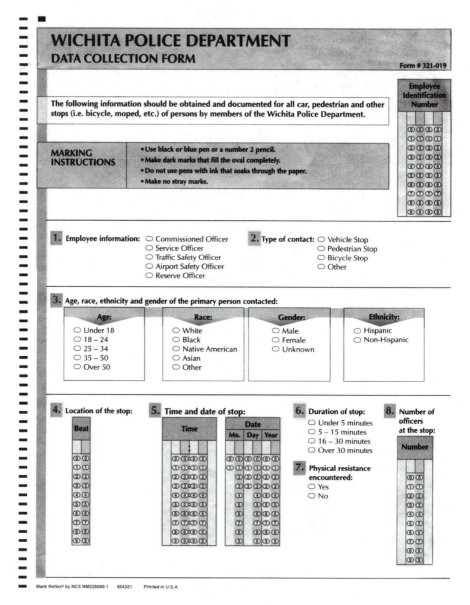

FIGURE 6–1 Wichita Police Department Contact Card

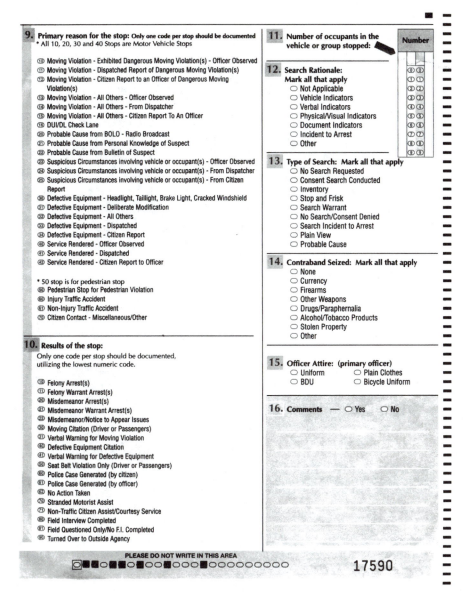

9. **Primary reason for the stop:** Only one code per stop should be documented
* All 10, 20, 30 and 40 Stops are Motor Vehicle Stops

⑩ Moving Violation - Exhibited Dangerous Moving Violation(s) - Officer Observed
⑪ Moving Violation - Dispatched Report of Dangerous Moving Violation(s)
⑫ Moving Violation - Citizen Report to an Officer of Dangerous Moving Violation(s)
⑬ Moving Violation - All Others - Officer Observed
⑭ Moving Violation - All Others - From Dispatcher
⑮ Moving Violation - All Others - Citizen Report To An Officer
⑯ DUI/DL Check Lane
⑳ Probable Cause from BOLO - Radio Broadcast
㉑ Probable Cause from Personal Knowledge of Suspect
㉒ Probable Cause from Bulletin of Suspect
㉓ Suspicious Circumstances involving vehicle or occupant(s) - Officer Observed
㉔ Suspicious Circumstances involving vehicle or occupant(s) - From Dispatcher
㉕ Suspicious Circumstances involving vehicle or occupant(s) - From Citizen Report
㉚ Defective Equipment - Headlight, Taillight, Brake Light, Cracked Windshield
㉛ Defective Equipment - Deliberate Modification
㉜ Defective Equipment - All Others
㉝ Defective Equipment - Dispatched
㉞ Defective Equipment - Citizen Report
㊵ Service Rendered - Officer Observed
㊶ Service Rendered - Dispatched
㊷ Service Rendered - Citizen Report to Officer

* 50 stop is for pedestrian stop
㊿ Pedestrian Stop for Pedestrian Violation
⑩ Injury Traffic Accident
⑪ Non-Injury Traffic Accident
⑫ Citizen Contact - Miscellaneous/Other

10. **Results of the stop:**
Only one code per stop should be documented, utilizing the lowest numeric code.

⑩ Felony Arrest(s)
⑪ Felony Warrant Arrest(s)
⑳ Misdemeanor Arrest(s)
㉑ Misdemeanor Warrant Arrest(s)
㉒ Misdemeanor/Notice to Appear Issues
㉚ Moving Citation (Driver or Passengers)
㉛ Verbal Warning for Moving Violation
㊵ Defective Equipment Citation
㊶ Verbal Warning for Defective Equipment
㊷ Seat Belt Violation Only (Driver or Passengers)
㊿ Police Case Generated (by citizen)
㊶ Police Case Generated (by officer)
㊷ No Action Taken
⑳ Stranded Motorist Assist
㉑ Non-Traffic Citizen Assist/Courtesy Service
㉚ Field Interview Completed
㉛ Field Questioned Only/No F.I. Completed
㎠ Turned Over to Outside Agency

11. **Number of occupants in the vehicle or group stopped:** | Number |

12. **Search Rationale:**
Mark all that apply
○ Not Applicable
○ Vehicle Indicators
○ Verbal Indicators
○ Physical/Visual Indicators
○ Document Indicators
○ Incident to Arrest
○ Other

⓪ ⓪
① ①
② ②
③ ③
④ ④
⑤ ⑤
⑥ ⑥
⑦ ⑦
⑧ ⑧
⑨ ⑨

13. **Type of Search:** Mark all that apply
○ No Search Requested
○ Consent Search Conducted
○ Inventory
○ Stop and Frisk
○ Search Warrant
○ No Search/Consent Denied
○ Search Incident to Arrest
○ Plain View
○ Probable Cause

14. **Contraband Seized:** Mark all that apply
○ None
○ Currency
○ Firearms
○ Other Weapons
○ Drugs/Paraphernalia
○ Alcohol/Tobacco Products
○ Stolen Property
○ Other

15. **Officer Attire:** (primary officer)
○ Uniform   ○ Plain Clothes
○ BDU   ○ Bicycle Uniform

16. Comments — ○ Yes   ○ No

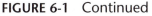
PLEASE DO NOT WRITE IN THIS AREA

17590

FIGURE 6-1   Continued

advantage of paper forms is their expense. They are relatively inexpensive, particularly when produced in large volume. Second, paper forms do not require major software changes to department information systems. In most cases the forms and the machine designed to read them are provided by an outside service in the form of a stand alone system. The major disadvantage to paper forms is that they take up a lot of room, both in patrol cars and in central filing systems. Second, the distribution of paper forms may be problematic. Third, the process by which the forms are transformed from the paper format to the database may adversely affect the accuracy of the data. Similarly, unlike electronic data collection mechanisms, real time data integrity checks are not possible with paper forms. Finally, there is sometimes a considerable lag time between when the data are collected via a paper form and entered into the database. This delay may diminish the opportunity for verification if the officer is particularly prolific and does not recall the details of every police-citizen contact.

The next most common form of data collection relies on mobile display terminals, laptops, or handheld computers. In some situations data is entered by dispatchers, per a patrol officer's instructions, onto a computer-aided dispatch system. Data collection in this format is analogous to paper forms. The only difference, if any, is that the required fields are displayed on pull down menus rather than organized into blocks as on a paper form. One advantage to this strategy is that it eliminates the need to transfer the data from a hard copy format to an electronic database. This may enhance the accuracy of the data and reduce the delay associated with paper forms. Second, data entry systems featuring real time integrity checks can reduce error. For example, in the Wichita study the officers were required to enter the context of the stop as either a vehicle, pedestrian, bicycle, or other. In nearly 60 percent of the pedestrian stops the officers reported the reason for the stop to be a motor vehicle violation. An appropriately designed data entry system would recognize this as an error and require the officer to correct the record before entering it into the database. Third, electronic data collection systems are not hampered by the problems associated with the distribution of paper forms. As long as officers have access to working data entry screens they can enter data.

Alternatively, electronic data entry may require considerable changes to a department's information system. In most departments this is not an easy process, particularly when one considers the rather onerous security and response time requirements imposed on departments by their information partners. Furthermore, given the rather temporary nature of racial profiling data collection, it may not be feasible to change a department's information system. Second, unless a department is currently equipped, stand alone data collection systems based on laptops and handheld computers may require a considerable capital expenditure.

Although rare, some departments may be able to produce appropriate stop data from their current information systems. In some cases this may require the merger of information from several sources. For example, if the department routinely collects driver's license numbers, by using a state maintained database it can determine the race, age, and gender of the people it contacts. This of course assumes that the state driver licensing authority collects this information. Not all state driver licensing authorities collect information relating to the race of the driver. The most important advantage to this method is its lack of reactivity. Because the data is already there, the officers are not required to complete a separate form. It is unlikely, however, that a police department's current information system is comprehensive enough to supply the data necessary for a rigorous racial profiling inquiry.

Regardless of the data collection method chosen, there are a few critical steps that must be taken to ensure the accuracy and completeness of police stop data. First, the data collection process, in particular the variables selected for collection, should be relevant to the department's analytical concerns. Consequently, data that is not necessary to respond to the department's analytical questions should not be included in the data collection process. Second, the date entry process should be as seamless and unobtrusive as possible. The racial profiling data collection exercise should appear as routine as possible within the context of the department's regular data collection mechanism (Ramirez, McDevitt, and Farrell 2000). Third, departments should commit considerable time and resources to training officers on how to collect the data. This necessarily includes informing officers of how the data will be maintained and analyzed. In most situations a three-to six-month pilot test is advisable to ensure that offices are responsive to the data needs of the racial profiling inquiry (Ramirez, McDevitt, and Farrell 2000). Finally, the department should determine the scope of the data collection process. If this process is intended solely to respond to a racial profiling inquiry, then an end date should be established and communicated to the officers. If, however, the data collection process is intended to support a more permanent strategy for addressing racially biased policing, then the department should prepare its officers accordingly (Fridell et al. 2001).

Measurement: Variables and Attributes

Before outlining the most appropriate variables for a racial profiling inquiry, it is important to review a few important methodological concepts. The first is the distinction between variables and attributes. A variable is generally defined as anything that varies or a logical collection of attributes. For example, race is a variable. Attributes are the categories or levels of a variable. For example, Caucasian, African-American, Native American, and Asian/Pacific Islander are attributes of the race variable. After determining which variables to collect, the researchers should give considerable attention to their attributes. Two rules are important. First, the attributes should be mutually exclusive. This means that an individual can be classified into one, and only one, attribute. This often becomes an issue when the classification "Hispanic" is included in an attribute within the race field, when in actuality it is an ethnicity. In many cases Hispanics may also be considered Caucasian. To overcome this, some researchers include a separate variable describing an individual's ethnicity. Second, the list of attributes should be exhaustive. This means that all reasonably possible categories of the variable are available for classification. This decision is driven primarily by the population of the locality in which the data are collected. For example, in New Jersey the researchers made a distinction between Asian Indians (e.g., Indians and Pakistanis) and Other Asians. Studies in Great Britain tend to define race more narrowly. One study included four separate categories for Black citizens (British, Caribbean, African, and Other). The same study also included three mixed race categories (Black/White, Asian/White, and Other) (Ramirez, McDevitt, and Farrell 2000). As a general but not absolute rule, an attribute list should include all racial and ethnic categories that represent more than 3 percent of a community. To account for less represented individuals, most researchers include "other" in their lists of attributes.

The second methodological issue is more analytical. The level at which a variable is measured ultimately determines the type of statistical analyses that can be conducted with the data. The higher the level of measurement, the more inferential (predictive) and informative the analysis will be. The lowest level of measurement is nominal. The attributes of a nominally measured variable are simply names. For example, race is a nominally measured variable. The attributes of this variable cannot be rank ordered. The second level of measurement is ordinal. Ordinally measured variables also name things and can be rank ordered. For example, the top three finishers in a bicycle race can be rank ordered into first, second, and third place. While this level of measurement is more flexible than the nominal level, it has a disadvantage. The distances between each of the levels may not be equivalent. There may be five seconds between the first and second place finishers' times, while a full minute may have lapsed between the second and third place finishers. The next level of measurement overcomes this. Interval level measures provide both a name and a rank order. In addition, the distances between levels in the rank order are equivalent. Height is an example of an interval level measure. The difference between 6′0″ and 6′1″ (one inch) is the same as the difference between 5′9″ and 5′10″. A ratio level measure has the same characteristics as an interval level measure and also includes an absolute zero. Age (in years) is an example of a ratio level measure. It is possible for an individual to be zero years old (see Table 6.1). For analytical purposes interval and ratio level variables are categorized into a single category called "scale." In other words, the analytical options for interval and ratio measured variables are identical.

TABLE 6.1   Levels of Measurement

Level	Name	Rank Order	Equal Distance	Absolute Zero
Nominal	Yes	No	No	No
Ordinal	Yes	Yes	No	No
Interval	Yes	Yes	Yes	No
Ratio	Yes	Yes	Yes	Yes

What to Collect and Why

Determining what information to collect is as important as the decision on the most appropriate data collection method. The variables selected for collection should be directly responsive to the analytical questions of the project and the particular concerns of the community, and nothing more. The data collection process is too onerous to be burdened by the collection of irrelevant information. On the other hand, regardless of the number of variables collected, the decision to collect stop data is a substantial commitment. Collecting ten variables is nearly as difficult as collecting twenty. As a result, the decision on which variables to collect should be based on the balance between what is necessary to conduct a comprehensive study and what might be interesting to measure.

The variables required by most data collection statutes and ordinances tend to be rather minimal. For example, the *Federal Traffic Stops Statistics Act* of 1997, if passed, would have required the collection of eleven variables. These include

1. The traffic violation alleged to have initiated the stop
2. The race and/or ethnicity of the individual stopped
3. The age of the individual stopped
4. The gender of the individual stopped
5. The immigration status of the individual stopped
6. Whether the stop included a search
7. Whether the officer asked for the individual's consent to search and if the consent was denied
8. The alleged criminal behavior that justified the search
9. Whether contraband was seized during the search
10. The disposition of the stop (warning, citation, or arrest)
11. The duration of the stop

In contrast, the stop data from the Wichita Stop Study (Withrow 2002) included thirty-two variables, and from these an additional ten variables were created.

At the outset the agency should determine exactly which stops will be measured. Most studies include vehicular stops. A few include stops involving pedestrians and bicyclists. Most agencies do not measure nondiscretionary contacts resulting from citizen calls for service and accident investigations. This seems appropriate because of the effect officer discretion appears to have on the racial profiling controversy. Regardless of which stops are measured, it is critical for officers to complete information on the totality of the stop. This includes the reason for the stop, its qualitative features (e.g., searches, physical confrontations), and its outcome (Cleary 2000; Smith and Alpert 2002). Generally, police stop data can be classified into three categories, but these categories are purely instructional.

Information about the persons stopped. Within this category the race and ethnicity of the individuals stopped are understandably the most important variables. At a minimum, the attributes of the race variable should include White, Black, Native-American, Asian, and Other. Additional attributes should be added according to the racial representation of the community in which the data are collected or in response to the particular issues surrounding a racial profiling inquiry. The actual labels are not analytically important, but they should have meaning to the individuals who collect the data. Strong consideration should be given to including a mixed race category. One of the most important findings of the 2000 U.S. Census is the surprisingly large proportion of mixed race citizens. In most cases ethnicity refers to either Hispanic or non-Hispanic. Some researchers include Hispanic as an attribute in the race variable. While this may make the analyst's job easier, it may be misleading. Some communities include significant populations of black-skinned Hispanics. These individuals may be difficult to classify unless the race and ethnicity variables are separate. Also, separating the race and ethnicity variables does not preclude the analyst from developing more descriptive designations. Both the race and ethnicity variables can be merged into a single variable that identifies Hispanics within each of the racial categories.

Because race and ethnicity are nominally measured, the analysis of differences in stops between racial and ethnic groups are often limited to simple cross-tabulations. This is primarily a descriptive technique. As a result, the analysis tends to simply compare the qualitative differences between stops involving various racial or ethnic groups and cannot make any direct or measurable inferences about how an individual's race affects an officer's performance. This may be overcome by either adding an additional variable or replacing the race and ethnicity fields with an indicator of the driver's skin color measured at the scale level. While not a valid indicator of race, this variable measured in this way may provide some insight into how skin color (as a proxy for race) may affect an officer's decision making. More importantly, with one exception (see Denver Police Department, 2002), the race or ethnicity of the driver is only measured after the stop. By then it is too late to honestly determine how race might have affected an officer's decision to initiate a traffic stop. The contact card used in Denver asked officers to enter what they though the citizen's race of ethnicity was prior to and after the stop.

A driver's age and gender are also important variables. Both are consistently found to be important correlates of certain behaviors. Males are more likely than females to commit traffic violations. Young drivers are more likely than older drivers to attract the attention of the police because of their driving behaviors. The overrepresentation of males and youths in police stop data is predictable. These variables are important analytical qualifiers. With some analytical models (e.g., regression) it is possible to measure the relative effects of several variables on a particular outcome. For example, it may be possible to calculate the relative impacts of age, gender, and race on the outcome of a stop. Gender is inherently a nominally measured variable. To support rigorous analyses, age should be collected at the scale level. The alternative is to classify individuals into one of a few age range categories producing an ordinally measured variable.

The number of occupants in the vehicle during the stop may also produce some interesting findings. In Wichita the analyst found that young Black men are far more likely to be stopped if they are driving a vehicle with three or more passengers (Withrow 2002). This finding actually caused a local minister to caution his youth against carpooling.

Variables relating to the height, weight, physical build, clothing, and demeanor of drivers, although interesting, do not appear to add appreciably to studies of this sort. It might, however, be interesting to know whether the outcome of the stop is affected in any way by differences between the officers' and drivers' size and gender. For example, are smaller framed officers less likely to arrest drivers who are larger than them? Are stops involving larger framed officers more likely to include incidents of physical confrontation? Studies that respond to these questions may not address the traditional racial profiling questions, but they do provide important insight into how contextual variations may affect an officer's behavior.

Information about the stop itself. Within this broad category, information relating to the reason and outcome of the stop are critically important. The reason or justification for the stop may provide some insight into the factors that affect an officer's decision to initiate a contact. It may also provide some insight into whether minorities are stopped for different reasons than nonminorities. For example, if minorities are stopped more frequently for equipment violations, then socio-economic status may be a more important predictor of stops than race. These variables are particularly valuable for the analyst interested in finding a relationship between the seriousness of the reason for the stop and the punitiveness of the outcome. One might expect that individuals stopped for flagrant violations are more likely to receive a citation and that individuals stopped for relatively minor violations are more likely to receive a warning. If stops involving minorities are more likely to result in a citation regardless of the seriousness of the reason for the stop, then one might conclude that officers are more willing to overlook the transgressions of nonminority drivers. Unfortunately, when the reason for the stop is recorded, it is usually measured nominally. As a result, it is not possible to rank order the justifications for stops in any logical manner. It may, however, be possible to develop a variable indicating an officer's level of discretion. Officers tend to have more discretion in stops predicated by officer-observed behaviors and less in citizen- or dispatch-directed stops. If possible, the reason for the stop should be measured at the scale level indicating the relative threat of the behavior to public safety.

At a minimum, the outcome of the stop should include whether the individual was arrested, cited, warned, referred to another agency, field interviewed, or let go. The more detail here, the better. The key analytical objective here is to determine the level of discretion afforded the officer while making a dispositional decision—for example, whether an arrest was for a suspected felony or misdemeanor violation, and if so, based on a warrant, would provide this important insight Warrantless misdemeanor arrests are nearly always an important analytical focus.

Information relating to searches is central to the racial profiling controversy. To facilitate the analysis, three distinct variable fields are necessary. The first is an indicator of whether or not a search occurred or was requested by the officer. The second includes information on the justification for the search. Attributes for this variable should at a minimum include vehicle, verbal, physical/visual, document, and other indicators or if the search was conducted incident to arrest. This particular variable informs the analyst what, if anything, led the officer to initiate or request the search. The third variable indicates the type of search. Attributes for this variable should include, consent, inventory, stop and frisk, warrant, incident to arrest, plain view, probable cause, and other. Within this analytical dimension the focus is on consent searches. From a purely racial profiling research perspective it is important to determine what factors an officer considers when requesting a consensual search. For administrative reasons it is important to determine whether hit rates from consensual searches differ with respect to race or ethnicity.

Search hit rates are among the most interesting findings in racial profiling research. In addition to measuring what percent of searches result in contraband seizures, it may also be advisable to determine what types of contraband are being seized. Attributes for this variable should include currency, firearms, other weapons, drugs/paraphernalia, alcohol/tobacco, stolen property, other contraband, and none. The key analysis is, however, the percentage of consensual searches that result in contraband seizures, or the hit rate. Some of the most important commentators on racial profiling have found that hit rates do not differ with respect to race or ethnicity (Harris 2002; Lamberth 2003a). In fact, in some situations hit rates are lower in searches involving racial minorities. To the extent that this is true, it fundamentally attacks the premise for targeting racial minorities based on the perception that they are more likely to be trafficking drugs.

Stops involving minorities may be more likely to include incidents of physical resistance or confrontation. Therefore, it is important to determine the percentage of stops that involve physical resistance or confrontation between officers and citizens. While the percentage of stops involving physical confrontation is generally very low, there may be a racial distinction. Data collected in this instance would be responsive to this allegation. It is, however, difficult to establish the temporal order of events during a stop using police stop data alone at its present level of sophistication. For example, it may be unclear whether or not the physical resistance was the cause or the result of an arrest. For some racial profiling researchers this may not matter. For police administrators it may be an important evaluative tool.

The location of the stop may provide important contextual insight into the stopping behavior of officers, particularly in a municipal policing context. Normally, this requires the officers to enter the beat number on the form. By itself the beat number is meaningless. However, using the beat number, the researcher can develop several key variables subsequent to the data collection process. For example, most departments calculate crime rates within beats. The crime rate of a beat may cause officers to conduct more discretionary stops and stop and frisk searches. The beat number, in conjunction with census tract information, may allow the researcher to develop demographic profiles for each beat that would include information on the proportional racial representation and socio-economic status of beat residents. Stops measured within beats are an acceptable proxy for measuring deployment emphasis to determine whether or not policing resources are concentrated in minority neighborhoods, an important alternative explanation. Finally, beat numbers enable the researcher to develop internal benchmarks. Using beat-specific data, the researcher can determine how individual officers perform compared with similarly situated officers.

Whether minorities are detained longer during stops has always been an important issue in the racial profiling controversy. Collecting this information at the scale level will enable the researcher to better determine how the race of the driver may affect the length of the stop. Here again, temporal order is important. Stops involving arrests or searches will, regardless of the race of the driver, be longer in duration. The analyst should account for these time-consuming outcomes when comparing the length of time individuals are detained with respect to their race or ethnicity.

Since the beginning of the racial profiling controversy the minority community has criticized police departments for dispatching large numbers of officers to stops involving minorities. This allegation is easily addressed by including this variable in the data collection process. It is best measured at the scale level. Here again, temporal order is important. The data collected should indicate whether the officers were dispatched prior to or after the individual's race became known to the initiating officer. Additionally, the data should provide some insight into whether the relative dangerousness of the police-citizen contact predicated the need for additional officers.

The actual time and date (day of week) of stops are likely not critical to a racial profiling study. They may be important administratively to evaluate the performance of the overall enforcement program or to determine workload demands. The time variable may be converted by the analyst to the department's shift schedule or used to determine the effect of darkness on the officer's decision to search.

The residency or immigration status of individuals stopped may also be an important indictor. Knowing the residency of the individuals stopped may provide some insight into the validity of a population-based benchmark. If a significant portion of stops involve residents from neighboring communities, then the benchmark can be imputed to account for a possible difference between the resident and driving populations (see Rojek, Rosenfeld, and Decker 2004).

Information about police officers. While very few studies (Novak 2004, Smith and Petrocelli 2001, and Withrow 2002 are the notable exceptions.) include demographic information about police officers, there are some potentially important explanatory variables available. This data is usually appended to the stop data set from human resources data maintained by the department subsequent to the data collection process. It is only available to the researcher if the stop data contain unique identifiers (i.e., badge numbers) that link individual officers with a stop records. These variables normally include the age, gender, race, and experience (in years) of the officer.

Collecting this data is rather controversial. Many officers, and their union representatives, object to the inclusion of an officer's identification number in the stop data set. Most are afraid that the data could be used for disciplinary purposes or as a means to single out individual officers for scrutiny. Some states prohibit the release of personal information about officers without their written permission.

All of this controversy may be for naught. There is no evidence that demographic differences between officers affect their stopping behaviors. Researchers usually find that minority officers stop equal or greater proportions of minority drivers and that younger officers are more likely to arrest individuals than older officers. It appears more likely that the officer's particular beat assignment has a greater effect on the racial proportions of the individuals stopped.

Improving Accuracy and Completeness

Researchers are typically wary of self-report data, especially when its accuracy and completeness cannot be verified independently. In most police departments a central repository of information relating to all police-citizen contacts normally does not exist. Citation, investigation, vehicle inventory, field inventory, and injury reports are normally judiciously recorded in police department information systems. Information relating to warnings, informal field interviews, citizen assists, and contacts not resulting in a formal record are seldom recorded. As a result, it is often not possible to determine whether officers are accurately and completely completing stop data reports on all designated police-citizen contacts. The importance of auditing police stop data cannot be overstated. In many legal proceedings during which police stop data were relevant, the accuracy of police stop data became important to the case. In most cases the department's inability to establish the accuracy and completeness of the data was directly responsible for their inability to prevail in a court of law (Smith and Alpert 2002; Susskind 1994).

Although problematic and likely not completely fool proof, there are a number of steps the researcher can take to enhance the accuracy and completeness of police stop data. Communicating to officers how the data will be maintained and reported may be the most effective way of ensuring compliance. If officers believe the data will be used to sanction them individually or that they will be publicly reported at the individual level, then they may be less likely to comply with the reporting requirements (Cleary 2000). Second, routine spot checks through the computer-assisted dispatch system, reviewing vehicle registration data, and regular customer satisfaction surveys may produce an important audit trail (Ramirez, McDevitt, and Farrell 2000). This of course assumes that the stop database includes the vehicle registration and driver's license numbers of the automobiles and individuals stopped. Some departments have attempted to tie stop data forms to citations or warnings. The feasibility of this may vary between departments and it may not be a conclusive measure.

In Rhode Island, Farrell (2003) reported that a steep decline in the number of tickets per officer per day (from an average of 25 to 4) occurred just after the implementation of the stop data collection process. Interviews with approximately 450 officers revealed limited supervisory support for and control of the data collection process. She implemented a two-step audit system based on two general types of stops. Stops resulting in citations were linked with a corresponding stop data report. Stops not resulting in citations were matched against dispatch data. Auditing these types of stops proved problematic because not all officers informed dispatch when a stop was initiated. Farrell also attempted to use video records of stops to verify the completeness of the stop data. This, however, proved to be time consuming. Ultimately, she was able to match from 90 to 93 percent of the stops to one of the three independent data sources. She makes the following recommendations:

- Develop an oversight system for data collection before gathering data.
- Know how to verify data before the external control issue is raised.
- Report the results of audits in traffic stop reports. This builds confidence and transmits a sense that we take this seriously.
- Officers should be aware that someone is looking at their traffic stop cards.
- Internal monitoring at both the first line supervisors and higher command levels is important.
- Use a lithocode (unique) number identifier.

Finally, a caution is in order. A reduction in overall productivity does not necessarily suggest a lack of compliance with the reporting requirements. In Wichita, Withrow (2002) reported a 30 percent reduction in overall stops during the data collection period. At the same time, using multiple indicators, he found compliance rates from 90 to 92 percent. The reduction in overall productivity appeared to be more directly related to an administrative change in departmental procedures involving the realignment of officers regularly assigned to traffic enforcement duties.

Data Analysis

The value of establishing a relationship with an objective research partner is evident during the analysis portion of the inquiry (Ramirez, McDevitt, and Farrell 2000). Most racial profiling research relies on relatively simple bivariate analyses. While interesting, these types of analyses cannot be used to infer or predict and generally cannot account for intervening causes of police behavior. Multivariate and hierarchal modeling techniques account for and measure the effects of various contextual features that surround most police stops (Batton and Kadleck 2004). The simple reality is that police stops are not simple. There are dozens of contextual issues that occur before, during, and after a police stop that affect an officer's professional judgment. The analytical methods used by the analyst should focus on and account for the complexities of police procedures and operational methods. In addition, the analysis should take into account the characteristics of the city and any events that could affect the validity of the data (McMahon et al. 2002).

Analysis at this level requires a high level of statistical skill. In addition, the analyst should be familiar with routine research methods. Knowing how to construct statistical models is one thing; interpreting the results in an effective manner is another. There are dozens of analytical nuances in racial profiling research that require the analyst to look behind the numbers and understand how the data were developed and the variables are measured. For example, one of the common mistakes made by racial profiling researchers is assuming that the benchmark is representative of the driving population. It may be, but the police do not focus much attention on the overall driving population. They pay attention primarily to the drivers who violate the traffic code. Therefore the estimate of the population of interest should be based on the racial proportion of traffic law violators.

The research partner should also be generally knowledgeable about routine police procedures. More specifically, the analyst should account for temporary changes in routine police procedures that may affect the data collection process. For example, during the data collection phase of the Wichita study a young girl was killed accidentally during a drive-by shooting. The suspects (based on witness statements) were young minority males known to frequent a predominantly Black neighborhood. The police conducted a ten-day saturation patrol procedure in and around this neighborhood. Ultimately, the suspects were caught and later convicted. During the ten-day period the police stopped a disproportionately high number of residents within a predominately Black neighborhood. Fortunately, the total number of cases in the stop data set was sufficiently large that the overall findings were not affected by this temporary change in police procedures (Withrow 2002).

Ultimately, the best analytical approach marries the skill of a competent analyst with the experience of a seasoned police officer. Because these are seldom found in a single person, many departments will assign a knowledgeable representative to work with the independent analyst. These collaborative situations often produce the most cogent results and offer relevant advice for policy makers.

Normally there are two general analytical procedures. The first is a comparison of the racial representation of individuals stopped (based on the stop data) against the racial representation of individuals at risk of being stopped (based on the benchmark). This comparison produces an odds ratio and is the information upon which the analyst bases the conclusion of whether racial profiling is occurring (Tomaskovic-Devey, Mason, and Zingraff 2004). In the absence of an alternative explanation to the contrary, if a racial group is overrepresented in police stops (as compared to the benchmark), then the analyst may conclude that racial profiling is occurring. In most studies racial disparity is evident, but is the level of disparity enough to conclude that racial profiling is occurring? Some disparity is normal, inconsequential, and due to pure chance. To respond to this, most analysts use either a chi-square or odds ratio technique. The critical decision component is significance, a statistical term indicating "that the results of a study are not simply a matter of chance" (Sprinthall 2003, 635). Normally, analysts conclude that the differences are statistically significant if the odds of a chance occurrence are 5 percent (.05) or less. The department should demand that the analyst conduct such tests.

The second general analysis focuses on poststop procedures. Within these analyses the benchmark used in the previous analysis is irrelevant. The benchmark for this portion of the analysis is developed by the police stop data and is more appropriately considered a baseline. For example, the police stop data will determine the proportion of stops involving Black drivers, say 20 percent. The stop data also measures what percent of stops, overall and by racial group, involve consent searches. One would expect that if

20 percent of the stops involve Black drivers, then 20 percent of the consent searches would involve Black drivers. If, however, 40 percent of the consent searches involve Black drivers, then one might conclude that, in the absence of an alternative explanation, the police are more likely to ask a Black motorists to consent to a search.

The department should insist that the analyst construct rigorous multivariate models using the police stop data that take into account as many factors associated with the stops as possible (see, e.g., Novak 2004; Smith and Petrocelli 2001; Withrow 2002). The most appropriate technique appears to be a logistic regression. This technique is the least demanding (in terms of its data assumptions), yet it produces the most instructive information on the relative influence of various factors within the police decision making process. Logistic regression requires the analyst to develop a binary dependent (outcome) variable. The technique produces coefficients for each independent (cause) variable that estimate "the probability that an event will occur or not" (Hair et al. 1992, 60). The statistical significance of the coefficients is tested using a Wald statistic. For example, let's say that the analyst wants to know what factors can predict whether a stop will include a physical confrontation. The dependent variable in this case (physical confrontation) is measured at two levels, "0" for no and "1" for yes. The independent variables may include

- The driver's race (Black or White)
- The driver's age
- The driver's gender (male or female)
- The officer's race (Black or White)
- The officer's age
- The officer's years of experience
- The officer's gender (male or female)
- The crime rate of the beat in which the incident occurred
- The number of occupants in the car
- The number of officers at the scene
- Whether or not an arrest occurred
- Whether or not a search occurred.

Using this model in the Wichita study, Withrow (2002) determined that stops involving searches and resulting in arrest are more likely to involve incidents of physical resistance or confrontation. Although less probable, stops involving Blacks appear more likely to include physical resistance than stops involving Hispanics or Whites. The model also predicts that as the number of officers at the scene increases, so does the likelihood of physical resistance. Unfortunately, the model cannot establish the temporal order of these relationships. For example, it is unclear whether the physical resistance is the cause or the result of an arrest or predicated by police-initiated abuse.

Identifying and communicating the limitations of the data is an important part of the process. Knowing what the data cannot determine is at least as important as knowing what the data can measure (McMahon et al. 2002). Ideally, this discussion should occur very early in the planning process. Stakeholders tend to get anxious in anticipation of a study's results. Many have personal expectations of what the study will accomplish. In a few cases stakeholders involved in the planning process have even made public promises about what a study will determine, only to be disappointed, and maybe a little embarrassed, when the study doesn't respond to their personal issues. To avoid this, the department, in cooperation with the analyst, should proactively communicate the limitations of the study early on, and often, during the data collection phase.

Finally, an often overlooked but potentially important issue is the ownership of the data. Clear guidelines should be developed, preferably in writing, on how the information will be used, maintained, and reported (McMahon et al. 2002). This is especially important if the database contains personal or sensitive information, like demographic data on police officers. Immediately after the publication of one study the analyst was approached by a citizen's advocacy group demanding a report on the stopping behaviors (racial proportions) of individual officers. The researcher flatly refused, arguing that to do so would violate a promise he made to the department's officers and might violate a state law prohibiting the release of a police officer's work history and personal information. Furthermore, the release of this information would have had a chilling effect on the department's overall enforcement efficiency and might have deteriorated officer morale. Undaunted, a representative of the group initiated a request for the stop data based on the premise that the analyses had been conducted by a state employee in a state supported university and was therefore a public record.

Fortunately, prior to receiving the data the researcher had done two things to avoid such a circumstance. First, he initiated a signed memorandum of understanding with the police department that, among other things, identified the department as the sole owner of the data. This memorandum specifically prohibited the researcher from releasing any information about the data without the written permission of the department. Second, using the memorandum as a guide, the researcher requested a formal review of the research plan from his university's office of research administration. This included a review of the research's potential harm to human subjects, specifically the police officers. This review process resulted in an additional prohibition against the release of information about individual officers.

It is important to consider that statistics and quantitative analyses alone may not be able to adequately account for all of the complexities associated with routine police procedures. Researchers should avoid a total reliance on quantitative information and welcome the introduction of qualitative information. Data collected from case studies, field observations, public surveys, and similar methods may be necessary to fully document and describe an enforcement practice or program.

Reporting the Results

The last formal step in the racial profiling research process is reporting the results. Usually, the long-term impact of a research project on positive change is directly related to its initial presentation. It is unlikely, given the pattern of findings in the current literature, that the results will be welcomed by the police, their political leaders, and the public. Furthermore, it is equally unlikely that the results of the report will change individual attitudes about the police. People who tend to be critical of the police will likely cite the report as additional evidence in support of their negative views of police officers and police departments. Individuals who tend to support the police will likely not be convinced that the police are guilty of wholesale discrimination and will point out the flaws in the research design. Reporting results under these adversarial conditions is indeed a daunting task. There are, however, a few general guidelines that can enhance the quality and effectiveness of the presentation.

First, preparation of the formal presentation is a critical step. In most cases the presentation will be a collaborative effort between the police department and the research partner. Often, interested political leaders and community advocates will be involved, or at the very least present. The stakeholders who developed or managed the process should be present and, if practical, play a visible role in the presentation of the results. Various instructional technologies are available and, if they improve the communicative quality of the message, they should be used. The preparation process should include a script designating the responsible person for each stage of the presentation. It is also important for the presenters to practice as a group several times before the final presentation. It may be cost-prohibitive to reproduce enough copies of the final report for distribution during the formal presentation. A shortened version in the form of an executive summary or results synopsis may be an appropriate alternative. Finally, the presenters will likely identify about a dozen questions that are likely to be asked during the presentation. If so, the responses to these questions should be developed prior to the formal presentation.

Second, after the department has internalized the report but before the formal public presentation, a series of preliminary presentations involving narrowly focused and small groups of stakeholders and community advocates should be considered. This intimate format facilitates a very frank discussion and produces alternative insights on the report not previously considered by the researchers. Also, it engages community support for the report and the policies designed to address the issues it identified before it becomes known to the media.

Third, the presenters should recognize that, beyond the obvious political ramifications of the research, a broad range of citizens are very concerned about racial profiling and will likely want to vent their frustrations publicly. This should not only be allowed to happen, but should be encouraged by the presenters. Allowing individuals to vent their concerns in a public forum is an important part of the problem solving process. Responding frankly and openly to their concerns goes a long way toward reestablishing ties with historically disenfranchised and disillusioned citizens. The key here is for the presenters not to be defensive. During one formal presentation of a racial profiling study (observed by the author) a particularly vocal community activist asked the chief of police a blistering question about why he hadn't done anything about "racism" in his department. The chief's response recognized the activist's concerns and then suggested that the reason he voluntarily decided to conduct this study, knowing that it might result in a finding of disparity, was to start the process of responding to community concerns about the practices of his officers. He then proceeded to outline the steps his department was initiating to respond to the report's findings. A response of this nature has two important advantages. First, it is wholly responsive to the immediate question. Second, and more importantly, it communicates in a very real way that the department's administration is aware of community concerns and has a plausible plan to address them.

Fourth, a major part of the presentation should be devoted to a description of what the department is doing or intends to do to address the problems identified in the research. Informing the audience of the department's newly minted prohibition of race-based stops and revised traffic stop policies are excellent examples of appropriate responses that should be communicated. Training programs developed to help officers understand cultural differences and racial prejudices should be summarized. Changes in citizen complaint procedures are also important steps to correcting deficiencies in a department's enforcement program. These and other solutions are discussed in the next chapter.

Finally, the report's findings should be presented in a brief and unqualified manner. The research partner, by virtue of his academic training, will likely want to qualify findings so that the consumer understands the limitations of the research. For example, the researcher may want to discuss the measurement error associated with the benchmark. While this is important in the text of the formal report, it should be avoided in the formal oral presentation. The general public consumers of research will likely not recognize the subtle nuances of research methods and may become frustrated unless they receive quick answers to their questions. This does not suggest that the important subtleties should be overlooked. What is does mean is that the report should get to the punch line very quickly and without unnecessary distraction.

SUMMARY

From a purely scientific perspective, racial profiling research is relatively simple. Once the researcher establishes the methodological plan, measurement criteria, and a priori analytical assumptions, the process is relatively straightforward and unremarkable until one considers that most racial profiling research occurs within an adversarial context. Few racial profiling research projects are initiated because someone thinks it would be a fun thing to do. Usually, there are several precipitating events that question the integrity of the police department or its officers.

Many important obstacles face the racial profiling researcher. Among these obstacles are the inability to measure race accurately and consistently, a lack of an independent information source to audit the accuracy and completeness of police stop data, and a palpable level of fear among police officers that the research will be used to their disadvantage. It appears from the literature that a police chief committed to understanding racial profiling in his department may be the most consistently successful key to overcoming these obstacles.

It is critical for the department interested in conducting racial profiling research to develop an association with an objective research partner. The research partner should be competently trained in research methodology and statistical analysis and generally familiar with routine police procedures. Often a well-informed member of the department is tasked with assisting the research partner. The research partner, in cooperation with a task force of community stakeholders should develop a series of initial analytical questions. In doing so, the task force can better identify the variables necessary to respond to the community's concerns.

The three principal strategies for collecting police stop data include paper forms, electronic data entry systems, and existing data. Primarily, researchers rely on machine-readable paper forms. Within each of these methods there are variations, and each method has its relative advantages and disadvantages. Because of the context in which police stop data are collected, there is concern about its accuracy and completeness. While it may be impossible to completely determine whether police stop data is accurate and complete, there are a number of steps the researcher can take to mitigate the potential for error.

The analysis of racial profiling data normally occurs in two phases. The first involves developing an odds ratio between the proportional racial representation of individuals stopped against the proportional racial representation of individuals at risk of being stopped. The second analytical component should focus on poststop behavior, using the stop data as a baseline. Departments should insist on rigorous statistical analyses by qualified individuals and, where possible, the use of multivariate models but be receptive to alternative methods of analysis when they would increase understanding of enforcement practices and procedures.

Reporting the results is the final step in the research process. The presentation should be a collaborative effort involving the police department, political leaders, the research partner, and the task force of community stakeholders. The presentation should be brief yet fully informative of the report's findings as well as the department's administrative responses.

DISCUSSION QUESTIONS

1. Discuss the process by which a police chief would be encouraged to conduct a racial profiling study.
2. What are some of the more effective ways of overcoming the obstacles of a racial profiling study?
3. What variables and attributes are necessary to appropriately measure a police department's search productivity?
4. Racial profiling research has been criticized as being overly empirical. What other methods of inquiry can be used to study racial profiling?
5. In addition to the seven salient questions outlined in this chapter, what other questions should be asked?
6. Discuss how the use of a broad-based and diverse citizen task force improves or diminishes the acceptance of a racial profiling study.

CASE STUDIES

1. Over the past decade your police department has actively recruited individuals with statistical training and improved its crime analysis section substantially. The chief wants to do a racial profiling study but cannot afford to hire an outside

research partner. He decides to use assign the racial profiling study to the crime analysis section. Advise the chief on the advantages and disadvantages of this decision.

2. The chief of police forms a citizen task force to oversee a racial profiling study. After the group is formed representatives from the local chapters of well-established juvenile gangs ask to be appointed to the oversight committee. They argue that because they are directly affected by police policy they should be at the table. How would you respond?

3. After the results of a racial profiling study are published, a local advocacy group asks for data on the racial representation of drivers stopped by each (by name) officer. What are the advantages and disadvantages of releasing this information?

chapter **7**

SOLUTIONS

OBJECTIVE

To outline and discuss the potential solutions to the racial profiling controversy.

CHAPTER OUTLINE

Introduction
Control Police Discretion
Control Consent Searches
Pay Attention to Deployment
Manage the Leader's Influence
Provide Proactive Training and Education
Recruit a Reflective Workforce
Use Technology
Change the Law
Make New Law
Make the Police More Accountable

INTRODUCTION

Talking honestly about racial profiling is difficult. Few people are neutral on the issue. Sometimes it seems that a lot of people are talking, blaming, and accusing and very few people are listening, understanding, and looking for real solutions. There is an air of political correctness surrounding the controversy that hampers an honest exchange of ideas that could lead to real solutions (Fredrickson and Siljander 2002). When the issue first arose the focus of the blame was exclusively on the police. Although not often explicitly stated, we were left with the overwhelming impression that the police are little more than a roving band of racist thugs. The police strongly denied the accusation, stating that no evidence of racial disparity existed in their routine enforcement programs (Fridell et al. 2001). They were correct. In fact, there was little evidence of anything about police patrol procedures until the racial profiling controversy. Then the story began to unfold. Study after study found an overrepresentation of minorities in traffic stops. In a short-lived effort to defend themselves, the police quoted the racial disparity in criminal behavior (based on the overrepresentation of minorities in the prison population) and intelligence reports (presumably based on empirical data) supplied by national law enforcement agencies. This proves, they argued, that the police are justified in focusing their attention on minorities. After all, we are rewarded for making drug seizures, and who wouldn't use this information to increase their odds of making a big bust? The researchers then demonstrated that hit rates are either equal to or lower for racial minorities.

Then, just when it seemed we were getting somewhere, the issue took a sinister turn. A number of social commentators began to fan the flames by suggesting that the overrepresentation of minorities in traffic stops is caused by cultural problems within the minority community. These commentators asked some rather provocative and insightful questions. Why we are so quick to blame the police? Shouldn't we focus our attention on the cultural problems that produced the racial disparity in criminal behavior in the first place? After all, aren't the police just doing their job? (MacDonald 2003).

This book is not about determining which side is right. In many ways both are, and in many other ways both sides are wrong. This book is about addressing the controversy in an intelligent way, free from the rhetoric and political correctness that have hampered its advancement. The rhetoric gets in the way of reason. As a result, we risk missing important opportunities to solve this and a host of other seemingly intractable social problems. "Presumably, race-neutral justice is a shared goal within communities throughout our nation. The very undertaking of a racial profiling study within a community is essentially a reaffirmation of this community value" (Cleary 2000, 36). Until the stereotypes that support racial profiling are addressed, critically analyzed, and ultimately found to be false, the practice of racial profiling will continue (Wise 2003). The practice of racial profiling cannot be solved simply or quickly. There are real social issues surrounding the controversy, and the criminal justice system is ill-equipped to address many of them in an effective way. This does not mean that a solution is impossible; far from it. There are a number of pathways out of this abyss, and this chapter discusses a few of the more promising ideas.

CONTROL POLICE DISCRETION

The discretionary authority of the police is an important factor in the racial profiling controversy. There are those who argue that the solution to the racial profiling controversy lies in the control of police discretion (Harris 1999a; Jernigan 2000). Most police officers readily admit that they can usually find some reason to stop almost any car if they just follow it long enough. Most police departments do not have formal written policies that establish the boundaries of discretionary power. In the absence of such policy, officers tend to develop personal enforcement policies. Enforcement decisions are rarely documented and officers are not likely to be held accountable for them. Holding officers accountable, especially for high discretion stops (minor, nonmoving, and equipment violations), may be the answer (Ramirez, McDevitt, and Farrell 2000).

On the other hand, controlling police discretion through strict policies may be more difficult than we think. Most police behavior, including enforcement policy, is based on informal interactions and subcultural expectations between officers, and not leadership constraints (Powell 1981). Nearly three-fourths of the stops the police make are discretionary. These include stops for relatively minor, nonmoving, and equipment violations. A motorist's failure to signal a lane change in a remote part of town is not likely a violation that demands the attention of the police, unless of course the officer has a bona fide reasonable suspicion that the motorist is guilty of a more serious violation. Low-discretionary stops involve flagrant violations or stops predicated by information from an external source. These account for about one-fourth of all traffic stops. It is not likely that the police will, or should, ignore a motorist's failure to signal a lane change if it directly impedes the progress of another motorist (Ramirez, McDevitt, and Farrell 2000). Denying the police the opportunity to use their discretion, even if it results in behaviors that we might label as racial profiling, may remove from them an important crime fighting tool that may be of particular benefit to the minority community (Trende 2003). For example, how should we respond to a police officer who, in response to credible information that a juvenile Hispanic gang is planning a drive-by shooting, focuses her attention on vehicles occupied by Hispanic youths? Is she guilty of racial profiling or is she being an attentive law enforcement officer?

Most police decisions are made at a distance from active supervision. A typical officer may go for days without the direct observation of a supervisor. As a result, most departments attempt to provide guidance proactively to officers through policy. While a well-stated enforcement policy is not likely to ensure full compliance, it does communicate the values of the department and provides the foundation upon which disciplinary action may be initiated on an individual basis. Generally speaking, enforcement policy comes in two forms: conceptual and operational. A conceptual policy is essentially a values statement. It provides general guidance to officers and communicates in a broad manner what the department believes to be appropriate behavior. The Police Executive Research Forum (PERF) recommends adopting policy that communicates the department's prohibition of racially biased policing and provides guidance to officers on the appropriate use of race and ethnicity in policing (Fridell et al. 2001). The following is

PERF's recommendation of a conceptual enforcement policy designed to address racial profiling:

> The initiation of traffic/pedestrian(s) stops must be based on reasonable and articulable suspicion or actual violation of the law committed by the occupant(s) of the vehicle or pedestrian(s). Safety reasons alone may justify the stop if the safety reasons are based upon specific and articulable facts. Members of the Department may not rely to any degree on the race, color, gender, disability or religion of the occupant(s) of the vehicle or pedestrian(s) as the sole deciding factor of whether to stop the vehicle/pedestrian(s), in taking enforcement action or conducting a search.

Operational policies provide more specific guidance. They attempt to inform the officer of appropriate procedures. These policies often outline the steps the officer should follow during a violator contact. The following seven-step violator contact provides such guidance. Imbedded in this procedure are the elements that support the perception of the stop's legitimacy and the officer's professional competence.

1. Identify yourself by name and department.
2. Inform the violator why he or she is being stopped.
3. Ask the violator to provide his or her driver's license and vehicle registration.
4. Determine whether or not the violator has a reason for violating the traffic law (e.g., on the way to a family emergency).
5. Inform the violator of your enforcement decision (i.e., ticket or warning).
6. If necessary, inform the violator of what he or she must do to resolve the matter (e.g., how to pay the fine, contact the judge, or correct the problem).
7. Leave.

The policy direction taken by a department should recognize that stops can cause embarrassment, anxiety, or even fear. Often the citizen's perception of the stop may be more important than its objective reality (Weitzer and Tuch 2002). Furthermore, the department should recognize that individuals' cultural perspectives or opinions of the police may affect their perceptions of the legitimacy of traffic stops (Withrow and Jackson 2002). The research reveals four factors that improve the perceived legitimacy of traffic stops. First, to ensure public trust and confidence, stops must be perceived to be carried out for good reasons. The reason for a stop should be perceived to be important and consistent with a real public safety need. This may also require the officer to offer a plausible explanation for the stop. Second, stops and searches must be predicated upon an appropriate legal or policy standard. They must adhere to the generally accepted guidelines of police procedure and not appear to be arbitrary or capricious. Third, stops must be perceived to be effective in pursuit of a legitimate law enforcement need. This means stops are targeted to maximize contact with active offenders and minimize contact with law abiding members of the public. Fourth, a violator's perception of an officer's attitudes and behaviors can affect the perceived legitimacy of the stop. Discourtesy, foul language, and incomplete explanations all appear to reduce the violator's perception of the stop's legitimacy (Quinton, Bland, and Miller 2000).

CONTROL CONSENT SEARCHES

When the police are right and evidence of criminality is found, seldom are the officer's motivations for requesting a consent search a concern (Oliver 2000). Even though the legality of a search cannot be established by its results, the courts are less sympathetic to a defendant alleging bias if the police actually find contraband during a consensual search. However, these are not the kinds of searches that are important in the racial profiling controversy. It is the thousands of searches conducted by officers based on nothing more than a mere hunch that are of particular concern. The potential for actual and perceived racial bias in this activity is substantial. As a result, controlling consensual searches may be an effective means to address the practice of racial profiling.

While the consent search is an important part of routine patrol procedures, there is a clear need to minimize the level of intrusion into the lives of the general public. Overly intrusive searches pose a risk to public confidence. There is a need to improve the reliability of the information upon which search decisions should be made (Engel and Calnon 2004a; Quinton, Bland, and Miller 2000). The New Jersey consent decree attempts to control the use of consensual searches by requiring officers to articulate a reasonable suspicion. This is an important first step, but the consent decree's provision does not have the force of the exclusionary rule. Furthermore, it lacks a remedial provision (Oliver 2000). The decree does not specify how officers would be sanctioned if found to be in violation of the court's order. Quinton, Bland, and Miller (2000) identified wide variations among officers in their concepts of reasonable suspicion. The grounds upon which searches are based are often poorly recorded or inconsistent with applicable legal requirements. They offer the following recommendations for managers interested in controlling consensual searches.

- Clear policies and procedures should outline acceptable practices.
- Officers should be well-schooled on the meaning of reasonable suspicion and probable cause.
- The legal framework for building grounds for a search should be clearly stated.
- Departments should provide accurate and timely intelligence to officers.
- Clarify the essential elements of an acceptable description. This means officers should not be allowed to use cryptic or incomplete suspect descriptions.
- Require officers to accurately and completely record their justification for seeking a suspect's consent.
- Proactively train officers on appropriate stop and search procedures. This includes improving communication skills.

In 1966, the Supreme Court handed down what is arguably the most significant case affecting police procedure in the history of the republic. In *Miranda v. Arizona* the Supreme Court was asked whether the police should inform a suspect during a custodial interrogation and prior to questioning of his constitutional rights relating to self-incrimination and access to legal representation. The Supreme Court said yes and proceeded to offer an unprecedented level of detail in its direction to police officers on the constitutionally proper way to conduct a custodial interrogation. The Court's opinion explicitly stated that evidence obtained during a custodial interrogation cannot be used in court unless the suspect is informed of the following rights prior to the asking of questions:

- The right to remain silent
- That any statement made may be used in a court of law
- The right to have an attorney present during questioning
- That if the suspect cannot afford an attorney, one will be appointed for him prior to questioning

The response to this ruling from the law enforcement community was predictable. The vast majority of police administrators felt that the ruling would have a profoundly negative effect on police procedures. Specifically, they predicted that if they were required to inform individuals of their rights, then nobody in their right mind would confess to a crime. Because most convictions are based on confessions, the police would be required to allocate additional resources to the criminal investigation process. *Miranda*, in their view, ended policing as they knew it. The police were both right and wrong. In the long term *Miranda* did not, as predicted, result in a sustained decrease in the number of confessions. Roughly the same percentages of suspects confess to their discretions now as did in 1965. *Miranda* did, however, end policing as we knew it. Prior to *Miranda* policing in America was brutal, particularly during custodial interrogations. Except for a few progressive municipal departments, police officers were not sufficiently trained in the practice of policing. *Miranda*, along with many of the criminal procedure decisions emanating from the activist Warren Court of the 1960s, focused the nation's attention on the brutality and lack of training of its police. It caused police departments to invest in officer training and development. Most policing practitioners and scholars agree that the practice of policing is better because of *Miranda*.

The path out of the racial profiling controversy may lie in our experience with *Miranda*. Consent searches are popular among officers for three reasons. First, they cost the department and the officer very little in terms of time and energy. Officers are not required to bother with articulating reasonable suspicion, or even worse, leaving the patrol beat to secure a warrant. Second, because most people are not aware that they can refuse, consent is nearly always given. Many people are shocked when they learn that it is their right to refuse a consensual search. Third, consent searches yield results. The number of individuals who readily consent to a search knowing they possess evidence of criminal behavior is alarming, and police officers know this. In short, consent searches are a highly effective and low cost way to increase an officer's productivity. Controlling consensual searches may require the development of a series of *Miranda*-like procedures:

- In a moment I am going to ask for your permission to search your car.
- Anything I find during this search can be used against you in a court of law.
- You have the right to refuse my request to search your car, and your refusal cannot be used against you.
- You also have the right to limit the area of your car I am allowed to search.
- You may also revoke your consent for me to search at any time, even after I have started.
- May I now have permission to search your car?

It is not clear whether the voluntary imposition of this procedure will, like a *Miranda* warning, create "a prophylactic rule . . . to discourage pretextual traffic stops" (Oliver 2000, 1415), but such a procedure appears consistent with fair and equitable policing (Harris 2002). If the consent search is sufficiently controlled or harder to do, then why bother with a pretextual stop?

Fortunately, we have some preliminary evidence that controlling searches may be an effective way to address racial profiling. In 1998, the United States Customs Service evaluated the efficiency of its search function. They identified two very important and now familiar themes within their searching practices. First, Customs Service employees were not very good at predicting whether a person entering the country is carrying contraband. Overall, only 1,251 of 22,857 searches (5.4 percent) resulted in the seizure of contraband. Given the personnel time allocated to this intrusive activity, this was not considered an acceptable level of performance. A business would be hard pressed to realize a profit at this level of performance. Second, there appeared to be differences in hit rates between racial and ethnic groups. Whites were the subject of 11,765 searches. Of these, 677 (5.75 percent) resulted in a contraband seizure. Blacks were the subject of 6,141 searches. Of these, 365 (5.94 percent) resulted in a contraband seizure. Hispanics were the subject of the most searches (14,951), but of these, only 209 (1.4 percent) resulted in a contraband seizure.

The Customs Service conducted a rigorous evaluation of its search criteria. They found little empirical foundation for their search practices. The evaluation resulted in a number of changes to their search criteria. For obvious reasons the Customs Service does not publicize its search criteria, but the results of the policy change are significant and instructive. In 2000, the Customs Service conducted only 8,099 searches, a 65 percent decrease overall, of which 1,204 (14.87 percent) resulted in the seizure of contraband. The new search criteria, based on empirically verified factors, substantially reduced the overall number of searches (and hence the personnel costs associated with them) and nearly tripled the hit rate. Of more relevance to the racial profiling controversy, the total number of searches and hit rates between racial and ethnic groups did not vary significantly. Whites were the subject of 2,931 searches, of which 462 (15.8 percent) resulted in a contraband seizure. Blacks were the subject of 2,437 searches, of which 384 (15.8 percent) resulted in a contraband seizure. Hispanics were the subject of 2,731 searches, of which 358 (13.1 percent) resulted in a contraband seizure.

PAY ATTENTION TO DEPLOYMENT

A department's deployment strategy may affect the proportional racial representation of individuals stopped. If officers are heavily deployed to predominantly minority neighborhoods, then we should not be surprised to find minorities overrepresented in police stops, especially when the results are evaluated citywide. At the very least, a department should evaluate enforcement practices at the neighborhood or beat level, taking into consideration factors that might affect a police officer's behavior. Evaluations at this level tend to find that deployment (measured by the number of total stops within a beat) is best predicted by crime rates and population rather than race. This means the police department allocates patrol services based on actual and legitimate demand. What this also indicates is a lack of institutional racism in police administrative decision making (Smith and Petrocelli 2001, Withrow 2002). Patrol resources should be concentrated in well-documented high crime areas and focus on bona fide high risk offenders (Cohen, Lennon, and Wasserman 2000).

Beyond this, administrators should recognize that there is clear evidence that neighborhood factors may be more important to the level of support for the police than race or ethnicity (Dunham and Alpert 1988). Attitudes toward the police tend to be consistent within neighborhoods. The literature suggests that opinions of the police tend to be consistent between residents of a neighborhood. This is likely due to informal communications between neighbors about experiences with the police. The best way for administrators to capitalize on this research is to proactively develop positive relationships with individuals who tend to view the police unfavorably.

MANAGE THE LEADER'S INFLUENCE

A leader's influence has a profound effect on behavior. Subordinates tend to behave in ways that they perceive are consistent with the leader's desires. Behavioral cues are sometimes communicated indirectly by the leader through offhand comments, nonverbal gestures, or side bar comments. Usually, behavioral cues communicated informally have more influence on employee behavior than published policy. When given the option, police officers will focus more on how leaders behave than what they say.

When Colonel Carl Williams of the New Jersey State Police attempted to justify the racial and ethnic disparity of his trooper's practices by pointing out that the presidents of the United States and Mexico (and not Ireland and Great Britain) met to discuss drugs, he was communicating an organizational value. It is likely that the troopers under Colonel Williams' command applauded him for speaking the truth (Harris 1999a).

Addressing racial profiling, however, requires far more than communicating appropriate organizational values. Police executives should conduct extensive audits of their department's mission statements, codes of ethics, policies, and procedures to ensure they do not inadvertently violate human rights. In addition, police leaders should routinely assess the organizational culture to determine if it is consistent with the American sense of fairness (Fridell et al. 2001). Unfortunately, police leaders focus too much attention on minor indiscretions of police officers. A substantial amount of administrative time is devoted to relatively minor violations like not wearing hats or eating meals outside of the beat. Very few agencies proactively investigate potential violations of civil liberties (Barlow and Barlow 2002). Police leaders should

- Focus on internal control mechanisms
- Encourage diversity
- Conduct regular reviews and audits of the complaint process
- Consider the use of an early warning system based on an internal benchmark
- Clarify expectations to middle managers
- Require compliance with rules
- Pay attention to the field training process and the performance of probationary officers
- Conduct spot checks of in-car videos
- Ensure that citizen complaints receive fair hearings (Fridell et al. 2001)

Administrators should consider a wholesale change in their department's incentive structure (Harris 2002). An emphasis on the war on drugs encourages officers to seek out drug couriers. Departments reward officers for major drug busts. The media focuses attention on them for significant seizures. Departments benefit financially from the seizure of assets. One reason the police inappropriately use race as an indicator of potential criminality is because they were led to believe, by various perceived authorities, that drug couriers are more likely to be minorities. It is a predictable response. Discounting the value of drug seizures may discourage officers from using inappropriate indicators of potential criminal behavior in their decision making. Unfortunately, it may also increase the available supply of illegal drugs.

Buerger (2002) offers six general supervisory solutions to the racial profiling controversy.

1. Equip the troops: Teach officers the importance (or lack thereof) of race.
2. Deal with monkey wrenching: Respond quickly and appropriately to work slow downs, defiance, depolicing, going underground, making off the record stops, balancing, ghosting, and badmouthing.

3. Mediate disputes and citizen complaints: Provide citizens with a means to complain. Develop a sense that the complainant has a legitimate concern.
4. Handle problem cases: Impose discipline now and deal with resulting morale problems later.
5. Distinguish racial disparity from racial profiling: Improve the quality of the analyses.
6. Sell the program: Invest time with officers to sell them on the importance of addressing the issue.

A great deal of a leader's time is spent balancing risks and rewards. There are two important risks for policing leaders associated with the racial profiling controversy. First, when allegations of racial profiling surface, the leader should recognize that the credibility of the department, as well as the leader's personal image, are on the line. A racial profiling inquiry has been for some a career-ending event. There is a real potential for federal intervention and the diminished control of the police department. O'Reilly (2002) offers the following steps for policing leaders.

- Improve communications and relationships with elected officials. This includes familiarizing them with routine police procedures and how records are maintained. Specifically, political leaders should recognize the risk associated with federal intervention and be enlisted to support the department, if possible.
- Conduct internal audits in the areas most likely to receive judicial attention. Prepare data and get analytical assistance if necessary.
- Candidly discuss the defensibility of the statistical information with administrators familiar with how the data are collected and maintained.
- Grant full access to information to anyone who wants it for whatever reason.
- Look for ways to actively deter a judicial review. This may include change policing procedures and data collection procedures.
- Search for an agreement without litigation. A settlement is nearly always a more appropriate option.

Litigation is unlikely. As of 2001, only three cases brought by the United States Department of Justice have advanced beyond an early settlement stage. The strength of the case will likely hinge on the quality of the statistical data, and as has been noted previously, this is indeed a shaky foundation. It is more likely that a case will result in some sort of prelitigation settlement. Even though there is considerable risk for political leaders (e.g., cost associated with the defense, the potential for a tarnished public image), they should recognize that there is more risk in not mounting a vigorous defense (O'Reilly 2002).

Second, addressing the racial profiling controversy directly, as in conducting a rigorous study, may produce unintended results. Very few racial profiling studies result in substantial changes to departmental policies and procedures. In their analysis Schultz and Withrow (2004) found that less than one third of the departments studied adopted new or changed existing policies as a result of a racial profiling study. The typical administrative response, if any, is to develop policies prohibiting racial profiling, require data collection, and implement various training programs designed to address potential cultural biases. None of these changes have been demonstrated to have any initial or lasting effect on racial profiling. In short, racial profiling studies seldom produce any substantive organizational change. This does not, however, mean that they do not affect the department in other unintended ways.

Nearly all departments experience some sort of reduction in overall productivity during a racial profiling study (Schultz and Withrow 2004). During the Wichita study officers conducted 30 percent fewer stops than during the same time in the previous year (Withrow 2002). Racial profiling studies were directly responsible for a 25 percent reduction of productivity in Los Angeles, a 55 percent reduction in New Jersey, and a 63 percent reduction in Minneapolis (MacDonald 2003). There is a risk that racial profiling studies and the attention they focus on police departments may adversely affect the community these studies are designed to protect. "Of equal concern in the long run is whether the changed policing practices resulting from racial profiling studies will impact crime rates. There is some fear that any reduction in police aggressiveness might result in increased crime" (Cleary 2000, 20) For example, in 1992, the city of Chicago passed an ordinance prohibiting known gang members from standing on public streets. It authorized officers to disperse crowds of suspected gang members and was used to make over 45,000 arrests of mostly Black and Hispanic youths. Because gang members are predominantly minorities, it effectively became against the law to "stand while Black." Some authors wondered what would happen if the police were told to ignore the law. There was a concern that doing so would cause an increase in gang violence (MacDonald 2003). Ultimately, the United States Supreme Court struck down the Chicago antiloitering ordinance during the summer of 1999. The Court found that the majority of people arrested under this ordinance were Black or Hispanic (*Chicago v. Morales* 1999).

A more ominous unintended result of racial profiling studies is emerging. After their departments were publicly chastised and legally sanctioned for alleged racial disparities in various police procedures, the officers in two major city departments developed an effective defense mechanism: disengagement. Sometimes referred to as depolicing, this occurs as a logical response when police officers become so fearful of being accused of impropriety that they do nothing at all. In one city this informal response is referred to as NCNC, meaning no contact, no complaint. In another it is referred to as FIDO, meaning fuck it, drive on. The result of this is a measurable decrease in enforcement activity in the parts of town that are likely to have a legitimate need for enhanced policing services (Kevin Gilmartin, personal communication with author February 27, 2003).

Of course, along with the risk there are some very important potential rewards for policing leaders. First, proactively addressing racial profiling expresses the police department's commitment to improving the perceived legitimacy of its actions. Often the creation of these initial measures is an important first step toward effective management of the issue. Second, the mere collection of data sends an important message that the department considers racial profiling a serious issue. Furthermore, data collection may also communicate the department's commitment to eradicating practices that are inconsistent with effective policing and a sense of equal protection. Third, having the data forces the issue beyond its rhetoric. It supports an informed discussion about officer deployment and the use of resources. Fourth, racial profiling studies often teach us a great deal about how the police patrol function works. In doing so, administrative opportunities are often identified. Finally, the data collection effort itself may improve police behavior. Sometimes merely studying a problem identifies a solution (Ramirez, McDevitt, and Farrell 2000).

PROVIDE PROACTIVE TRAINING AND EDUCATION

Usually, when things go bad police departments look to the training academy for a solution. Training may sensitize officers on the "subtle and unintended ways in which broad based racial assumptions and stereotypes may lead to racial profiling" (Cleary 2000, 36). Training may help police officers understand the complexities of the racial profiling controversy in a nonaccusatory context (Carter and Katz-Bannister 2004; Fridell et al. 2001; Harris 2002). Training should be tailored to an agency's specific needs and integrated into a wide range of curricula. It must be precise in defining the problem and outlining its solution. The message should include how racial profiling affects the community and explore its theoretical explanations (Fridell et al. 2002). Mediation, or the ability to resolve conflict, should be an important teaching objective (Buerger 2002). Cooper (2001) observed that the police are generally ill-equipped for mediation, a highly cognitive skill, because they are generally unaware of how culture affects individual motivation. The police must learn to view issues from multiple cultural perspectives. More importantly, the police should learn not to define the behaviors of others through their own cultural lenses.

Although training is important, it is not a panacea. There is no universal recognition of the effectiveness of training to address racial profiling. More importantly, there is some indication that training may do more harm than good, especially if it relies too much on lecture. Walker, Spohn, and Delone (2000) recommend that teaching should focus on behavioral motivation. Engel and Calnon (2004a) argue that training may not be effective, because racial profiling is so entrenched within the institutions of policing. Training, by itself, is not likely to be very effective at reducing officer prejudice.

The effectiveness of training for changing officer behavior is not fully understood. At the very least, training offers a department a context in which to communicate important values in an effective way. It should not be overlooked as an important component in the problem solving process. Training should focus on changing the interactions between officers and citizens. This can be achieved by educating officers about how traffic stops and routine police procedures are perceived by citizens from various cultures (Harris 2002).

RECRUIT A REFLECTIVE WORKFORCE

Actively recruiting a racially reflective police force has long been suggested as an effective strategy for ensuring equal justice (Cleary 2000; Fridell et al. 2001). It seems logical that the public is more willing to view the police as fair if the force mirrors the racial representation of the community at large. There are likely real advantages for police departments that increase the diversity of their ranks.

Unfortunately, while racial diversity is an important organizational goal, its effect on overall police decision making is unclear. The value of a racially diverse police organization may lie primarily in public perception. If historically disenfranchised groups observe representatives from their own race or cultural background as successful participants in the policing function, then their overall support for the police department may be enhanced substantially. Regardless of whether recruiting racial and ethnic minorities improves the law enforcement function, it remains an important goal in the broad sense of social justice.

USE TECHNOLOGY

It is an understatement that police officers were initially resistant to in-car video systems. When these systems were first installed many police officers objected to them. More than a few refused to be assigned a patrol car equipped with a video. Police unions, taking cues from their members, even negotiated the use of video cameras in labor contracts. A decade later, the opposite is true. The police have learned that a videotape of a stop or police-citizen contact is more likely to exonerate them than convict them. Some internal affairs investigators report that citizens will even drop complaints when they find out a videotape of the incident is available.

Technology may offer a solution to the racial profiling controversy (Carter and Katz-Bannister 2004; Harris 2002). Video and audio recordings of police-citizen contacts provide the best documentation of police behavior available. They also provide researchers with a means, albeit time-consuming, to evaluate the accuracy and completeness of police stop data (Farrell et al. 2004). Beyond this, recent improvements in information technology may efficiently provide accurate and timely information about criminal behavior and suspects (Cohen, Lennon, and Wasserman 2000).

CHANGE THE LAW

In 1994, David Harris offered a series of potential legal remedies to the racial profiling controversy. First, he advocated a return to the pre-*Terry* law by requiring officers to articulate probable cause for all searches, particularly cursory or pat-down searches. Second, the amount of evidence necessary for an officer to establish reasonable suspicion should be increased. Third, the courts should not allow officers to conduct searches on the basis of objectively innocent, but contextually threatening, behaviors like walking the other way when the police arrive. Two years after Harris' remarks the Supreme Court in deciding the *Whren* case substantially reduced the likelihood that any of these recommendations would occur in the near future. While some experts advocate the reversal of *Whren* (Jernigan 2000) most agree that this is unlikely in our current legal environment.

Harris (2002) advocates for an expansion of Section 14141 (pattern and practice) prosecutions. In these legal proceedings the officers' actual intent is not as essential to the case as in a cause based on a violation of the Equal Protection Clause of the Fourteenth Amendment. Unfortunately, because only the United States Department of Justice can initiate such a prosecution, the efficacy of this approach is hampered by limited resources and maybe political ideology in control of the Department of Justice.

The exclusionary rule is a judge-made rule and was developed over many years of jurisprudence as a mechanism to control the behavior of police officers (del Carmen 1998). Simply stated, the exclusionary rule disallows the use in a criminal prosecution of any evidence that is seized in violation of the Constitution. A similar rule that would disallow evidence seized during a pretextual stop may produce the same level of control (Oliver 2000). If the police know that any evidence obtained through a pretextual stop will be inadmissible, then they will likely avoid such behavior.

Regardless of the legal approach taken, the inadequacies of the current research remain an issue. Carter and Katz-Bannister (2004), Harris, (1999b, 2002), and Jernigan (2000) advocate an expansion in the number of racial profiling studies as well as an improvement in their technical accuracy. These studies are particularly necessary in the nation's largest cities, where the largest proportion of racial minorities reside. This recommendation includes passing federal and state legislation requiring the collection of racial profiling data.

MAKE NEW LAW

Passing a prohibitive statute is one of the most widely discussed alternatives for addressing the racial profiling controversy. As previously mentioned, with varying levels of success, several legislative bodies at the federal, state, and local levels have attempted to pass racial profiling laws. Many statutes simply require departments to collect information. Some specifically prohibit the practice of racial profiling as defined by the statute. Given the viability of the Fourteenth Amendment (specifically the Equal Protection Clause), some may question the necessity of an additional statute prohibiting racial profiling. Others view the passage of such a statute as an important message about state or local policy. Regardless of their necessity or legislative intent, it is clear that many of the current statutes are somewhat lacking in their ability to control the practice of racial profiling.

Amnesty International USA (2004) suggests that an effective racial profiling statute should have eight key elements. (1) The statute should include a comprehensive ban on racial profiling. This ban should include profiling on the basis of race, ethnicity, national origin, and religion. The use of these factors as an enforcement criterion should only be allowed in the presence of "trustworthy information, relevant to the locality and time frame, that links persons belonging to one of the aforementioned groups to an identified criminal incident or scheme" (p. 29). (2) The statute should prohibit pretextual stops. This means the police would be prohibited from using a minor traffic violation as an excuse to stop someone they suspect (but have no probable cause) of violation of a more serious law. (3) A criminal penalty should be established for anyone found to be guilty of racial profiling. (4) The statute should require routine data collection of all stops (pedestrian and traffic) and searches. This data should also include information on the outcome of the stop and the perceived race, gender, age, and immigration status of the individual stopped. (5) The data should be analyzed and reported publicly. (6) An independent commission should be appointed to oversee the data collection process, review complaints of racial profiling, and publicize the results of the investigations of the allegations. (7) The statute should allow an individual to "seek court orders to stop individual departments from continuing to engage in racial profiling" (p. 29). (8) The statute should provide funds for training officers and installing in-car video systems to monitor traffic stops.

MAKE THE POLICE MORE ACCOUNTABLE

Since the mid-1990s Professor David Harris has been one of the most outspoken critics of police procedures surrounding the racial profiling controversy. A central theme of his work (summarized here) is the necessity for the police to be accountable for their actions to the larger society (see Harris 2002). This accountability starts with the recognition of the costs—all the costs—associated with racial profiling, and there are quite a few. While it may not be readily apparent, there are costs associated with the overuse of pretextual stops and consent searches. When a police officer is wrong and finds no contraband— and they usually don't in the absence of bona fide and empirically verified indicators— the officer's time is wasted. Racial profiling reinforces segregation because it deters minorities from traveling to or living in certain parts of the community. Finally, racial profiling supports a distorted view of social reality. The unchecked practice of racial profiling may diminish the overall effectiveness of the law and the legal system. Whether racial profiling is real or not is irrelevant. Perception is often more important than objective reality. If the public perceives the police to be unfair, they will discount the validity of police testimony, decline to participate as witnesses in police investigations, or refuse to serve as jurors in legal proceedings.

Solutions to the racial profiling controversy will require a focus on how an officer's behavior is perceived by others. We know that individual perception is governed by experience and that not all experience is the same. The police should recognize that while they enjoy consistently high levels of public support within some communities, they are the subject of ridicule and scorn within others. Enabling the police to see themselves through various cultural lenses can only be achieved through appropriate education and cultural sensitivity training.

The police should focus on what works in policing. Not all policing programs are equally successful. Few undergo rigorous evaluation, and some are have a substantial disparate effect. Policing programs should focus on a particular and legitimate public safety need. Finally, police departments should set realistic goals in their pursuit of a solution to racial profiling. Absolute elimination is unlikely. Administrators should focus first on bringing the practice under control. Then attention should focus on making racially disparate behaviors uncommon and then rare.

CAN WE REALLY MAKE A DIFFERENCE?

There is a possibility that the solutions to the racial profiling controversy may not work. While most responsible administrators are not ready to admit defeat, there are a number of obstacles to an effective solution. David Cole (1999) identified three principal obstacles. First, to what extent can a system that improperly focuses on race be corrected by paying attention to race? This is the perennial problem associated with affirmative action. By assisting historically disadvantaged groups, we inadvertently disadvantage others. As a matter of public policy, this may be appropriate, at least until the social problems that caused the problem in the first place are adequately addressed. The real question therefore is not if we should to it—we clearly should—but when should we stop doing it?

Second, racial profiling may be bigger than the criminal justice system. Racial inequality has its roots in a broad range of social problems. Unemployment, poverty, and limited access to educational opportunities are all causes and results of racial discrimination, none of which are caused by or likely solved by the criminal justice system, at least as we know it. Criminal justice agencies for about a decade have been criticized for widening their net. They, like the public education system, have been tasked either directly or indirectly with addressing a broad range of social problems. When the courts ruled that the institutionalization of mentally ill individuals was inappropriate, state departments of mental health simply opened the doors of their mental hospitals and walked away. In many cases care was replaced by a bus ticket out of town. Some patients became inmates, and the criminal justice system was and still is ill-equipped to address the problem appropriately.

Finally, attempts to control police behavior may adversely affect the individuals they intend to help. There is considerable evidence that the police will disengage from addressing many of the intractable problems associated with crime and urban decay. The travesty is that many minority neighborhoods truly need and want help from the police. If the police are fearful that their assistance may be viewed as racist, then they are understandably reluctant to allocate their services in a meaningful way. Ultimately, we must be very careful that our attempts to address the racial profiling controversy do not inadvertently harm the people we are attempting to help.

SUMMARY

Some issues (e.g., sex, politics, and religion) should never be discussed in polite company. It seems that racial profiling may have the same conversational qualities. With the exception of the abortion issue, there are few more polarizing issues than racial profiling. Despite this, racial profiling is important enough to risk alienating a few friends. It demands our attention, our reason, and our sincere attempt to find a solution. What it does not deserve is our rhetoric.

The roots of racial profiling run deep in the American culture. This does not mean that nothing can be done to address racial profiling. There are a number of potentially promising solutions. First, it appears that most of what we regard as racial profiling occurs during one of two rather discrete police procedures: discretionary stops and consent searches. Although not likely to completely address the problem, police discretion can be controlled somewhat effectively through appropriate policy, active supervision, and adequate training. During the 1960s the activist Warren Court was quite effective at controlling many historically abusive police practices. *Miranda* effectively controlled police brutality and ultimately caused the police to devote considerable attention to officer training and development. In a similar way we can voluntarily control consent searches. The manner in which the police are deployed may affect the proportional racial representation of individuals stopped by the police.

Paying attention to how police resources are allocated may partially address the racial profiling controversy. Patrol allocation should be based on empirically verified facts that indicate a bona fide and present need for police resources.

Leadership plays a key role in organizational change. Leaders should never underestimate the influence they have on their organizations. Proactively studying racial profiling in spite of its risks, communicating values consistent with our sense of fairness, and addressing errant behavior are key leadership responsibilities.

When the police are faced with serious challenges they often turn toward the academy for a solution. Training can address a host of policing problems and it plays some role in addressing the racial profiling controversy. Empirical research suggests that training programs should be comprehensive, focused on cultural sensitivity, and integrated broadly throughout the curriculum.

Actively recruiting a diverse workforce communicates a powerful message to the larger community. When members of historically disenfranchised groups see one of their own in a position of authority and respect, it goes a long way toward creating a feeling of legitimacy.

Although police departments and officers are often slow to accept technology, once they do, they tend to invest heavily. Video and audio recordings of police-citizen contacts may produce the most compelling and accurate documentation of police procedures.

We are after all, a nation of laws. The minority community has in the last half century made great strides through legal change. The legal chapter of the racial profiling controversy has yet to be written. Regardless of which direction it takes, it is likely that it will depend on our ability to define and measure the policing process. Our way out of the racial profiling controversy may lie in the extent to which the police are willing to accept responsibility for their actions. Accountable policing requires that the police recognize the cost, both social and economic, of their actions. Unchecked police authority may result in the diminished effectiveness of our legal system. Finally, we should be cognizant that the racial profiling controversy may be bigger than the criminal justice system. Furthermore, the criminal justice system by itself may be ill-equipped to respond appropriately to broad-range social problems. However, this does not preclude us from at least making a valiant attempt.

DISCUSSION QUESTIONS

1. Can, or should, we effectively control police discretion? If so, how?
2. What effect would the imposition of a *Miranda*-like warning have on consent searches?
3. Do leaders really influence an officer's behavior?
4. Beyond monitoring public order through crime control, to what extent can or should the police address social issues (i.e., poverty, unemployment, illiteracy) that tend to correlate with criminal behavior?
5. Would a racial profiling study conducted by a police department that is truly reflective of the city's population (in terms of race and ethnicity) produce results different from what we usually have found?

6. Would the use of videotaped traffic stops expand our knowledge of racial profiling? If so, how?

Case Studies

1. The chief of police, at the request of the city council, implemented a *Miranda*-style procedure (as outlined in this chapter) to control consent searches. This resulted in a substantial reduction in traffic stops and consent searches conducted by the police department. It also resulted in an increase in the supply of illegal drugs (as evidenced by a reduction in price) in the community. The city manager has asked you to develop an alternative policy that would keep the level of consent searches low yet reduce the supply of illegal drugs.

2. Police officers in your city are deployed on the basis of demand (calls for service). This results in a higher proportion of police patrol resources in parts of town predominantly populated by racial and ethnic minorities and in turn an overrepresentation of minorities in traffic stops. Develop an alternative deployment strategy that would also reduce the representation of minorities in traffic stops.

3. The local judges in your jurisdiction have implemented a rule. The rule states that evidence seized during a consensual search will be admissible only if the officer can prove that the search was (1) voluntary and (2) the individual searched was informed of his or her right to refuse to give consent to be searched. What effect would this rule have on enforcement?

chapter

WHAT'S NEXT?

OBJECTIVES

To identify the anticipated direction and trends of the racial profiling controversy.

To discuss how the racial profiling controversy will be relevant to our national war on terrorism.

CHAPTER OUTLINE

Introduction

Patterns in Research

Scholars and Police Administrators Will Partner to Produce Important Research

A Measurable Definition of Racial Profiling Will Remain Controversial

The Collection of Police Stop Data Will Become More Routine

Benchmarks Will Become More Accurate

INTRODUCTION

Three hundred years ago, before the dawn of the Industrial Age, most parents could teach their children nearly all they needed to know to lead a successful adult life. Except for the occasional war or political upheaval, life was predictably centered on an agrarian calendar. Crops were planted, tilled, harvested, and then planted again year after year after year. Today, no social commentator can rationally predict the future with any reasonable degree of accuracy. Who could have predicted that the computers we literally carry in our pockets would be more powerful than the mammoth machines we fed punched cards into just a quarter century ago? American society is literally at a cultural crossroads. We live in an age of immense political, social, and cultural division where the old rules don't seem to apply anymore (Greenberg 2004). It seems that as a nation we are unable to agree to disagree and that every issue is a blood sport. Predicting the future of the racial profiling controversy, or any social issue for that matter, is folly.

We do, however, as participants in the social dialogue, have an obligation to at least try. Over the past decade countless hours have been devoted to the study of racial profiling by some of the most competent and committed social scientists, legal experts, police administrators, and political leaders of our time. Much work has been done. Much work has yet to be done. A pattern of sorts has emerged. Some parts of this pattern are well developed, and others have yet to be explored. The purpose of this chapter is to survey this pattern and identify the parts of it that are likely to receive the most attention in the coming years.

PATTERNS IN RESEARCH

Racial profiling will continue well into the future as a distinct research agenda for several reasons. First, the researcher garners a great deal of attention. Getting a racial profiling article published is relatively easy. Publishers are interested in including such works in academic journals and trade publications. Second, there is a great deal more to do. The current research produces far more questions than answers. Academics are inherently curious people. There is a great deal of professional satisfaction associated with being a part of an emerging research agenda. Third, racial profiling research nearly always directly affects the administration of justice. Much of what most academics do seldom directly impacts practitioners, at least within any reasonable time frame. The effects of a racial profiling study are nearly always immediate.

Scholars and Police Administrators Will Partner to Produce Important Research

During the past decade at least 400 racial profiling studies have been conducted in municipalities, counties, and states throughout the nation (McMahon et al. 2002). A few of these studies were conducted to comply with state statutes or municipal ordinances. Some are the result of external political pressure imposed on departments to address the racial profiling controversy. Most were conducted voluntarily by police administrators who sincerely wanted to evaluate their departments' performance. In most cases the entire research projects are managed by competent internal specialists within the policing organization. Their work represents some of the most creative contributions to racial profiling research available. Police department researchers developed the first stop data collection systems. It is also important to note that the application of a benchmark based on accident records, now an emerging trend among scholars, was the idea of researchers at the Washington State Police, more than four years before the academic community recognized the potential value of this measure. The result of this is an immensely important body of literature upon which future researchers will no doubt benefit.

Expanding the body of knowledge is usually the task of the university. The process is relatively straightforward. Scholars conduct research, normally at a theoretical level, and then report their findings to an academic audience. Eventually, the results of the research find their way into practitioner training and become a part of the professional knowledge. Within the racial profiling controversy the expansion of knowledge appears to be cyclical. It started at the practitioner level and has moved slowly into the scholarly arena. Legal scholars were the first to recognize the racial profiling controversy. Substantial academic recognition of the racial profiling research agenda did not occur until well after the bulk of the practitioner-based research became well known. The first special issue of an academic journal (*Police Quarterly*) devoted exclusively to racial profiling research was not published until June 2002. The first comprehensive book on the subject, *Profiles in Injustice* (Harris 2002), was published the same year.

This has resulted in a marriage of sorts between policing scholars and administrators, and a productive marriage it is. Few issues have resulted in such a prolific and interdependent relationship. Scholars are increasingly interested in the racial profiling research agenda. The volume of scholarly research on the subject is expanding rapidly. The second special issue of an academic journal on racial profiling was published by the same journal just two years after the first. Except for the community policing philosophy (which offered scholars access to considerable resources from federal grants), no other recent controversy in policing has garnered as much academic attention. Police administrators are increasingly more cognizant of the value of an academically trained research partner. Even when specialists within their departments appear to have adequate analytical training, some administrators are reluctant to conduct studies without some assistance from an objective outsider. They appear to recognize the value of peer review, something that has been a part of the scientific community for generations. There is also a more pragmatic reason. Unlike scholarly articles, racial profiling studies are seldom overlooked. The racial profiling research process is inherently public. Along with their objectivity and analytical skills, police administrators are aware that research partners bring a critical air of legitimacy to the project.

Racial profiling research in the future will likely be conducted simultaneously in both the practitioner and scholarly communities. Scholars will continue to work as research partners. After responding to the analytical demands of the agency, they will likely transform their work into scholarly articles. This research will no doubt benefit from rigorous peer review. Because police administrators are paying so much attention to the issue, scholarly research will find its way into the professional knowledge base more quickly. This can result in an overall expansion of the literature quantitatively, as well as qualitative improvements in the research.

In addition to an increase in the frequency and sophistication of racial profiling studies, it is highly likely, especially post-9/11, that the scope of inquiry will expand. New studies will probably consider the effect of race, ethnicity, and religious appearance on police office decision making in airports and shopping malls. Innovative researchers will consider how socioeconomic status or perceived immigration status affect how a police officer selects individuals to be confronted.

A Measurable Definition of Racial Profiling Will Remain Controversial

While there appears to be some agreement among researchers, a universally accepted definition of racial profiling has not yet emerged. In fact, there is not even a consensus on what to label the controversy or even if it is a single controversy. Is it racial profiling, race-based policing, or racially biased policing? Much of this disagreement is purely semantic, and maybe a little provincial. The controversy does not lie in the label, the conceptual definition, or even the operational definition of the issue. It lies in their confluence. The research conceptually defines racial profiling one way and operationally measures it in another.

For example, most researchers agree that racial profiling occurs when a police officer uses race as a primary indicator of criminal tendency. A police officer, based on prejudicial bias, believes minorities are more likely to be drug couriers. The officer then stops minorities for relatively minor violations of the traffic code and proceeds to find a legal justification to conduct a search. The impropriety of this behavior is indisputable, but to prove the case the researcher must determine to what extent the officer's racial prejudice, if any at all, actually influenced the decision to initiate a traffic stop and conduct a more thorough search. It may be that a disparity with respect to race in an officer's enforcement behavior may not be based on a prejudicial attitude at all. The officer may simply be responding to what he believes is valid information, supplied by seemingly qualified experts, suggesting that minorities are more likely to be in possession of illegal drugs.

Instead, most researchers make a methodological leap and use aggregate level data as evidence of individual behavior. The process is analogous to that used by plaintiffs in an affirmative action challenge. Within this context the plaintiff need only prove a disparate effect, not discriminatory intent. Fortunately for the plaintiffs, they have an accurate measure of the individuals, by race or ethnicity, who approach the employer for a job and an accurate measure of the individuals, by race or ethnicity, who actually get a job. These measures produce an odds ratio that is recognized by any court as a valid indicator of discriminatory hiring practices. Racial profiling researchers are not so fortunate. They rely on relatively inaccurate measures of the individuals who might be subject to routine police observation.

Researchers who define racial profiling with respect to the influence of race on police officer decision making seldom conclude that racial profiling is occurring based on aggregate level data indicating an overrepresentation of minorities in traffic stops. They can't. Aggregate data of this sort does not measure police officer decision making and the relative influence race or ethnicity has upon on it. Researchers who define racial profiling as an overrepresentation of minorities in traffic stops always conclude that racial profiling is occurring when presented with evidence of such overrepresentation. Unfortunately, these researchers fail to consider alternative explanations (e.g., differential offending rates or officer deployment patterns) of the findings and may be guilty of circular reasoning.

A case study approach may be the way out of this problem. Many profiles were developed from extensive observations and interviews with officers who are particularly skilled at identifying drug couriers. Nearly every department has at least one officer who is prolific at catching drug couriers. To benefit from these officers' expertise, researchers spent countless hours observing them at work in the field and asking them why they stopped certain cars or drivers and not others. Eventually, a pattern emerged. This pattern was essentially an expert system analogous to those used by physicians to diagnose disease. Factors were then identified and empirically tested by hundreds of officers. Eventually they became a dynamic part of routine policing practice. A similar methodology could be applied to racial profiling research using a broader range of police officers. Although time consuming, and likely expensive, a pattern will emerge that may allow us to measure the relative influence of race in police officer decision making.

The Collection of Police Stop Data Will Become More Routine

Until the racial profiling controversy emerged, few departments routinely collected the data necessary to respond intelligently to the accusations being leveled against them. With the exception of a few national or regional studies, our knowledge of police patrol procedures was virtually nonexistent. If racial profiling research has done one thing, it has vastly improved our understanding of the dynamics of patrol procedures.

Admittedly, most data collection mechanisms are suspended once sufficient data are collected to respond to a racial profiling inquiry, but police departments are beginning to recognize the value of extensive evaluative data within this critical functional area. Stop data sets have become a valuable tool in administrative decision making. This data produces the information necessary to determine patrol allocation needs, officer deployment strategies, training deficiencies, shift differentials, and many other systems affecting the patrol function. As a result, many departments are exploring the feasibility of integrating their racial profiling data collection mechanisms into the routine information gathering systems of their departments.

To achieve this, departments will have to overcome many of the obstacles associated with extensive data collection. Chief among these obstacles is reactivity. If officers believe that collecting such information will provide their departments with data that may be used to hold them accountable for their behaviors, then they may change their behavior in deference to departmental expectations. From a research perspective, this is a critical threat to the validity of the results. From an administrative perspective, this may not be such an undesirable outcome.

Second, to be effective, data collection must be associated with an independent audit mechanism. Most departments do not maintain a central repository of records on all police-citizen contacts. Furthermore, many potentially abusive contacts do not produce a record. To establish the credibility of the data, a comprehensive repository of information relating to a broad range of police-citizen contacts must be developed and maintained.

Third, many of the logistical problems associated with data collection can be solved if the various informational needs are integrated into a seamless process. This process must prioritize the critical information needs in the form of required data fields. In addition, the process should include a series of internal audit subroutines to reduce the potential for error. Finally, the data collected should support a detailed analysis of the contextual factors of every stop. There are dozens of factors that enter into a police officer's decision to initiate a traffic stop. For example, the time of day may be important, but so might the time left on the officer's shift. Traffic conditions, weather, suspect demeanor, incongruity, and many other factors affect an officer's decision to initiate a stop. The general objective should be to collect as much contextual information with as much detail as is feasibly possible. In doing so the department ensures itself access to the rigorous multivariate analytical tools that can empirically evaluate the performance of its officers.

Benchmarks Will Become More Accurate

Unquestionably, the most serious threat to the advancement of the racial profiling research agenda is the lack of an accurate benchmark. The inability of a benchmark to accurately estimate the racial proportions of individuals accessible to police observation adversely affects racial profiling research in three principal ways. First, the perceived value (validity) of a racial profiling study's overall findings is directly influenced by the perceived accuracy of the benchmark. For example, if a population-based benchmark is unable to determine differential exposure rates within the population, it may not accurately estimate the driving population. We know that certain racial minorities tend to own fewer cars, utilize public transportation more frequently, and drive fewer miles per day. Unless the benchmark accounts for this, the perception of the entire study's findings may be in jeopardy. Second, with rare exceptions (New Jersey, Maryland), the statistical information from most racial profiling studies, which is in part based on a benchmark, does not satisfy the evidentiary requirements necessary for a legal remedy. The current law, in particular the Equal Protection Clause of the Fourteenth Amendment, is already in place and capable of effecting a change in police behavior. What is missing is an effective mechanism to measure disparate effect, much less discriminatory intent. This is in large part due to our inability to develop generally acceptable estimates of the at-risk population. Third, using an inaccurate benchmark may result in a police department being falsely accused of racist behavior. The current benchmarks cannot eliminate important alternative explanations like deployment patterns and differential offending rates. Unfortunately, when the results of the study are released, only the alleged disparity is reported. It is an effective sound bite, but it may unjustly label a department.

In addition to improving the primary benchmarks (population, field observation, accident records) used in racial profiling research, the creation of new benchmarks is likely. A number of studies that use multiple or competing benchmarks will likely be published in academic journals within the next year. These studies will enable researches to critically evaluate the efficacy of each benchmark. In doing so, the capabilities, as well as the inadequacies, of the available benchmarks will be demonstrated. Similarly, it is likely that future researchers will focus their attention solely on benchmarks outside the context of a narrow racial profiling study.

Second, one of the most promising benchmarks is based on the not-at-fault drivers in two-vehicle accidents. This benchmark has an extensive history of use in traffic engineering and is generally recognized (within this field) to be an accurate estimate of the driving population, that is, the population at risk of police observation. In addition, this benchmark is generally simple and inexpensive to obtain. Unfortunately, the validity of this benchmark has yet to be established. For it to be considered an accurate estimate of the driving population, it will be necessary to conduct extensive reliability and validity tests. These may include field observations and the analysis of driver trip logs.

Third, internal benchmarks will likely receive more attention from researchers. Cities are not homogenous with respect to their proportional racial representation. Most are still highly segregated. The proportional racial representation of individuals stopped by a particular officer is more usually influenced by the proportional racial composition of the neighborhood in which the officer is assigned to work. It would not be particularly alarming if 90 percent of the individuals an officer stops are Black if 90 percent of the residents in the neighborhood in which the officer works are Black. On the other hand, if 90 percent of the individuals an officers stops are Black and only 10 percent of the residents in his beat are Black, then it may be necessary to devote some serious supervisory time to the officer. In addition to identifying potential disparities in enforcement programs, internal benchmarks have the capacity determine the exact location of a potential problem.

Finally, benchmarks will only be substantially improved when they are able to differentiate between the driving and offending populations. Differential offending rates (by race) are currently the most plausible alternative explanation for the overrepresentation of minorities in traffic stops. The work of Lamberth (1994) and Lange, Blackman, and Johnson (2001) in New Jersey notwithstanding, we do not know whether offending rates are equivalent between racial and ethnic groups. Until we do, we will never be able to evaluate the plausibility of this alternative explanation.

PATTERNS IN POLICE ADMINISTRATION

The police are victims of a stubborn myth. They are often portrayed as uneducated, clannish, and inflexible. While this may have been an accurate assessment of American policing a generation ago, it is far from true today. The police are among the most creative, sophisticated, and responsive public administrators working today, and they are paying attention to the racial profiling controversy. They recognize the threat racial profiling poses to their agencies and are, for the most part, willing to address the issues associated with it in a meaningful way.

Police Departments May Recognize
Their Role in Addressing Racial Injustice

Police departments have a successful track record of proactively addressing critical issues. Recently, police departments have effectively addressed such issues as high speed pursuits and the use of force. In addition, in the past fifteen years American policing has experienced substantial ideological change. As a whole, police departments are measurably more responsive to the needs of their communities than they were just one generation ago. The majority of police departments in this nation have accepted responsibility for a broader range of social issues. While some may view this widening of the police task with disdain, and even with a bit of suspicion, the facts reveal a more responsive and socially aware level of policing.

The 1992 Los Angeles riots following the acquittal of the Rodney King defendants, the 1996 riots in St. Petersburg, Florida, after the shooting of a Black motorist, and many other similar incidents are evidence of what can happen if we ignore the hopelessness, frustration, or police abuse within the inner city and among racial minorities (Davis 1997). The police realize that they can no longer be complacent and that they have an important role to play in improving the quality of life within many communities.

We know that the police are capable of addressing racial injustice. We know that the police recognize the need. We know that the police in general believe they have an important role to play in addressing racial injustice. What we do not know is what the genesis of change will be. In most cases it takes a bit of convincing for the police to allocate the necessary resources and administrative will to address racial injustice. For example, police departments were reluctant to address high speed pursuits until they realized their substantial liability exposure. Whether or not a similar level of realization will be necessary for the police to address racial injustice is unknown.

Police Departments Will Avoid Legal
Intervention at All Costs

It is immensely difficult to explain what American policing was like prior to the 1960s. For example, most people cannot imagine a police department that actively supported the brutal treatment of racial minorities, failed to provide training to its officers, and prohibited its employees from intervening in domestic violence conflicts. These were characteristics of American policing prior to the 1960s. During the 1960s three factors merged to effectively transform American policing. First, the activist Warren Court handed down several landmark rulings (*Mapp*, *Gideon*, and *Miranda*) that resulted in wholesale changes to routine police procedures. Second, the Law Enforcement Assistance Administration provided considerable financial incentives for scholars to conduct evaluations of police procedures. Third, the Law Enforcement Education Program encouraged officers to partake in higher education. Of these, legal intervention produced the swiftest, most comprehensive, and longest-lasting change. It also was involuntary. The police are generally afraid of legal intervention, and they have good reason. Legal intervention often results in a loss of administrative flexibility, a diminished capacity to manage the department, and potentially serious threats to an individual's career.

The tendency to avoid intervention may manifest itself in one of four ways. First, A few police administrators may be reluctant to voluntarily collect racial profiling data. Conducting a racial profiling study may be viewed by some as little more than an evidence gathering activity for the plaintiff. This is precisely what happened in New Jersey, Illinois, and Maryland. It is more likely that the police will want more control over the racial profiling study and will therefore opt to conduct it proactively. Second, the police are far more sophisticated than most people think. They are increasingly aware of the methodological inaccuracies of racial profiling studies. It is likely that some police administrators will capitalize on the inadequacies of the current research and force plaintiffs to more rigorously argue their position. Third, some administrators, or their political leaders, will probably adopt a more pragmatic approach and accept a pretrial settlement, usually in the form of a consent decree. Given the cost and potential political damage associated with a legal proceeding, this may be the more prudent course. Finally, proactive police administrators likely see change in the wind. These administrators will seriously evaluate the research and consider the feasibility of various solutions to the problem. In some cases these administrators may recognize that they can do a lot proactively to address the controversy and thereby avoid legal intervention.

Police Departments Will Implement
Proactive Citizen Complaint Procedures

A citizen who approaches a police department with a complaint about one of its officers is indeed a brave soul. The police are skilled at evaluating the potential of an allegation. They know what levels of proof are required to convict a suspect and will be damned if they let anyone get by with less when accusing one of their own of impropriety. Typically, complainants are required to make a formal complaint in person and in the form of a sworn affidavit. Usually, the complaint form includes a warning that false statements will be prosecuted. In addition, the complainant suffers the burden of proof. In due time, the department will assign an internal affairs, often now called a professional standards, investigator to the case. The investigator will interview the officer, the complainant, witnesses, and other officers; review the physical evidence, if any; and write a final report. If the complaint is sustained (found to be true), the department will initiate a disciplinary action ranging from a verbal reprimand to suspension to termination. Depending on the size of the department, the nature of the complaint, and the workload of the internal affairs section, the process will require from a few days to several weeks. In far too many departments there is a lack of follow-up, and the complainant never knows, unless he asks, the result of the complaint. It is, for all parties involved, a stressful situation.

In addition, an onerous complaint process may effectively deter individuals from making bona fide complaints against officers. Less educated and economically deprived complainants may lack the knowledge, experience, or courage to take on the police department in a significant way.

To circumvent this, some police departments have implemented proactive citizen complaint programs. While these programs vary considerably between departments, they have a few common characteristics. First, in most cases complainants are not required to make the complaint in person or in writing. Supervisors or professional standards investigators are authorized to take the complaint over the phone. Second, the department assumes the burden of proof and must gather evidence to disprove the charge. Third, and likely most effective, officers are required to inform their supervisor anytime a citizen accuses them of racial prejudice or racial profiling. Supervisors are then required, by policy, to contact the individual and determine the specific basis for the claim. Informal interviews by the author suggest that most initial claims do not result in a formal charge. Usually, the citizen is simply frustrated. Even so, merely taking this proactive step may communicate that complaints of this sort are serious and warrant the department's undivided and unfiltered attention.

Police Departments Will Develop Extensive Cultural Sensitivity Training Programs

There is considerable support for the effectiveness of training on officer behavior. Training is particularly effective on officer behavior in highly stressful situations that threaten the life or safety of the officer. The importance of training is also demonstrated by the fact that in nearly every case where an officer's actions are under review, such as in a legal proceeding, how the officer was (or was not) trained is an issue. As a result, since the late 1960s police departments have devoted considerable time and resources to the pre- and in-service training of their officers, as well as documenting the performance of their officers in an academy setting.

Police departments typically respond to a crisis by implementing training programs. Doing so produces several important advantages. First, through a formal training program, the department can at least attempt to identify and correct errant behavior. Second, a well-documented training program demonstrates a department's level of commitment to addressing a community issue. Third, training programs offer an opportunity for the police department to communicate desired values and outcomes in a relatively proactive manner. Finally, training programs establish a series of behavioral expectations in a positive manner. In short, training is a considerably more efficient means to manage officer behavior than the disciplinary system.

In some cases departmental training is proactive. For example, when problem- and community-oriented policing became popular many department invested considerable training resources to teach officers the highly cognitive skills necessary for these approaches to policing. Most training, however, is reactive. For example, when departments realized their liability exposure in high speed pursuit driving, the use of nonlethal weapons, and officer street survival they invested heavily in training. In a similar way police departments recognize the potential risk associated with officers who are unable to effectively communicate with individuals from other cultures. It is likely that training programs will be developed to teach officers how to view their behavior from alternative cultural perspectives. Undoubtedly, some of this training will be relatively short (one-day) sensitivity exercises. These nominal responses are likely designed to simply demonstrate an attempt to address the issue, albeit half-heartedly. It is more likely that multicultural teaching objectives will find their way into a broad range of police academy subjects. Given the current and anticipated demographic trends in American society, police leaders can afford little less.

Police Officers Will Learn To Clearly Articulate Their Motivations

A substantial portion of the racial profiling controversy could be effectively addressed if officers did a better job articulating the exact reasons for stops, thereby justifying their behavior. In addition, clearly articulating how the suspect's behavior adversely affects public safety accomplishes two important objectives. First, it forces the discussion into an objective reality. In effect, it informs the suspect of why his behavior is potentially threatening to public safety. Second, and more importantly, it encourages officers to be introspective and to evaluate their personal enforcement approach. No doubt, after a short while the officer, unless he is completely devoid of a conscience, will recognize the folly and potential harm of his or her behavior.

There is no empirical evidence on whether or not issuing a citation to every driver who is stopped has any effect on the perception of racial profiling. It is, however, reasonable to predict that police officers will recognize the potential for a suspect to question the legitimacy of a stop when no ticket is issued. It is also likely that administrators will require officers to more completely articulate their justifications for initiating a stop or conducting a search.

LEGAL PATTERNS

How the legal community will respond to the racial profiling controversy is largely unknown. While we have witnessed compelling rulings in New Jersey, Maryland, and Illinois, we have yet to fully explore all of the legal remedies available to address racial profiling. There are, however, a few predictable trends.

Whren is Not Likely To Be Reversed in the Near Future

The Supreme Court may have missed an opportunity to end, or at least diminish, a common police activity with a potential for racial profiling. Pretextual stops are unquestionably one of the most potentially abusive, yet potentially effective, police procedures. Given the breadth of the traffic code and the inevitability of violation, anyone, at any time, and for any reason is subject to heightened police officer scrutiny regardless of whether the police have any reasonable suspicion that a crime (other than the one for which the individual was stopped) has been committed (Harris 2002). The Court in *Whren* applied an objective test and ruled that as long as the police have an objective reason to stop someone (e.g., a violation of the traffic code) then the stop, and anything emanating from the stop (assuming the search is legal), is admissible. Some scholars suggest that the Court should have applied a subjective test. This would have required the officers in *Whren* to articulate their actual reasonable suspicion for following, stopping, and subsequently searching the defendants. The Court closed the door on a Fourth Amendment challenge to a pretextual stop. More importantly, the Court validated the practice of pretextual stops in a unanimous decision. A reversal of *Whren* is one avenue out of the racial profiling controversy, but it is an unlikely avenue.

Legal Remedies Based on the Equal Protection Clause Will Not be Feasible Until the Statistics are Better

The Equal Protection Clause of the Fourteenth Amendment may become a more feasible, and productive, legal remedy. The Equal Protection Clause enjoys an immensely rich legal history. It has been used successfully to correct a broad range of social problems. Furthermore, it seems to have some potential as a remedy in racial profiling. Unfortunately, the evidentiary requirements necessary to prevail in such a cause are onerous. Plaintiffs are usually able to prove an overall disparate effect, but even that may be difficult in court given the inability of the current benchmarks to conclusively determine the qualitative dimension of "similarly situated" individuals. Furthermore, and more challenging, the available statistics are not able to establish discriminatory intent. All a defendant has to do is demonstrate that each and every one of the stops are initiated by a bona fide violation of the traffic code. The current sophistication of the statistics is not sufficient, at least at this point, to consistently convince courts of the plaintiff's position. The current studies, for the most part, are unable to discount alternative explanations of the disparity, at least to the satisfaction of most courts. As a result, this remedy will only be feasible when, or if, statistically based evidence becomes more inferential.

Legal Remedies Based on 42 U.S.C., Section 14141 May Become More Frequent

42 U.S.C., Section 14141 may become the most viable legal remedy. The evidentiary requirements associated with this statute are less of a barrier than those associated with the Equal Protection Clause. Furthermore, they do not require a plaintiff to demonstrate that he or she was harmed by the behavior of the police department. Two factors will determine the effectiveness of this law as a legal remedy for racial profiling. First, for the United States Department of Justice to initiate actions under Section 14141 in a significant way, it must have sufficient resources. Second, the political ideology within the department must be supportive of such causes. The current emphasis at the Department of Justice is on homeland security, corporate fraud, and to some extent abortion rights. Unless and until the department's emphasis changes, it is unlikely that Section 14141 will be used to address racial profiling at a substantial level.

POST-9/11 AND THE WAR ON TERROR: ARE WE MAKING THE SAME MISTAKE?

Prior to September 11, 2001, racial profiling had, as an issue, coalesced to the point where nobody could legitimately defend it as a practice. It was universally viewed with disdain. "By September 10, 2001, virtually everyone from Jesse Jackson, to Al Gore, to George W. Bush, to John Ashcroft, agreed that racial profiling was bad" (Heumann and Cassak 2003, 154). National opinion polls consistently reported strong opposition to racial profiling, even among nonminorities and individuals not likely to be subjected to it. That all changed when nineteen Arab-Muslim terrorists hijacked four commercial jetliners and caused the deaths of thousands of innocent individuals. It then seemed an easy thing for people to suggest that Middle Eastern–looking individuals should receive more scrutiny at airports. Immediately after 9/11 and for several months thereafter opinion polls reported that as high as 71 percent of Blacks, 63 percent of non-Whites, and 57 percent of Whites supported ethnic profiling specifically targeting Arabs and Muslims in airports. Many people began to wonder whether or not we were too quick to condemn the practice of racial profiling. After all, we had just witnessed the slaughter of thousands of innocent Americans on our soil. Are we really supposed to ignore the one consistently identifiable feature of the terrorists? (Heumann and Cassak 2003). After 9/11 the rules changed and everything we had learned about the social costs and ineffectiveness of racial profiling was largely ignored.

We have been to this place before. In 1942, shortly after the bombing of Pearl Harbor by the Japanese Imperial Navy, California Attorney General Earl Warren (who later, as Chief Justice of the United States Supreme Court, became an unyielding advocate for civil rights) supervised the preparation of maps indicating Japanese-owned land in California and by the end of the year advocated the enforcement of the state's Alien Land Law. He did this despite delivering a speech in 1940 in which he cautioned his listeners against bigotry based on national origin. In this speech he stated, "It should be remembered that practically all aliens have come to this county because they like our land and our institutions better than those from whence they came" (Siggens 2004). The internment of Japanese-Americans, many native born, followed and became one of our nation's most infamous examples of racial bigotry. In many ways the events following 9/11 are similar. Our government's selective enforcement of the immigration laws, in an effort to identify potential terrorists, has resulted in the wholesale deportation of Arab and Muslim men and boys, causing disruptions in family life and economic devastation within the Arab-American community. Even United States citizens have not escaped this dragnet. More than 1,200 United States citizens have been detained, but not publicly charged with terrorism, since 9/11. The National Security Entry/Exit Registration System was initially applied to visiting males between the ages of 16 and 24 from predominantly Muslim countries and North Korea. Thousands of long-term residents of the United States fled to Canada to avoid deportation. The system has resulted in more than 13,000 deportations and massive backlogs in United States Immigration and Naturalization offices. Even though the Immigration and Naturalization Service intended to expand the program to include nationals from additional countries, it has now been abandoned (AIUSA 2004).

The effects of additional scrutiny of individuals based primarily on their ethnicity or religious preference are substantial. At the individual level feelings of humiliation, helplessness, anger, and fear are common within the Arab-American community. There exists a diminished trust in law enforcement and a reluctance to rely on the police for help among even the most law-abiding Arab- and Muslim-Americans. At the community level this fear and mistrust has resulted in a lack of cooperation with police officers and a reluctance to report crime. This further segregates and alienates ethnic minorities and could adversely affect the ability of our government to identify and apprehend potential terrorists (AIUSA 2004).

In 2003, Amnesty International USA conducted a series of public hearings across the nation to assess the impact of our nation's post-9/11 immigration policies. The comments made by individuals at these hearings are heart wrenching and communicate a sense of despair and rage within the Arab and Muslim community. In many ways these stories are remarkably similar to the stories of racial profiling victims published by newspapers in the mid-1990s. Whether or not these stories will heighten the general public's awareness of the plight of the victims and result in a comprehensive evaluation of enforcement programs that have a disparate effect remains to be seen.

After 9/11 our nation developed a series of profiles designed to identify potential terrorists at airports and other public facilities. For national security reasons the elements of these profiles are not well publicized, so it is not possible to know how prominent factors relating to an individual's race, ethnicity, national origin, religion, or religious appearance are within them, but it appears that these profiles are having a disparate effect on Arab and Muslim travelers. It is important for us to ask whether the new profiles will improve our national security. It is clear that race-based profiles are largely ineffective at accurately identifying drug couriers, so what makes us believe that a similar profile will be any more effective at identifying potential terrorists? Even if they prove to be initially productive, there is no guarantee that those who have our demise as their objective are not willing to amend their behaviors enough to pass under our national radar screen.

Our experience with the racial profiling controversy suggests that the next logical step is to conduct rigorous studies in airports to determine whether our national security measures are having their intended effect. This type of research will likely be similar, in terms of its methodology, to the previous research. One potential advantage is that benchmarks will be based on a more defined population of individuals, that is, travelers. Whether or not our national leaders will allow such an inquiry remains to be seen. It is, however, the most likely extension of the racial profiling controversy. Our national security requires, and indeed demands, that we avoid repeating the same mistake. The danger is that despite our best intentions we are not likely to enhance the nation's security by using ethnically based profiles (Harris 2002). It may make us feel better, as if we are proactively defending ourselves, but we may be fooling ourselves into a false sense of security.

SUMMARY

More than any other time in our history, we are concerned about the future. Unfortunately, at no time in the history of mankind have we been less able to predict our fate. This does not release us from an ethical responsibility to at least attempt to predict the future of important social issues. Racial profiling, as a distinct research agenda, will probably remain important to the scholarly community for the foreseeable future. The issue commands our attention, and there is much to be done. Advances in the accuracy of measures and estimates will likely be the focus of future researchers. Given what we have learned in the recent past about patrol procedures, within the context of racial profiling research, it is likely that police departments will, in partnership with the academic community, play a significant role in future research. Police departments, as they have in the past, will allocate substantial training time and resources to address the racial profiling controversy. The greatest opportunity for change may be within the legal community. Legal challenges to the practice of racial profiling, despite the accomplishments in New Jersey, Maryland, and Illinois, are in their infancy. Much work needs to be done in this arena.

Finally, in a very real way history may be repeating itself. Post-9/11 efforts to enhance our national security are to some degree dependent on the application of a profile that attempts to identify potential terrorists. At this point the efficacy of these profiles is unclear. What is clear is that affected groups, predominantly the Arab community, are beginning to levy some of the same accusations against law enforcement that were levied by racial minorities during the height of the war on drugs. We are at risk of tricking ourselves into a false sense of security unless we learn from the mistakes of our past.

DISCUSSION QUESTIONS

1. Discuss the factors that may cause either an increase or decrease in future racial profiling research.
2. Can, or should, the police play a key role in addressing racial injustice?
3. Is there any evidence that the current profiles used to detect terrorists will be any more or less effective than any of the previously developed profiles?
4. Would a de-emphasis on drug interdiction reduce the overrepresentation of minorities in traffic stops?
5. Anecdotal evidence suggests police officers are seldom aware of a driver's race or ethnicity prior to a stop or when making a decision to stop. If this is true, then how would cultural sensitivity training reduce the overrepresentation of minorities in traffic stops?
6. Other than race, ethnicity, national origin, religion, or religious appearance, what factors are common among known terrorists in sufficient frequency to justify the scrutiny of airport screeners?

CASE STUDIES

1. At the end of an exhaustive racial profiling study the police chief decides to formalize the data collection process and make it a part of the routine data collection protocols of the department. Discuss how you (the patrol captain) would accomplish this.

2. Your department's new proactive citizen complaint process reduces the level of proof necessary to sustain a complaint against an officer. How would you ensure that the officers' rights are protected in such a system?

3. During a speech to local Muslim religious leaders a popular police chief stated, "Don't worry about all this extra scrutiny we are giving to Muslims and Arabs. It will die down after all this hysteria and hype over the War on Terror ends, just as it did for the Japanese after Pearl Harbor. For now, just deal with it." How would you as the city manager respond?

REFERENCES

Ajzen, I., and Fishbein, M. 1977a. Attitude-behavior relations: A theoretical analysis and review of empirical research. *Psychological Bulletin* 84:888–918.

Ajzen, I., and Fishbein, M. 1977b. *Understanding Attitudes and Predicting Social Behavior.* Englewood Cliffs, NJ: Prentice Hall.

Alpert, G. 1997. *Police Pursuit: Policies and Training.* Washington, DC: U.S. Government Printing Office.

Alpert, G. P., and Dunham, R. G. 1988. *Policing Multi-Ethnic Neighborhoods.* Westport, CT: Greenwood Press.

Alpert, G. P., Kenney, D. J., Dunham, R. G., and Smith, W. C. 2000. *Police Pursuits: What We Know.* Washington, DC: Police Executive Research Forum.

Alpert, G. P., Smith, M. R., and Dunham, R.G. 2003 (March). Toward a Better Benchmark: Assessing the Utility of Not-at-Fault Traffic Crash Data in Racial Profiling Research. Paper resented at Confronting Racial Profiling in the 21st Century: Implications for Racial Justice. Boston, MA: Northeastern University.

American Civil Liberties Union (ACLU). 1999 (January 15). Driving while Black or Brown Questionnaire. Washington, DC: Author. Retrieved September 16, 1999, from http://www.aclunc.org/dwb-question.html.

American Civil Liberties Union (ACLU). 2000. Plaintiff's Fifth Monitoring Report: Pedestrian and Car Stop Audit. Retrieved January 13, 2004, from aclyupa.ort/repot.htm.

Amnesty International USA (AIUSA). 2004. *Threat and Humiliation: Racial Profiling, Domestic Security and Human Rights in the United States.* New York: Amnesty International USA.

Asim, J. 2001. Black man standing. In *Not Guilty: Twelve Black Men Speak Out on Law, Justice and Life,* ed. J. Asim, 24–40). New York: Harper Collins.

Babbie, E. 1999. *The Basics of Social Research.* Belmont, CA: Wadsworth.

Banks, R. R. 2001. Race-based suspect selection and colorblind equal protection doctrine and discourse. *UCLA Law Review* 48:1075–115.

Banton, M. 1964. *The Policeman and the Community.* New York: Basic Books.

Barlow, D. E., and Barlow, M. H. 2002. Racial profiling: A survey of African American police officers. *Police Quarterly* 5(3):334–58.

Bast, C. M. 1997. Driving while Black: Stopping motorists in a subterfuge. *Criminal Law Bulletin* 33:457–86.

Batton, C., and Kadleck, C. 2004. Theoretical and methodological issues in racial profiling research. *Police Quarterly* 7(1):30–64

Bernard, T. J., and Egnel, R. S. 2001. Conceptualizing criminal justice theory. *Justice Quarterly* 18(1):1–30.

Bittner, E. 1970. *The Functions of the Police in Modern Society.* Washington, DC: U.S. Government Printing Office.

Bittner, E. 1979. *The Functions of the Police in Modern Society.* Chevy Chase, MD: National Institute of Mental Health.

Black, D. J. 1971. The social organization of arrest. *Stanford Law Review* 23:1050–111.

Black, D. 1976. *The Behavior of Law.* New York: Academic Press.

Black, D. 1980. *The Manner and Customs of the Police.* New York: Academic Press.

Black, D. J., and Reiss, A. J., Jr. 1970. Police control of juveniles. *American Sociological Review* 35(1):63–77.

Blumenson, E., and Nelson, E. 1998. Policing for profit: The drug war's hidden economic agenda. *University of Chicago Law Review* 65:76–84.

Brooks, L. W. 1997. Police discretionary behavior: A study in style. In *Critical Issues in Policing: Contemporary Readings,* ed. R. G. Dunham and G. P. Alpert, 3d ed., 149–66. Prospect Heights, IL: Waveland Press.

Brown, M. K. 1981. *Working the Street: Police Discretion and the Dilemmas of Reform.* New York: Russell Sage Foundation.

Buerger, M. E. 2002. Supervisory challenges arising from racial profiling legislation. *Police Quarterly* 5(3):380–408.

Buerger, M. E., and Farrell, A. 2002. The evidence of racial profiling: Interpreting documented and unofficial sources. *Police Quarterly* 5(3):272–305

California Highway Patrol (CHP). 2000. *CHP Public Contact Demographic Data Summary.* Sacramento: California Highway Patrol.

Campbell, J. P., and Pritchard, R. D. 1976. Motivation theory in industrial and organizational psychology. In *Handbook of Industrial and Organizational Psychology,* ed. M. D. Dunnett, 63–130. Chicago: Rand McNally.

Carr, B. R. 1969. A statistical analysis of rural Ontario's traffic accident using induced exposure data. *Accident Analysis and Prevention* 1:343–57.

Carter, D. L., and Katz-Bannister, A. J. 2004. Racial profiling: Issues and implications for police policy. In *Contemporary policing: Controversies, challenges, and solutions,* ed. Q. C. Thurman and J. Zhao, 235–47. Los Angeles: Roxbury.

Chambliss, W. J. 1994. Policing the ghetto underclass: the politics of law and law enforcement. *Social Problems* 41:177–94.

Chambliss, W. J., and Seidman, R. 1971. *Law, Order and Power.* Reading, MA: Addison-Wesley.

Cleary, J. 2000. *Racial Profiling Studies in Law Enforcement: Issues and Methodology.* St. Paul: Minnesota House of Representatives, Research Department.

Cohen, J. D., Lennon, J., and Wasserman, R. 2000. Eliminating racial profiling: A "third way." *Law Enforcement News* 26(530):12–15.

Cole, D. 1999. *No Equal Justice.* New York: New Press.

Cooper, C. 2001. Mediation in black and white. In *Not Guilty: Twelve Black Men Speak Out on Law, Justice and Life,* ed. J. Asim, 126–41. New York: Harper Collins.

Cordner, G., Williams, B., and Zuniga, M. 2000. *San Diego Vehicle Stops: Executive Summary.* San Diego, CA: San Diego Police Department.

Cordner, G., Williams, B., and Zuniga, M. 2002. *Vehicle stops in San Diego: 2001.* San Diego, CA: San Diego Police Department.

Covington, J. 2001. Round up the usual suspects: Racial profiling and the War on Drugs. In *Petit Apartheid in the United States Criminal Justice System: The Dark Figure of Racism,* ed. D. Milovanivic and K. K. Russell, 27–42. Durham, NC: Carolina Academic Press.

Cox, S. M., Pease, S. E., Miller, D. S., and Tyson, C. B. 2001. *Interim Report of Traffic Stops Statistics for the State of Connecticut.* Rocky Hill, CT: Division of Criminal Justice, Office of the Chief State's Attorney.

Crank, J. P., and Langworth, R. 1992. An institutional perspective of policing. *Journal of Criminal Law and Criminology* 83: 338–63.

Davis, A. J. 1997. Race, cops and traffic stops. *Miami Law Review* 51:425–443.

Davis, K. C. 1975. *Police Discretion.* St. Paul, MN: West.

DeJong, C., Mastrofski, S. D., and Parks, R. B. 2001. Patrol officers and problem solving: An application of expectancy theory. *Justice Quarterly* 18:31–61.

DeYoung, D. J., Peck, R. C., and Helander, C. S. 1997. Estimating the exposure and fatal crash rates of suspended/revoked and unlicensed drivers in California. *Accident Analysis and Prevention* 29(1):17–23.

del Carmen, R. V. 1998. *Criminal Procedure: Law and Practice,* 4th ed. Belmont, CA: West.

Denver Police Department (DPD). 2002. *First Annual Report: Denver Police Department Contact Card Data Analysis.* Denver, CO: Denver Police Department.

Donohue, B. 2000. 10 Troopers cleared of charges as Dunbar sees profiling ending. *Star Ledger,* April 15, A1.

Donohue, J. J., III, and Levitt, S. D. 1997. The Impact of Race on Policing, Arrest Patterns, and Crime. ABF Working Paper #9705, American Bar Association.

Donzinger, S. R. 1996. *The Real War on Crime.* New York: Harper Collins.

Dunham, R.G., and Alpert, G. P. 1988. Neighborhood differences in attitudes toward policing: Evidence for a mixed-strategy model of policing in a multi-ethnic setting. *Journal of Criminal Law and Criminology* 79(2):504–23.

Engel, R. S., and Calnon, J. M. 2004a. Examining the influence of drivers' characteristics during traffic stops with police: Results from a national survey. *Justice Quarterly* 21(1):50–90.

Engel, R. S., and Calnon, J. M. 2004b. Comparing benchmark methodologies for police-citizen contacts: Traffic stop data collection for the Pennsylvania state police. *Police Quarterly* 7(1):97–125

Engel, R. S., Calnon, J. M., and Bernard, T. J. 2002. Theory and racial profiling: Shortcomings and future directions in research. *Justice Quarterly* 19(2):249–273.

Farrell, A. 2003. Auditing Municipal Traffic Stop Data: Implications for Racial Profiling Analysis. Paper presented at Confronting Racial Profiling in the 21st Century: Implications for Racial Justice. Boston, MA: Northeastern University.

Farrell, A., McDevitt, J., Bailey, L., Andresen, C., and Pierce, E. 2004. *Massachusetts racial and gender profiling final report.* Boston, MA: Institute on Race and Justice, Northeastern University.

Farrell, A., McDevitt, J., and Buerger, M. E. 2002. Moving police and community dialogues forward through data collection task forces. *Police Quarterly* 5(3):359–79.

Frank, J., Brandl, S. G., and Cullen, F. T. 1996. Reassessing the impact of race on citizens' attitudes toward the police: A research note. *Justice Quarterly* 13(3):231–324.

Fredrickson, D. D. and Siljander, R. P. 2002. *Eliminating the confusion between racial and criminal profiling and clarifying what constitutes unfair discrimination and persecution.* Springfield, IL: Charles C. Thomas.

Fridell, L., Lunney, R., Diamond, D., Kubu, B., Scott, M., and Laing, C. 2001. *Racially biased policing: A principled response.* Washington, DC: Police Executive Research Foundation.

Fyfe, J. 1979. Administrative interventions on police shooting discretion: An empirical examination. *Journal of Criminal Justice* 7(Winter):309–232.

Gardiner, J. 1969. *Traffic and the police.* Cambridge, MA: Harvard University Press.

Garrett, B. 2000. Standing while Black: Distinguishing *Lyons* in racial profiling cases. *Columbia Law Review* 100(7):1815–46.

Gallup. 1999. Racial Profiling Seen as Widespread Particularly among Black Males. Princeton, MA: Gallup News Service. Retrieved November 19, 2003, from http://www.gallup.com.

Geller, W. A., and Scott, M. 1992. *Deadly Force: What We Know.* Washington, DC: U.S. Government Printing Office.

Gieryn, T. F. 2000. A space for place in sociology. *Annual Review of Sociology* 26:463–95.

Goldberg, J. 1999. The color of suspicion. *New York Times Magazine,* June 20, Section 6, p. 51.

Goldman, N. 1963. *The Differential Selection of Juvenile Offenders for Court Appearance.* New York: National Council on Crime and Delinquency.

Goldstein, H. 1990. *Problem Oriented Policing.* New York: McGraw-Hill.

Greenberg, S. B. 2004. *The Two Americas: Our Current Political Deadlock and How to Break It.* New York: St Martin's Press.

Greenwald, H. P. 2003. *Police Vehicle Stops in Sacramento, California.* Los Angeles: University of Southern California, School of Policy, Planning and Development.

Haight, F. A. 1970. A crude framework for bypassing exposure. *Journal of Safety Research,* 2(1):26–29.

Hair, J. F., Anderson, R. E., Tatham, R. L., and Black, W. C. 1992. *Multivariate data analysis.* New York: Macmillan.

Harris, D. A. 1994. Factors for reasonable suspicion: When Black and poor means stopped and frisked. *Indiana Law Journal* 69:659–88

Harris, D. A. 1997. Driving while Black and other traffic offenses: The supreme court and pretextual traffic stops. *Journal of Criminal Law and Criminology* 87:544–82.

Harris, D. A. 1999a. Driving while Black: Racial profiling on our nation's highways. Washington, DC: American Civil Liberties Union. Retrieved December 22, 1999, from http://www.acly.org/profiling/report/ndex.html.

Harris, D. A. 1999b. The stories, the statistics, and the law: Why "driving while black" matters. *Minnesota Law Review* 84:265–326.

Harris, D. 2000 (March 30). Data collection: the first step in coming to grips with racial profiling. Testimony before United

States Senate Subcommittee on Constitution, Federalism, and Property Rights, Washington, DC.

Harris, D. A. 2002. *Profiles in Injustice: Why Racial Profiling Cannot Work.* New York: New Press.

Hemmons, C., and Levin, D. 2000. Resistance is futile: The right to resist unlawful arrest in an era of aggressive policing. *Crime & Delinquency* 46(4):472–96.

Herszenhorn, D. M. 2000. Police and union chiefs meet to address racial profiling. *New York Times,* October 22, Section 1, p. 41.

Heumann, M., & Cassak, L. 2003. *Good Cop, Bad Cop: Racial Profiling and Competing Views of Justice.* New York: Peter Lang.

Jernigan, A. S. 2000. Driving while Black: Profiling in America. *Law & Psychology Review* 24:127–38

Johnson, R. M. 2001. Fear of a blue uniform. In *Not Guilty: Twelve Black Men Speak Out on Law, Justice and Life,* 81–91. New York: Harper Collins.

Kennedy, R. 1997. *Race, Crime and the Law.* New York: Vintage.

Kennedy, R. 1999. Suspect policy. *New Republic,* September 13, 30.

Kinsley, M. 2001. When is racial profiling OK? *Washington Post,* September 30, B7.

Klinger, D. A. 1994. Demeanor or crime? An inquiry into why "hostile" citizens are more likely to be arrested. *Criminology* 32: 475–93.

Klinger, D. A. 1997. Negotiating order in patrol work: An ecological theory of police response to deviance. *Criminology* 35:277–306.

Knowles, J., Persico, N., and Todd, P. 1999. Racial Bias in Motor Vehicle Searches: Theory and Evidence. Cambridge, MA: Working Paper Series #7449, National Bureau of Economic Research.

Lamberth, J. 1994. Revised Statistical Analysis of the Incidence of Police Stops and Arrests of Black Drivers/Travelers on the New Jersey Turnpike between Exits or Interchanges 1 and 3 from Years 1988 through 1991. West Chester, PA: Author. Retrieved July 7, 1999, from www.lamberthconsulting.com/research_articles/asp.

Lamberth, J. 1996. Report of John Lamberth, Ph.D. Washington, DC: American Civil Liberties Union. Retrieved July 7, 1999, from www.aclu.org/court/lamberty.html.

Lamberth, J. 2003a. *Racial Profiling Data Analysis: Final Report for the San Antonio Police Department.* Chadds Ford, PA: Lamberth Consulting.

Lamberth, J. (2003b, March). Enhancing Community and Police Trust. Paper presented at Confronting Racial Profiling in the 21st Century: Implications for Racial Justice. Boston, MA: Northeastern University.

Landsdowne, W. M. 2002. *Vehicle Stop Demographic Study.* San Jose, CA: San Jose Police Department.

Langan, P. A., Greenfield, L. A., Smith, S. K., Durose, M. R., and Levin, D. J. 2001. *Contacts between Police and Public: Findings from the 1999 National Survey.* Washington, DC: Department of Justice.

Lange, J. E., Blackman, K. O., and Johnson, M. B. 2001. *Speed Violation Survey of the New Jersey Turnpike: Final Report.* Calverton, MD: Public Services Research Institute.

Lanza-Kaduce, L., and Greenleaf, R. G. 1994. Police-citizen encounters: Turk on norm resistance. *Justice Quarterly* 11:605–23.

Leitzel, J. 2001. Race and policing. *Society* 38(3):38–42.

Leo, R. A. and Thomas, G. C., III. 1998. *The Miranda Debate.* Boston, MA: Northeastern University Press.

Lundman, R. J. 1994. Demeanor or crime? The Midwest City police-citizen encounter study. *Criminology* 32:651–656.

Lundman, R. J., and Kaufman, R. L. 2003. Driving while Black: Effects of race, ethnicity, and gender on citizen self-reports on traffic stops and police actions. *Criminology* 41(1):195–220.

Lyles, R. W., Stamatiadis, P., and Lighthizer, D. 1971. Quasi-induced exposure revisited. *Accident Analysis and Prevention* 23(1):275–85.

MacDonald, H. 2001. The myth of racial profiling. *City Journal* July 13, 11(2).

MacDonald, H. 2003. *Are Cops Racist?* Chicago: Ivan R. Doe.

Magee, R. K. 1994. The myth of the good cop and the inadequacy of Fourth Amendment remedies for Black men: Contrasting presumptions of innocence and guilt. *Capital University Law Review* 23(151):161–213.

Manning, P. K. 1997. *Police Work: The Social Organization of Policing,* 2d ed. Prospect Heights, IL: Waveland Press.

Mastrofski, S. D., Ritti, R. R., and Snipes, J. B. 1994. Expectancy theory and police productivity in DUI enforcement. *Law & Society Review* 28:113–48.

McCorkle, R. C. 2003. *A.B. 500: Traffic Stop Data Collection Study.* Carson City, NV: Office of the Attorney General.

McMahon, J., Garner, J., Davis, R., and Kraus, A. 2002 (October). How to Correctly Collect and Analyze Racial Profiling Data: Your Reputation Depends on It! Final Project Report for Racial Profiling data Collection and Analysis. Washington, DC: United States Department of Justice, Office of Community Oriented Policing Services.

Meeks, K. 2000. *Driving while Black.* New York: Broadway Books.

Meehan A. J. and Ponder, M. C. 2002. Race and place: The ecology of racial profiling African-American motorists. *Justice Quarterly* 19(3):399–430.

Miller, J. 2000. Profiling Populations Available for Stops and Searches. Police Research Series Paper 131. London: Home Office.

Minnesota Department of Public Safety (MDPS). 2003. *Minnesota Racial Profiling Report: All Jurisdictions Report.* St. Paul, MN: Council on Crime and Justice.

Mitchell, R. R. 1974. Expectancy models of job satisfaction, occupational preference and effort: A theoretical, methodological, and empirical appraisal. *Psychological Bulletin* 81:1053–77

Muharrar, M. 1998 (September/October). Media Blackface: "Racial profiling" in News Reporting. Retrieved January 13, 2004, from www.fair.org/extra/9809/media-blackface.html.

Muir, W. K., Jr. 1977. *Police and Street Corner Politicians.* Chicago: University of Chicago Press.

National Institute of Justice. 2002. *Satisfaction with the Police: What Matters?* Washington, DC: United States Department of Justice, Office of Justice Programs.

Navarro, M. 2003. Going beyond black and white, Hispanics in census pick other. *New York Times,* November 9, a-1.

Neuman, W. L. 2004. *Basics of Social Research: Qualitative and Quantitative Approaches.* Boston, MA: Allyn & Bacon.

New York Attorney General's Office. 1999. *The New York City Police Department's "Stop and Frisk" Practices.* Albany: New York State Attorney General's Office.

Norris, C., Fielding, N. Kemp, C., and Fielding J. 1992. Black and blue: An analysis of the influence of race on being stopped by the police. *British Journal of Sociology* 43:207–24.

Novak, K. J. 2004. Disparity and racial profiling in traffic enforcement. *Police Quarterly* 7(1):65–96.

Oaks, D. 1970. Studying the exclusionary rule in search and seizure. *University of Chicago Law Review* 37(Summer): 665–757.

Office of National Drug Control Policy. (2002). *National Drug Control Strategy.* FY 2003 Budget Summary. Washington, DC: Author. Retrieved July 1, 2003, from http://www.whitehousedrugpolicy.gov/publications/pdf/budget2002.pdf.

Oliver, W. M. 2000. With an evil eye and an unequal hand: Pretextual stops and doctrinal remedies to racial profiling. *Tulane Law Review* 74 (4):1409–81.

O'Reilly, J. T. 2002. *Police Traffic Stops and Racial Profiling.* Springfield, IL: Charles C. Thomas.

Pallone, N. J., and Hennessy, J. J. 1999. Blacks and whites as victims and offenders in aggressive crime in the U.S.: Myths and realities. *Journal of Offender Rehabilitation* 31(1/2):1–33.

Petrocelli, M., Piquero, A., and Smith, M. R. 2003. Conflict theory and racial profiling: An empirical analysis of police traffic stop data. *Journal of Criminal Justice* 31(1):1–12.

Piliavin, I., and Briar, S. 1964. Police encounters with juveniles. *American Journal of Sociology* 70(2):206–414.

Police Foundation. (2003). *A Multi-Jurisdictional Assessment of Traffic Enforcement and Data Collection in Kansas.* Washington, DC: Author.

Powell, D. D. 1981. Race, rank, and police discretion. *Journal of Police Science and Administration* 9(4):383–89.

Quinney, R. 1980. *Class, State and Crime.* New York: Longman.

Quinton, P., Bland, N., and Miller, J. 2000. *Police Stops, Decision Making and Practice.* London: The Policing and Reducing Crime Unit, Research, Development and Statistics Directorate, Home Office.

Ramirez, D., McDevitt, J., and Farrell, A. 2000. *A Resource Guide on Racial Profiling Data Collection Systems: Promising Practices and Lessons Learned.* Washington, DC: United States Department of Justice, Bureau of Justice Assistance.

Roberg, R., Crank, J., and Kuykendall, J. 2000. *Police and Society,* 2d ed. Los Angeles: Roxbury.

Roberg, R, and Kuykendall, J. 1993. *Police and Society.* Los Angeles: Roxbury.

Rojek, J., Rosenfeld, R., and Decker, S. 2004. The influence of drivers' race on traffic stops in Missouri. *Police Quarterly* 7(1):126–47.

Ross, H. L. 1960. Traffic law violations: A folk crime. *Social Problems* 8:231–241.

Rubinstein, J. 1973. *City Police.* New York: Random House.

Sacks, H. 1972. Notes on the police assessment of moral character. In *Studies in Social Interaction,* ed. D. Sudnow, 280–93. New York: Free Press.

Schultz, M., and Withrow, B. L. 2004. Racial profiling and organizational change. *Criminal Justice Policy Review* 15(4): 462–85.

Sherman, L. 1989. Hot spots of predatory crime: Routine activities and the criminology of place. *Criminology* 27:27–55.

Siggens, P. 2004. Racial Profiling in an Age of Terrorism. Speech delivered at the Markkula Center for Applied Ethics on March 12, 2002. Retrieved September 9, 2004, from http://www.scu.edu/ethics/publications/ethical perspectives/ profiling.html.

Skolnick, H. 1994. *Justice without Trial,* 3d ed. New York: Macmillan.

Smith, D. A., Graham, N., and Adams, B. 1991. Minorities and the police: Attitudinal and behavioral questions. In *Race and Criminal Justice,* ed. M. J. Lynch and E. B. Patterson, 22–35. New York: Harrow and Heston.

Smith, D. A., and Visher, C. A. 1981. Street-level justice: Situational determinants of police arrest decisions. *Social Problems* 29(2):167–77.

Smith, D. A., Visher, C. A., and Davidson, L. A. 1984. Equity and discretionary justice: The influence of race on police arrest decisions. *Journal of Criminal Law and Criminology* 75(1):234–49.

Smith, M. R., and Alpert, G. P. 2002. Searching for direction: Courts, social science, and the adjudication of racial profiling claims. *Justice Quarterly* 19(4):673–703.

Smith, M. R. and Petrocelli, M. 2001. Racial profiling? A multivariate analysis of police traffic stop data. *Police Quarterly* 4:4–27.

Sprinthall, R. C. 2003. *Basic Statistical Analysis*, 4th ed. Boston: Allyn & Bacon.

Spitzer, E. 1999. *The New York City Police Department's "Stop and Frisk" Practices: A Report to the People of the State of New York from the Office of the Attorney General.* Albany, NY: Office of the State Attorney General.

Stamatiadis, N., and Deacon, J. A. 1997. Quasi-induced exposure: Methodology and insights. *Accident Analysis and Prevention* 29(1):37–52.

Statistical Assessment Service (STATS). 1999. Race and Crime: Is "Profiling" Reasonable? Retrieved September 24, 2001, from http://www.stats.ort/newsletters/9904/profile.htm.

Susskind, R. S. 1994. Race, reasonable articulable suspicion, and seizure. *American Criminal Law Review* 31(1-2):327–439.

Taylor, J., and Whitney, G. 1999. Crime and racial profiling by the U.S. police: Is there an empirical basis? *Journal of Social, Political, and Economic Studies* 24(4):485–510.

Tedeschi, J. T., and Felson, R. B. 1994. *Violence, Aggression, and Coercive Actions.* Washington, DC: American Psychological Association.

Texas Department of Public Safety (TDPS). 2000. *Traffic Stop Data Report.* Austin: Texas Department of Public Safety.

Thorpe, J. T. 1967. Calculating relative involvement rates in accidents without determining exposure. *Traffic Safety Research Review* 11(2):3–8.

Thompson, A. C. 1999. Stopping the usual suspects: Race and the Fourth Amendment. *New York University Law Review* 74: 957–1013.

Tomaskovic-Devey, D., Mason, M., and Zingraff, M. 2004. Looking for the driving while black phenomena: Conceptualizing racial bias processes and their associated distributions. *Police Quarterly* 7(1):3–29.

Tonry, M. 1995. *Malign Neglect: Race, Crime, and Punishment in America.* New York: Oxford University Press.

Trende, S. P. 2003. Why modest proposals offer the best solution for combating racial profiling. *Duke Law Journal* 50:331–50.

Turk, A. T. 1969. *Criminality and Legal Order.* Chicago: Rand McNally.

United States General Accounting Office (U.S. GAO). 2000 (March). *Racial Profiling: Limited Data Available on Motorist Stops.* Washington, DC: United States General Accounting Office.

Van Maanen, J. 1974. Working the street: A developmental view of police behavior. In *The Potential for Reform of Criminal Justice,* ed. H. Jacob, 83–130. Beverly Hills, CA: Sage.

Van Maanen, J. 1978. The asshole. In *Policing: A View from the Street,* ed. P. K. Manning and J. Van Maanen, 221–38. Santa Monica, CA: Goodyear.

Van Maanan, J. 1983. The boss: First-line supervision in an American police agency. In *Control on the Police Organization,* ed. M. Punch, 275–317). Cambridge, MA: MIT Press

Van Maanen, J. 1984. Making rank: Becoming an American police sergeant. *Urban Life* 13:155–76

Verniero, P. and Zoubeck, P. H. 1999. *Interim Report of the State Police Review Team Regarding Allegations of Racial Profiling.* Trenton, NJ: Attorney General's Office.

Walker, S. 2001. Searching for the denominator: Problems with police traffic stop data and an early warning system solution. *Justice Research and Policy* 3(1):63–95.

Walker, S. 2003. *Internal Benchmarking for Traffic Stop Data: An Early Intervention System Approach.* Omaha: Police Professionalism Initiative, University of Nebraska at Omaha.

Walker, S., Spohn, C., and DeLone, M. 2000. *The Color of Justice: Race, Ethnicity, and Crime in America.* Belmont, CA: Wadsworth.

Washington State Patrol (WSP). 2001. *Report to the Legislature on Routine Traffic Stop Data.* Olympia: Washington State Patrol.

Webb, G. 1999. *Report on Operation Pipeline prepared for California Legislature Task Force on Governmental Oversight.* Retrieved April 1, 2002, from www.aclunc.org/discriminatin/webb-report.htm.

Weitzer, R. 1999. Citizen perceptions of police misconduct: Race and neighborhood context. *Justice Quarterly* 16:820–46.

Weitzer, R. 2000. Racialized policing: Residents' perceptions in three neighborhoods. *Law and Society Review* 34:129–55.

Weitzer, R., and Tuch, S. A. 2002. Perceptions of racial profiling: Race, class, and personal experience. *Criminology* 40(2):435–56.

West, M. H. 2001. *Community-Centered Policing: A Force for Change.* Oakland, CA: PolicyLink.

Westly, W. A. 1953. Violence and the police. *American Journal of Sociology* 59:34–41.

Wilson, J. Q. 1968. *Varieties of Police Behavior: The Management of Law and Order in Eight Communities.* Cambridge, MA: Harvard University Press.

Wilson, J. Q. and Kelling, G. 1982. Broken windows: The police and neighborhood safety. *Atlantic Monthly* 127:29–38.

Wise, T. 2003. Racial profiling and its apologists. In *Annual Editions: Criminal Justice,* 27th ed., ed. J. L. Victor and J. Naughton, 91–94). Guilford, CT: McGraw-Hill/Duskin.

Withrow, B. L. 2002. *The Wichita Stop Study.* Wichita, KS: Wichita State University, Midwest Criminal Justice Institute.

Withrow, B. L. 2003. *Racial Profiling in Sedgwick County, Kansas.* Wichita, KS: Wichita State University, Midwest Criminal Justice Institute.

Withrow, B. L. 2004a. Driving while different: A potential theoretical explanation for race-based policing. *Criminal Justice Policy Review*. 15(3):344–64.

Withrow, B. L. 2004b. A comparative analysis of commonly used benchmarks in racial profiling research: A research note. *Justice Research and Policy* 6(1):61–62.

Withrow, B. L., and Jackson, H. 2002. Race based policing: Alternatives for assessing the problem. In *Crime and Justice in America: Present Realities and Future Prospects,* 2nd ed., ed. W. R. Palacios, P. F. Cromwell, R. Dunham, 183–90. Upper Saddle River, NJ: Prentice Hall.

Zingraff, M. T., Mason, H. M., Smith, W. R., Tomaskovic-Devey, D., Warren, P., McMurray, H. L., and Fenlon, C. R. 2000. *Evaluating North Carolina State Highway Patrol Data: Citations, Warnings, and Searches in 1998.* Raleigh: North Carolina State University, Center for Crime and Justice Research.

CASES CITED

Brown v. Board of Education, 347 U.S. 483 (1954).

Brown v. City of Oneonta, 235 F. 3d 769 (2nd Cir. 2000).

Chavez v. Illinois State Police, 231 F 3d 612 CA7 Ill. 2001.

Chicago v. Morales, 527 U.S. 41 1999.

Florida v. Royer, 460 U.S. 491, 103 S. Ct. 1319 (1983).

Gideon v. Wainwright, 372 U.S. 335 (1963).

Hibel v. Sixth Judicial District Court of Nevada, Humboldt County 2003.

Hughes v. State, 269 Ga. 269 Ga. 258 (1998).

Illinois v. Wardlow, 528 U.S. 119, 120 S. Ct. 673 (2000).

Maryland State Conference of NAACP Branches v. Maryland Department of State Police, 72 F. Supp. 2d 560 (D. Md. 1999).

Lyons v. City of Los Angeles, 461 U.S. 95, 103 S. Ct. 1660 (1983).

Mapp v. Ohio, 367 U.S. 643 (1961).

McClesky v. Kemp, 481 U.S. 279 (1987).

Minnesota v. Dickerson, 508 U.S. 366 (1993).

Miranda v. Arizona, 384 U.S. 436 (1966).

Ohio v. Robinette, 519 U.S. 33 (1996).

Reid v. Georgia, 448 U.S. 438 (1980).

Rodriquez v. California Highway Patrol, 89 F. Supp. 2d 1131 (N.D. Cal. 2000).

Schneckloth v. Bustamonte, 312 U.S. 218 (1973).

State of New Jersey v. Pedro Soto, 734 A. 2d 350 (N.J. Super. Ct. Law Div. 1996).

Terry v. Ohio, 392 U.S. 1 (1968).

United States v. Armstrong, 116 S. Ct. 1480 (1966).

United States v. Avery, FED App. 0059A (6th Cir.) (1997).

United States v. Bautista, 684 F. 2d 1286 (9th Cir. 1982).

United States v. Brignoni-Ponce, 422 U.S. 873, 95 S. Ct. 2574 (1975).

United States v. Jones, FED App. 232 (2nd Cir. 2001).

United States v. Martinez-Fuente, 428 U.S. 543 (1976).

United States v. Mendenhall, 466 U.S. 544 (1980).

United States v. Montero-Camaro, 208 F. 3d 1122 (9th Cir. 2000).

United States v. Smith, 799 F.2d 704 (11th Circuit, 1986).

United States v. Sokolow, 490 U.S. 1 (1989).

United States v. Travis, FED App. 0253P (6th Cir.) (1995).

Whren, et al. v. United States, 517 U.S. 806 (1996).

Wilkins v. Maryland State Police, Civ. No. CCB-93-468 (D. Md.). (1993)

Winfield v. Board of County Commissioners of Eagle County Colorado, 837 F. Supp. 338 (D. Colo. 1993).

Wilson v. Tinicum Township, (Civ. No. 92-6617, 1993 U.S. Dist, LEXIS 9971)E.D. Pa. July 20, 1993).

INDEX